STRATEGIC TEACHING AND LEARNING

Standards-Based Instruction to Promote
Content Literacy in Grades Four Through Twelve

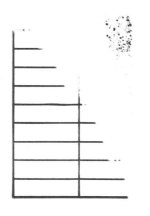

Publishing Information

Strategic Teaching and Learning: Standards-Based Instruction to Promote Content Literacy in Grades Four Through Twelve was developed under the direction of the California Department of Education. This publication was edited by Faye Ong, working in cooperation with Beth Breneman, Consultant, Professional Development and Curriculum Support Division. It was designed and prepared for printing by the staff of CDE Press, with the cover and interior design created and prepared by Juan Sanchez. Typesetting was done by Carey Johnson and Gloria Barreiro. It was published by the Department of Education, 721 Capitol Mall, Sacramento, California (mailing address: P.O. Box 944272, Sacramento, CA 94244-2720). It was distributed under the provisions of the Library Distribution Act and *Government Code* Section 11096.

ISBN 0-8011-1472-1

Special Acknowledgment

The Professional Development and Curriculum Support Division extends its appreciation to the principal writers of this document: Robert Pritchard, Professor of Education and Coordinator of the Reading/Language Arts Program, California State University, Fresno, and Beth Breneman, Language Arts Consultant, California Department of Education.

Ordering Information

Copies of this publication are available for $12.50 each, plus shipping and handling charges. California residents are charged sales tax. Orders may be sent to CDE Press, Sales Office, California Department of Education, P.O. Box 271, Sacramento, CA 95812-0271; FAX (916) 323-0823.

An illustrated *Educational Resources Catalog* describing publications, videos, and other instructional media available from the Department can be obtained without charge by writing to the address given above or by calling the Sales Office at (916) 445-1260.

Notice

The guidance in *Strategic Teaching and Learning: Standards-Based Instruction to Promote Content Literacy in Grades Four Through Twelve* is not binding on local educational agencies or other entities. Except for the statutes, regulations, and court decisions that are referenced herein, the document is exemplary, and compliance with it is not mandatory. (See *Education Code* Section 33308.5.)

Prepared for publication
by CSEA members.

CONTENTS

A MESSAGE FROM THE STATE SUPERINTENDENT OF PUBLIC INSTRUCTION

I BELIEVE IN THE POWER OF LANGUAGE. IT IS THROUGH THIS POWER, BOTH SPOKEN AND WRITTEN, that we preserve our principles, practices, and institutions as a democracy. For our students, literacy is a key to academic success, higher education, career development, citizenship, and personal enrichment. If we wish to provide all students an equal opportunity to learn, it is essential that we do whatever it takes to ensure success in literacy for *every* student.

When students advance from the third to the fourth grade, they often encounter a brand new set of expectations—particularly in the area of reading. The emphasis shifts from a focus on *learning to read* to *reading to learn.* Upper-grade teachers expect students to know how to read and use their reading abilities for acquiring new knowledge and competencies. These ever-increasing expectations continue as students move from grade to grade. To help students succeed, instruction in the use of reading, writing, and oral language should continue across the grades and in all content areas.

Fortunately, during the last 25 years, the pool of research-based strategies for promoting comprehension and learning has expanded. Before students can benefit from this research, teachers need access to it. The primary purpose of *Strategic Teaching and Learning: Standards-Based Instruction to Promote Content Literacy in Grades Four Through Twelve* is to provide teachers with a theoretical foundation as well as comprehension, vocabulary, and basic skill strategies to support student learning from literary and informational texts.

The second purpose of this document is to delineate strategies that might be incorporated into interventions for beginning and struggling readers. Despite our best efforts, there will probably always be some students in grades four and beyond who have been unsuccessful the first time around in learning how to read. The challenges for them are daunting. In addition to powerful interventions, underachieving students also need the strategic and explicit instruction provided by programs of reading and writing across the curriculum so that they will continue to expand their content knowledge as they catch up in reading skills.

Designed for teachers of California's diverse student population, *Strategic Teaching and Learning* contains 55 strategies evaluated for quality by California teachers and anchored in the *English–Language Arts Content Standards,* indices highlighting the appropriate uses and benefits of each strategy, examples of student work, and linkages to the *Reading/Language Arts Framework for California Public Schools.*

I wish to thank all the educators who served on the three advisory committees that helped to develop this document. Their thinking shaped the nature of the document, ensured that the needs of English learners and students at risk of failing to read were seamlessly addressed, and guided the strategy-selection process. I also want to acknowledge the contributions of the many teachers and researchers whose work is reflected in the following pages.

I hope that you will find this document useful as a handbook, an effective resource for professional development, and a catalyst for creating schoolwide programs across the curriculum to ensure literacy for every student.

DELAINE EASTIN
State Superintendent of Public Instruction

PREFACE

LTHOUGH LITERACY IN THE PRIMARY GRADES IS THE FOUNDATION OF SUCCESS IN later schooling, the quality of literacy instruction in the upper grades is equally essential. Students must be able to handle increasingly difficult texts and tasks if they are to achieve high standards across the curriculum. All teachers in grades four through twelve need resources and support to make academic success a reality for students.

In 1995 State Superintendent of Public Instruction Delaine Eastin convened the California Reading Task Force and charged it with the task of preparing a set of specific recommendations to help all children learn to read by the end of grade three. The task force produced the report *Every Child a Reader* (1995) and the reading program advisory *Teaching Reading* (1996), which offered programmatic guidelines for teaching beginning reading. At that time the Department of Education recognized the plight of struggling readers in the upper grades as a serious concern, and efforts to prepare a book were authorized. The *English–Language Arts Content Standards for California Public Schools* was adopted by the California State Board of Education in December 1997 and was published in 1998. The rigor of these standards underscored the need for a reading-to-learn resource to help teachers foster comprehension of both literary and informational texts in grades four through twelve.

Strategic Teaching and Learning: Standards-Based Instruction to Promote Content Literacy in Grades Four Through Twelve was designed to help address students' needs in the upper grades and the needs of all teachers in grades four through twelve who endeavor to:

1. Help students read to learn across the curriculum and comprehend at grade level; and

2. Accelerate the development of beginning and struggling readers.

This book was under development when the *Reading/Language Arts Framework for California Public Schools* (1999) was released for publication. The framework provides a standards-based description of a K–12 language arts program and serves as the basis for evaluating reading/language arts instructional materials.

The curricular foundation of both the framework and this book is the *English–Language Arts Content Standards. Strategic Teaching and Learning* has been reviewed for alignment with the *Reading/Language Arts Framework* and contains cross-references to it throughout.

Although the book is consistent with the *Reading/Language Arts Framework* and is based on the same set of standards, it was designed to be useful for instruction in the full spectrum of content areas and not exclusively for language arts instruction. As is stated in the framework: "When students advance from the third grade to the fourth grade, they make a critical transition from learning to read to reading to learn in subject-matter content" (page 101).

The primary audiences of this handbook are teachers across the curriculum in grades four through twelve; reading, library media, resource, special education, English-language development, and Title 1 teachers; teachers of juvenile offenders; and administrators and other instructional leaders who wish to use this handbook in conjunction with the *Reading/Language Arts Framework* as the basis for professional development. Parents, students, tutors, school site councils, teacher trainers, and other members of the educational community may also find uses for this handbook.

The first step in the development of *Strategic Teaching and Learning* was to create an Interdisciplinary Blue Ribbon Committee composed of highly regarded experts representing a variety of disciplines, organizations, and communities throughout California. In 1996 the following educators came together to serve on the Blue Ribbon Committee to help create a broad vision of the document so that it might serve the needs of all teachers of students in grades four through twelve:

Interdisciplinary Blue Ribbon Committee

Carol Becker, Mathematics Teacher, Lodi Unified School District; Representative of the California Mathematics Project

Roger Bylund, Curriculum Specialist in Language Arts, Mt. Diablo Unified School District

Carla Cherry, Project Director, Kern Health Careers Consortium, Kern Union High School District

Kathi Cooper, Language Arts Director, Sacramento City Unified School District

Chris Davis, History/Social Science Teacher, Glendale Unified School District

Marian Doss, Elementary Teacher, Hanford Elementary School District; Representative of the California Teachers Association

Nancy Farnan, Professor, School of Teacher Education, San Diego State University; Representative of the California Association of Teachers of English

Rhonda Farber, Director of Human Resource Development, Campbell Union High School District

Paul Giganti, Mathematics Educator, Representative of the Bay Area Mathematics Project, Lawrence Hall of Science, Berkeley

Stephanie Kloss, Secondary Career Vocational Education Teacher, Woodland Joint Unified School District

Gary Kroesch, Codirector of the History Social Science Project, University of California, San Diego

Kathleen McCreery, Director of Elementary Education and Categorical Programs, Baldwin Park Unified School District; Representative of the Association of California School Administrators

Jane Murray, K–12 Staff Development Resource Teacher, Torrance Unified School District; Representative of the California Reading and Literature Project

Suzanne Nakashima, Teacher/Associate Director, California Science Project; English Language Development Teacher, Yuba City Unified School District

Carrie Oretsky, Elementary Teacher, Oakland Unified School District; Representative of the California Arts Project

Mary Purucker, Head Library Media Specialist, Santa Monica High School, Santa Monica-Malibu Unified School District

Armin Schulz, Associate Professor, Department of Teacher Education, California State University, Stanislaus; President (1997–98), California Reading Association

Karen Smith, Program Specialist, Migrant Region III, Merced County Office of Education

Billie Jean Telles, Reading Consultant, Los Angeles County Office of Education

Laura Watson, English Teacher, Sheldon High School, Elk Grove Unified School District; Representative of the California Reading and Literature Project

Lincoln Westdal, Literacy Specialist, Training and Reading Site, Southridge Middle School, Fontana Unified School District; Reading Consultant, R.E.A.D.

Pam Wilson-Willmore, Language Arts Coordinator, Westminster High School, Huntington Beach Union High School District

Facilitator: Charlotte Keuscher-Barkman, Consultant, Elementary Education Division, California Department of Education

The following California Department of Education staff consultants collaborated in bringing together the Interdisciplinary Blue Ribbon Committee: Rod Atkinson, Judy Brown, Jennifer Ekstedt, Mae Gundlach, Barbara Jeffus, Les Pacheco, Jean Landeen, Patty Taylor, and Barbara Weiss.

The committee was convened under the direction of Glen Thomas, Executive Director, California County Superintendent Educational Services Association (former Director, Elementary Teaching and Learning Division, California Department of Education).

The Focus Group on Students with Special Needs was convened because it was essential to address the needs of beginning and struggling readers in the upper grades. The group reviewed the advisory *Teaching Reading* and analyzed similarities and differences between beginning readers in the primary grades and those in the upper grades. It identified critical research and relevant literature that would be useful for the development of this book. This group also created a set of considerations for struggling English learners and concluded that the issue of helping students with special needs should be addressed systemically throughout the document. With the needs of all struggling learners in mind, the group created a set of considerations for selecting exemplary classroom strategies to include in this book.

Focus Group on Students with Special Needs

The Focus Group on Students with Special Needs, whose members gave generously of their time and expertise, consisted of the following persons:

Roger Bylund, Curriculum Specialist in Language Arts, Mt. Diablo Unified School District

Edda Caraballo, Consultant, Language Policy and Leadership Office, California Department of Education

Diane Chapman, Facilitator, Success for All, WestEd

Fred Dobb, Consultant, Language Policy and Leadership Office, California Department of Education

Nancy Farnan, Professor, School of Teacher Education, San Diego State University; Representative of the California Association of Teachers of English

Holly Johnson, Title 1 Teacher, Littlejohn (Leighton) Elementary School, San Juan Unified School District

Kate Kinsella, Professor, Department of Secondary Education and Step to College Program, San Francisco State University

Adele V. Martinez, Second Language Specialist and Bilingual Consultant (*deceased*)

Louisa Cook Moats, Literacy Consultant, Sacramento County Office of Education; Author of *Implementing the Components of the California Reading Initiative*

Dennis Parker, Manager, District and School Program Coordination, California Department of Education

Nadeen T. Ruiz, Associate Professor, Bilingual/ Multicultural Education Department, College of Education, California State University, Sacramento

Armin Schulz, Associate Professor, Department of Teacher Education, California State University, Stanislaus; President (1997-98), California Reading Association

Lincoln Westdal, Literacy Specialist, Training and Reading Site, Southridge Middle School, Fontana Unified School District; Reading Consultant, R.E.A.D.

Facilitator: Lorna Sheveland, Consultant, Secondary Education Division, California Department of Education

Facilitator: Jim Miller, Consultant, Secondary Education Division, California Department of Education

Once a preliminary set of teaching and learning strategies had been compiled, a committee of educators was convened to review the strategies. Each strategy was evaluated on the basis of the following criteria: (1) usefulness to teachers at intermediate, middle, and high school levels; (2) usefulness to teachers across the curriculum; (3) usefulness to teachers of English language learners; (4) usefulness to teachers of students with special needs; (5) helpfulness to students in achieving high standards in reading as set forth in the *English–Language Arts Content Standards;* and (6) consistency with approaches recommended in *Teaching Reading.* Determinations of which strategies to include in *Strategic Teaching and Learning* were primarily based on that evaluation. Checks for consistency with successive drafts of the *Reading/Language Arts Framework* provided another set of considerations for the development of this document. The organization of both documents is based on the *English–Language Arts Content Standards.*

Strategy and Document Review Committee

The following educators gave generously of their time to participate in the evaluation of the section on instructional strategies and the subsequent first draft of the document:

Marilyn Astore, Assistant Superintendent, Instructional Support Services, Sacramento County Office of Education

Eleanor Black, Reading/Language Arts Specialist, Roosevelt Elementary School, Lawndale Elementary School District; Faculty Member, California State University, Los Angeles; and International Teacher Trainer

Helena Camilo, Spanish and French Teacher, Lee Junior High School, Woodland Joint Unified School District

Judy DeCoudres, Chair of English Department and Reading Specialist, Jordan High School, Long Beach Unified School District

Nancy Farnan, Professor, School of Teacher Education, San Diego State University; Representative of the California Association of Teachers of English

James Graham, Coordinator, American Indian Education Program, Marysville Joint Unified School District

Vicky Hoag, Reading Teacher (grades nine through twelve), Sierra High School, Sierra Unified School District

Cindy Lenners, History/Social Science Teacher, Harden Middle School, Salinas Union High School District

Sarah Martinez, Resource Teacher, Lee Junior High School, Woodland Joint Unified School District

Jane Murray, K–12 Staff Development Resource Teacher, Torrance Unified School District; Representative of the California Reading and Literature Project

Sandra Murphy, Professor, Division of Education, University of California, Davis

Becky Pastor, Literacy Specialist, Training and Reading Site, Southridge Middle School, Fontana Unified School District

Marilyn Robertson, Library Media Specialist, Los Angeles Unified School District

Nadeen Ruiz, Associate Professor, Bilingual/ Multicultural Education Department, College of Education, California State University, Sacramento

John Shacklett, Resource Specialist and Manager of Second Chance Reading Program, Morse High School, San Diego City Unified School District

Armin Schulz, Associate Professor, Department of Teacher Education, California State University, Stanislaus; President (1997-98), California Reading Association

Eleanor Thonis, Second-Language Specialist and Author

Terry Underwood, Assistant Professor of Reading Education, School of Education, California State University, Sacramento

Laura Watson, English Teacher (grades nine through twelve), Elk Grove Unified School District; Representative of the California Reading and Literature Project

Aida Walqui, Professor, School of Education, Stanford University

Lincoln Westdal, Literacy Specialist, Training and Reading Site, Southridge Middle School, Fontana Unified School District; Reading Consultant, R. E. A. D.

Sandy Williamson, Coordinator, Language Arts Curriculum and Instruction, Alameda County Office of Education

Facilitator: Lorna Sheveland, Consultant, Secondary Education Division, California Department of Education

Facilitator: Kristin Warriner, Consultant, Elementary Education Division, California Department of Education

Members of the Strategy and Document Review Committee were provided with overviews and draft copies of documents supporting the California Reading Initiative during the development of this document. For example, all members were provided copies of *Teaching Reading,* which was used in the review and evaluation of instructional strategies. Jan Chladek, Consultant, Elementary Education Division, California Department of Education, gave the committee an overview of the *English–Language Arts Content Standards* prior to the strategy review process. Diane Levin and Nancy Brynelson, Consultants, Elementary Education Division, California Department of Education, provided timely updates and draft copies of the *Reading/ Language Arts Framework.* Ada Hand and Debby Lott, Consultants, Elementary Education Division, provided ongoing support throughout the document development process. All names and titles of committee members and Department staff were current at the time of the production of this document.

Writers

Appreciation is extended to the principal writers of this document: Robert Pritchard, Professor of Education and Coordinator of the Reading/Language Arts Program at California State University, Fresno, and Beth Breneman, Language Arts Consultant, California Department of Education.

Appreciation is also extended to Laurie Goodman, English Teacher, Pioneer Middle School, Pioneer Union Elementary School District, for much of the illustrative material in Part II.

Beth Breneman served as the coordinator of this project. This handbook was prepared under the direction of the California Department of Education.

Sonia Hernandez
Deputy Superintendent
Curriculum and Instructional
Leadership Branch

William W. Vasey
Director
Professional Development and
Curriculum Support Division

Robert Cervantes
Manager
Professional Development and
Curriculum Support Division

INTRODUCTION

INCE THE RELEASE OF THE *NAEP 1994 READING REPORT CARD* BY THE NATIONAL Assessment of Educational Progress (Campbell and others 1996) and the publication of *Every Child a Reader* in 1995, education in general and reading in particular have become the focus of legislative and political initiatives in California.[1] As a result educators in this state have had an unprecedented opportunity to effect significant change in the way reading is conceptualized, taught, and assessed. Understandably, literacy in kindergarten through grade three has been at the forefront of these initiatives. Credential program revisions, external funding opportunities, and class size reduction efforts have mostly targeted the primary grades. Unfortunately, this emphasis on early literacy has left many educators who work with students in grades four through twelve feeling as though their needs and the needs of their students are being neglected. Richard Vacca, former president of the International Reading Association, has characterized this situation as the "benign neglect of adolescent literacy." He believes that "the public, and even professional, attitude is one of benign neglect [despite the fact that] the literacy development of a 12-year-old in middle school or a 17-year-old in high school remains as critical a concern as the literacy development of a preschool child or a child in the primary grades."[2]

> *Content literacy is the ability to use reading and writing to acquire new content in a given discipline.*

This lack of attention to the reading needs of students in grades four through twelve is all too common despite growing evidence that reading and writing instruction should continue with increased sophistication beyond the primary grades and should be incorporated in every content area. The NAEP report and results of statewide tests of reading proficiency clearly indicate that significant percentages of students in grades four through twelve experience difficulty learning from texts.[3] Some of these students are reading at or above grade level and still experience difficulty because of the task demands inherent in the increasingly complex and varied materials they regularly encounter in grade four and above. Other students are reading below grade level and need more basic reading intervention before they can comprehend these new materials.

Ultimately, the goal for both groups of students is to develop their content literacy; that is, the ability to use reading and writing to acquire new content in a given discipline.[4] Content literacy instruction is extremely important as teachers struggle to make their instructional materials accessible, relevant, and interesting to an increasingly diverse student population. Fortunately, research in reading comprehension indicates that with proper instruction students can develop content literacy and can apply this knowledge in the classroom, in the workplace, and in civic and social settings.[5]

This book provides teachers of students in grades four through twelve with a variety of research-based, instructional strategies to address their students' content literacy needs. These strategies can help students by providing them with the scaffolding they need to bridge the gap that too often exists between their reading ability and the difficulty of the text. When teachers across the curriculum—*not just those teaching English–language arts*—use these strategies regularly and consistently, they will reduce the amount of frustration-level reading occurring in grades four through twelve and increase the reading achievement and motivation of their struggling readers.

Achieving this goal requires teachers to have an understanding of theoretical and pedagogical issues related to reading development, among them the importance of a balanced approach to reading instruction. Therefore, in *Strategic Teaching and Learning,* great care was taken to present a balanced view of the reading process and a wide variety of instructional strategies. More specifically, parts I and II contain:

- A synthesis of what is known about relevant theoretical issues related to the reading development of students in grades four through twelve

- Specific suggestions and concrete examples of practical ways in which teachers can help facilitate that development

As challenging and rigorous content standards continue to be developed and implemented across the curriculum, teachers at all levels will need to seek solutions, meet challenges, and embrace changes necessary to ensure quality education for their students. This book is intended to contribute to that effort.

Notes

1. J. Campbell and others, *NAEP 1994 Reading Report Card for the Nation and the States.* Washington, D.C.: U.S. Department of Education, 1996; and *Every Child a Reader: The Report of the California Reading Task Force.* Sacramento: California Department of Education, 1995.

2. Richard Vacca, "The Benign Neglect of Adolescent Literacy," *Reading Today* (February/March 1997), 3.

3. J. Stewart, "The Blackboard Jungle: California's Failed Reading Experiment," *L.A. Weekly,* Vol. 18, 22–29.

4. Michael C. McKenna and Richard D. Robinson, "Content Literacy: A Definition and Implications," *Journal of Reading,* Vol. 34 (November 1990), 184–86.

5. Linda G. Fielding and P. David Pearson, "Reading Comprehension: What Works," *Educational Leadership* (February 1994), 62–67.

THEORETICAL BACKGROUND

Understanding the Reading Process

UNDERSTANDING THE READING PROCESS IS A KEY TO HELPING STUDENTS USE reading and writing to acquire new content in a given discipline. Fortunately, substantial progress in understanding this process and how it operates in content classes has been made in the past 25 years.[1] A number of influential scholars in the field, representing a range of theoretical perspectives, maintain that a strong consensus has emerged regarding the basic nature of reading; in general, reading is now viewed as a complex process of making meaning from print.[2]

One scholar, Marilyn Jager Adams, states, "Skillful reading is not a unitary skill."[3] She goes on to suggest that reading is a complex process involving skills and knowledge. In this process, the knowledge and activities involved in visual recognition of individual printed words are useless in and of themselves and are valuable only as the reader guides and receives them with complementary knowledge and activities of language comprehension. On the other hand, the entire process is likely to break down unless the reader controls the skills involved in individual word recognition. For instance, to read the word *cat* one must be able to connect the letters *c-a-t* with the sounds /k/ /a/ /t/ and understand that the word *cat* refers to a furry, household pet. Both kinds of knowledge—decoding ability and knowing what a cat is—are indispensable for comprehension.

The consensus about basic reading processes includes the premise that the ultimate goal of reading is comprehension. Most theorists distinguish the word recognition level of the reading process from comprehension and acknowledge the need for decoding, which in turn leads to rapid and automatic word recognition.[4] When readers develop a high degree of automatic word recognition (automaticity) with print, their cognitive capacity is free to focus on comprehension. If a reader lacks automaticity, then less cognitive capacity will be available for comprehension. For example, if it takes all of a reader's problem-solving ability to sound out the words in the sentence, "Cats have long been domesticated by man as carnivorous pets for catching rats and mice," the reader will be distracted from a focus on its meaning.

Fluent and accurate decoding alone, however, does not guarantee understanding. As one scholar points out:

> *It's . . . easy to lull oneself into believing that if kids can read the words with some degree of fluency and accuracy, they can read effectively enough to handle the conceptual demands inherent in texts. Often they can't, because they were never shown how. . . . Although they had developed fluency, the ability to read print smoothly and automatically, they didn't know what to do with texts beyond just saying the words.[5]*

Consider the following sentences: "Coulomb's law has a form remarkably similar to Newton's law of gravity. The force in both laws depends on the inverse square of the distance between two objects and is directed along the line between them." One might pronounce the words in these sentences fluently and accurately with little or no understanding of their meaning.

Thus, there is widespread agreement that most students will benefit from explicit instruction that promotes control of fluent decoding, vocabulary, and comprehension strategies. Recent Department publications—*Every Child a Reader* (1995), *Teaching Reading* (1996), and *Reading/Language Arts Framework for California Public Schools* (1999)—offer specific recommendations about reading instruction, including guidance on development of fluent decoding, vocabulary, and comprehension. These aspects of reading are discussed in parts I and II.

The three Department publications collectively emphasize the importance of learning to read by the end of grade three.

To that end, *the Reading/Language Arts Framework* offers the following description of beginning reading:

> *The dimensions of beginning reading are like the strands of a strong rope. Like such a rope, the strength of the reading process depends on the strength of the individual strands, the strategic integration of all the strands, and the effective binding or connecting of the strands. . . . First, it is critical that the strands, including vocabulary acquisition, concepts about print, phonemic awareness, decoding and word recognition, knowledge of the structure of stories, and listening comprehension are robust, stable, and reliable. Next, the strength of the reading process depends on strategic integration of the strands to produce readers who can apply their skills in a variety of contexts and tasks.[6]*

As students move through the grades, the range of tasks and contexts expands year by year. In applying their skills in this expanding array of contexts and tasks, readers are guided by their purposes for reading, their background knowledge and experience, and their proficiency in the language of the text. These factors, as well as the nature of the text and the context in which the reading occurs, interact to create the quality of comprehension experienced by the reader. The following subsections provide a description of the factors related to the *reader*, the *text*, and the *context* in which the reading occurs. (See figure 1, "The Reading Process.")

The Reader

Readers bring to reading situations specific reading abilities, such as fluency and automaticity with print, knowledge of word meanings, and the ability to identify explicit textual information.[7] However, because most texts are not completely self-explanatory, readers use what they

Prior knowledge is the strongest predictor of a student's ability to make inferences about text.

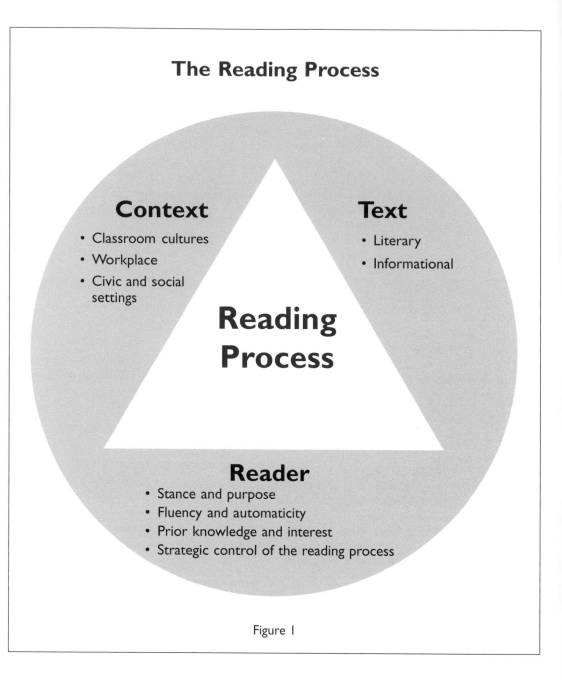

The Reading Process

Context
- Classroom cultures
- Workplace
- Civic and social settings

Text
- Literary
- Informational

Reading Process

Reader
- Stance and purpose
- Fluency and automaticity
- Prior knowledge and interest
- Strategic control of the reading process

Figure I

already know about a topic to make inferences and integrate information across a text. In general, the more students know about a topic, the better students comprehend and learn when reading about that topic. In fact, prior knowledge is the strongest predictor of a student's ability to make inferences about text.[8]

In addition to prior knowledge, other factors that affect comprehension are a reader's degree of interest in the topic, level of motivation for the task, strategic control of the reading process, purposes for reading, and perceptions of himself or herself as a reader. These factors contribute to the comprehension process by engaging students more actively in their reading, an involvement that research clearly shows enhances comprehension.[9]

Also influencing any reading event is the reader's stance or "mind-set." On the one hand, the reader may be seeking information, directions for action, or a logical conclusion. All such reading is focused on what is to be carried away at the end of the reading and has been termed the *efferent* stance, from the Latin word meaning "to carry away." This stance is appropriate for many classroom reading assignments. If, on the other hand, the reader encounters a story, a poem, or a play, attention will center on memorable characters, imagined events, and the sound and rhythm of words. From those images and ideas, a new experience, the story or poem, is shaped in the mind of the reader, giving rise to the *aesthetic* stance, from the Greek word meaning "to sense" or "to perceive." Any reading falls somewhere on the continuum between the aesthetic and efferent poles. Its place on the continuum will be influenced by the reader's mind-set in response to the text.[10]

The Text

Several factors related to the text need to be considered to predict how individual students will react to reading a specific text. One of the most important considerations is the nature and structure of the text. Because content area materials are predominantly expository or *informational* in nature, students who have learned to read by using primarily narrative or *literary* materials are exposed to new and unfamiliar patterns of organization.[11] Reading difficulty is also affected by other text features: the density of concepts; the size of the print; the amount of white space on a page; and the extent to which the text contains study aids, such as headings and subheadings, vocabulary, and highlighted marginalia.

Perhaps the most basic feature to consider is the match (or mismatch) between the language in which the text is written and the language of instruction, obviously a crucial issue for English learners. Unfortunately, even when the language of the text and the language of instruction match, the text may be too difficult for the readers.[12] Sentence length and word difficulty are the most commonly used criteria in the readability formulas designed to estimate text difficulty. However, such factors as the coherence, unity, and format of the text often have as much impact on the comprehensibility of a text.

The Context

Another integral aspect of the meaning-making process is the context in which the reading occurs. Context for reading includes the following components: physical setting, classroom environment, instructional task, and expected outcomes.[13] It is important to remember that these components are not limited to the school. Workplace environments and civic and social settings provide students with additional contexts for reading. Regardless of the setting, each of these components does in fact contribute to the situational context, which in turn influences the reading process. Instead of considering each of these components in isolation, it seems best to focus on the characteristics of the classroom cultures that result when these components have been integrated.

Research on classroom cultures that promote students' cognitive growth and ability to learn from reading indicates the following characteristics:[14]

- Large amounts of time for reading interesting, varied materials of appropriate difficulty
- Time to write about what was read
- Time for students to talk about their responses to reading
- Opportunities for collaborative learning
- Instruction that helps students connect the text with background knowledge
- Instruction that is explicit and models comprehension and text-handling strategies

Classrooms that foster students' motivation to read are characterized by the following conditions:

- The presence of people (e.g., teachers, older students, community volunteers, authors) who talk about good books, the benefits of reading, and the relationship between effort and achievement.
- A book-rich classroom environment.[15]
- Opportunities for self-selected reading. Students who choose their own reading

material expend more effort in learning and understanding the material.[16]

- Opportunities to interact socially with others on the basis of their reading. Social collaboration promotes achievement, higher level cognition, and an intrinsic desire to read.[17]
- Opportunities to become familiar with a wide variety of books.
- Appropriate incentives related to reading, such as books or bookmarks.[18]

Clearly, classrooms that promote academic learning and motivation share many common characteristics.

Summary

Finding the appropriate balance of factors related to the reader, the text, and the context is critical because students will learn more effectively from printed material when classroom instruction:

- Promotes rapid and automatic word recognition and fluency
- Provides adequate background knowledge about a topic prior to students' reading
- Promotes student understanding of vocabulary and concepts
- Encourages students' active involvement in and control over the reading process
- Models behavior that promotes ownership of reading and comprehension-monitoring strategies

This emphasis on practices that facilitate comprehension and strategic reading is consistent with the following provision in a supporting document of the California Reading Initiative: "Teachers need to know a framework for understanding the components of comprehension [and] a repertoire of interactive, constructive techniques to foster comprehension."[19] The characteristics of students who have developed these abilities are discussed in the following section.

Notes

1. Keith E. Stanovich, "Twenty-Five Years of Research on the Reading Process: The Grand Synthesis and What It Means for Our Field." Oscar S. Causey Research Award address presented at the National Reading Conference, Scottsdale, Arizona, December 1997.

2. P. David Pearson and others, *Developing Expertise in Reading Comprehension.* Technical Report No. 512. Champaign: University of Illinois, Center for the Study of Reading, 1990.

3. Marilyn J. Adams, *Beginning to Read: Thinking and Learning About Print.* Cambridge, Mass.: MIT Press, 1990, p. 3.

4. Stanovich, "Twenty-Five Years."

5. Richard Vacca, " The Benign Neglect of Adolescent Literacy," *Reading Today* (February/March 1997), 3.

6. *Reading/Language Arts Framework for California Public Schools, Kindergarten Through Grade Twelve.* Sacramento: California Department of Education, 1999, p. 29.

7. *Teaching Reading: A Balanced, Comprehensive Approach to Teaching Reading in Prekindergarten Through Grade Three.* Sacramento: California Department of Education, 1996.

8. Marilyn J. Adams and Bertram C. Bruce, "Background Knowledge and Reading Comprehension," in *Reader Meets Author/ Bridging the Gap.* Edited by Judith A. Langer and M. T. Smith-Burke. Newark, Del.: International Reading Association, 1982, pp. 2–25.

9. *Reading Engagement: Motivating Readers through Integrated Instruction.* Edited by John T. Guthrie and Allan Wigfield. Newark, Del.: International Reading Association, 1997.

10. Louise M. Rosenblatt, *Writing and Reading: The Transactional Theory.* Technical Report No. 13. Berkeley: Center for the Study of Writing, University of California, Berkeley, 1988.

11. *Reading/Language Arts Framework.*

12. Joseph L. Vaughn and Thomas H. Estes, *Reading and Reasoning Beyond the Primary Grades.* Boston: Allyn and Bacon, 1986.

13. Doris M. Cook, *Strategic Learning in the Content Classroom.* Madison: Wisconsin Department of Public Instruction, 1989.

14. Linda G. Fielding, and D. David Pearson. "Reading Comprehension: What Works," *Educational Leadership* (February 1994), 62–67.

15. Richard Allington and Anne McGill-Franzen, "What Are They to Read? Not All Children, Mr. Riley, Have Easy Access to Books," *Education Week* (October 3, 1993), 26.

16. U. Schicfele, "Interest, Learning, and Motivation," *Educational Psychologist,* Vol. 16 (1991), 299–323.

17. J. Almasi, "The Nature of Fourth Graders' Sociocognitive Conflicts in Peer-led and Teacher-led Discussions of Literature," *Reading Research Quarterly,* Vol. 29 (October, November, December 1994), 304–7.

18. Linda B. Gambrell, "Creating Classroom Cultures That Foster Reading Motivation," *The Reading Teacher,* Vol. 50 (September 1996), 14–23.

19. *Implementing the Components of the California Reading Initiative: A Blueprint for Teachers of Early Reading Instruction* (Second edition). Prepared by the California County Superintendents Educational Services Association—Curriculum and Instructional Steering Committee. Sacramento: CCSESA, 1996.

Developing Strategic Readers

Research data consistently indicate that the coordinated use of comprehension strategies is a critical component of effective reading.[1] Competent, proficient readers use a wider range of strategies more effectively and more flexibly than do less proficient readers. Proficient readers also know when and how to use a particular strategy and how to orchestrate its use with other strategies.[2] Strategic readers typically exhibit the following characteristics:

1. They are actively involved in the reading.
2. They often have a running dialogue with the text.
3. They visualize scenes and characters.
4. They make predictions about what they are reading.
5. They relate their prior knowledge to the topic they are reading about.
6. They read with a specific purpose in mind.
7. They monitor their comprehension and, when necessary, apply appropriate fix-up strategies (metacognition).
8. They accept ambiguity and push on; that is, when they come to a portion of the text that they do not understand, they go on, confident that they will eventually figure it out or be able to comprehend the overall meaning.[3]

Less proficient readers, on the other hand, have a relatively limited range of strategies for learning from text and coping with reading difficulties. These students may have difficulty recognizing the importance of using a strategy, fail to adjust strategy usage according to subject area, and may be unable to monitor their level of understanding.[4] Fortunately, research in strategy instruction provides educators with the information they need to help students with such difficulties.

Definitions of Strategies

Before considering research on the use of strategy instruction to help struggling readers, it is necessary to distinguish between the strategies readers use to construct meaning and the ones teachers use to facilitate learning. *Reading strategies* are the deliberate, cognitive acts learners use to bring meaning to a text.[5] *Instructional strategies* are the teaching techniques teachers model and use to help students become more independent readers and learners.[6] Although all the instructional strategies in this book are designed in some way to make students better readers, some of the instructional strategies help students become better readers *without* trying to teach them how to use the strategies independently. Other instructional strategies have the concomitant purpose of developing student ownership of the strategies. *Instructional* strategies become *reading* strategies when a student can independently select an appropriate one and use it effectively to construct meaning from a text.

Studies indicate that the behavior and achievement of low-achieving students may be influenced by explicit strategy instruction.[7] This finding is noted in the *Reading/Language Arts Framework for California Public Schools, Kindergarten Through Grade Twelve:*

> *Direct teaching and modeling of the strategies and readers' application of the strategies to the text they hear and read increase the ability of students to develop literal and inferential understanding, increase vocabulary, and make connections between parts of a text, between separate texts, and between text and personal experience.[8]*

Types of Strategic Knowledge

Research findings also provide specific guidance regarding what students need to know about strategies and how

Instructional strategies become reading strategies when a student can independently select an appropriate one and use it effectively.

teachers can most effectively facilitate students' use of them. In regard to the *what* of strategy instruction, researchers Paris, Lipson, and Wixson have demonstrated that students become more strategic readers and develop greater proficiency when they acquire three types of knowledge:[9]

- *Declarative knowledge* (what the strategy is)
- *Procedural knowledge* (how it should be used)
- *Conditional knowledge* (when and why it should be used)

When any one of these pieces is omitted from the strategy puzzle, students are much less likely to use appropriate processing behavior.

For example, a middle school student may know that PLAN stands for the reading-study strategy *Predict, Locate, Add, Note*. In other words he or she knows *what* the strategy is. However, having *declarative knowledge* about PLAN does not mean the student will understand how to use PLAN. That *procedural knowledge* is usually acquired from direct modeling and guided practice. However, *declarative knowledge* and *procedural knowledge* about PLAN alone cannot guarantee that the student will use the strategy effectively. For that to happen the student must also possess *conditional knowledge*—an understanding of when and why one would logically use the strategy.

Framework for Strategic Instruction

Guidance regarding the *how* of strategy instruction can be found in the work of a number of researchers. The reliability of their findings is enhanced by the fact that researchers from a variety of disciplines concur on some of the most basic aspects of strategy instruction.[10] Three researchers whose work is most relevant to language and literacy development are Michael Pressley, Anna Chamot, and Michael O'Malley. These researchers have made significant contributions to an understanding of the most effective ways to teach students (both English-speaking and English learners) to be strategic and to use strategic knowledge to develop their language and literacy abilities.

The primary focus of their approach is represented in the "Framework for Strategic Instruction" (figure 2). Although this model was developed by Chamot and O'Malley in their work with English learners,[11] it shares the same basic characteristics of models that Pressley and others have developed.[12] This one was chosen for inclusion here because of the clear, concise manner in which each step in the model is depicted. Two basic elements that are common to the previous models are as follows:

- Students must be explicitly taught how to use the strategies teachers want them to acquire.
- The instructional process gradually evolves from one that is teacher-directed to one that is student-directed.

In other words a gradual release of responsibility occurs once the teacher has explained and modeled the strategy. As instruction continues and the teacher's role is more akin to that of a coach, teacher and student responsibilities are more equal. Eventually, the students assume primary responsibility for practicing the strategies and trying to apply them in new situations.

Summary

Ideally, the students' strategic abilities and teachers' instructional approaches described in this chapter should begin to develop as a part of the *learning-to-read* process in the primary grades. However, even when this happens, teachers in grades four through twelve need to understand how to deliver strategic instruction. Fortunately, in the past 25 years, there has been a proliferation of research related to various aspects of this process. Educators concerned with strategic teaching for strategic learning

Students must be explicitly taught how to use the strategies teachers want them to acquire.

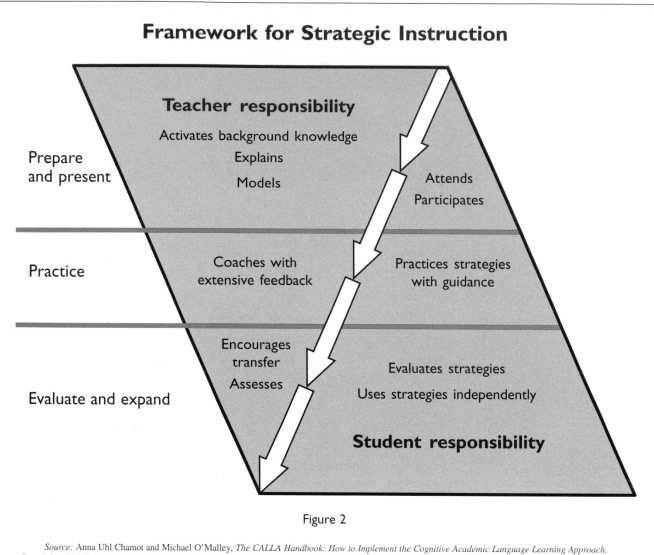

Framework for Strategic Instruction

Prepare and present

Teacher responsibility

Activates background knowledge

Explains

Models

Attends

Participates

Practice

Coaches with extensive feedback

Practices strategies with guidance

Evaluate and expand

Encourages transfer

Assesses

Evaluates strategies

Uses strategies independently

Student responsibility

Figure 2

Source: Anna Uhl Chamot and Michael O'Malley, *The CALLA Handbook: How to Implement the Cognitive Academic Language Learning Approach.* Copyright 1994. Reprinted by permission of Addison-Wesley Longman.

now have a strong empirical and pedagogical base to guide them in their efforts. Additional aspects of this research and implications for teachers are discussed in the following section.

Notes

1. Michael Pressley and Peter Afflerbach, *Verbal Protocols of Reading: The Nature of Constructively Responsive Reading.* Hillsdale, N.J.: Erlbaum, 1995.

2. N. Anderson, "Individual Differences in Strategy Use in Second Language Reading," *Modern Language Journal*, Vol. 75 (1991), 460–72.

3. Scott G. Paris, Marjorie Y. Lipson, and Karen K. Wixson, "Becoming a Strategic Reader," *Contemporary Educational Psychology*, Vol. 8 (1983), 293–316.

4. M. L. Simpson, "The Status of Study Strategy Instruction: Implications for Classroom Teachers," *Journal of Reading*, Vol. 28 (1984), 136–42.

5. Paris, Lipson, and Wixson, "Becoming a Strategic Reader."

6. Doris Cook, *Strategic Learning in the Content Areas.* Madison: Wisconsin Department of Public Instruction, 1989.

7. Rachel Brown, Pamela Beard El-Dinary, and Michael Pressley, "Balanced Comprehension Instruction: Transactional Strategies Instruction," in *Balanced Instruction: Strategies and Skills in Whole Language.* Edited by Ellen McIntyre and Michael Pressley. Norwood, Mass.: Christopher-Gordon Publishers, Inc., 1997.

8. *Reading/Language Arts Framework for California Public Schools, Kindergarten Through Grade Twelve.* Sacramento: California Department of Education, 1999, p. 25.

9. Paris, Lipson, and Wixson, "Becoming a Strategic Reader."

10. *Strategic Teaching and Learning: Cognitive Instruction in the Content Areas.* Edited by Beau Fly Jones, Annemarie S. Palincsar, Donna S. Ogle, and Eileen G. Carr. Alexandria, Va.: Association for Supervision and Curriculum Development, 1987.

11. Anna U. Chamot and J. Michael O'Malley, *The CALLA Handbook: How to Implement the Cognitive Academic Language Learning Approach.* Reading, Mass.: Addison-Wesley Longman, 1994.

12. Brown, Beard El-Dinary, and Pressley, "Balanced Comprehension Instruction: Transactional Strategies Instruction."

Delivering Strategic Instruction

Early literacy initiatives, the *English–Language Arts Content Standards* (1998), and the *Reading/Language Arts Framework for California Public Schools* (1999) have been designed to create a shared vision of what California students are expected to attain in the language arts and what the school community can do to ensure that the vision is realized. However, recent data indicate that many students are not yet realizing the vision.[1] In some schools and school districts, the number of students in grades four through twelve reading below grade level far exceeds the number reading at or above grade level.[2] If educators are to meet this challenge successfully, it is necessary to identify:

- The range of reading abilities within a school
- The percentage of students reading above and below grade level
- The nature of the reading difficulties students face

Various assessment procedures and instruments, both formal and informal, are available and can be used to obtain these data.[3] Assessments will vary with the age and reading ability of students, the students' special needs, the academic content, the instructional context, the goals of the class, and the standards for assessing student progress. Teachers may need to rely on specially trained professionals for the correct use of these assessment tools needed for planning both group and individualized instruction. Although a description of assessment procedures and instruments is beyond the scope of this book, knowledge of reader strengths and needs forms the instructional base of teachers committed to supporting the development of their students' reading abilities. See Chapter 6 of the *Reading/Language Arts Framework for California Public Schools* for a discussion of assessment procedures.

Knowledge of reader strengths and needs forms the base for supporting the development of students' reading abilities.

Range of Reading Abilities

Regardless of the specific instruments or procedures used, one fact consistently emerges from the data: students in grades four through twelve exhibit a wide range of reading abilities.[4] This range can be grouped into three broad levels of achievement:

- Students reading at or above grade level
- Students reading below grade level
- Beginning readers who are reading significantly below grade level

These groups exist at nearly every school. What varies from school to school is the percentage of students in each group. The challenge is obviously greater when the percentage of students reading below grade level is high.

An important factor in understanding how this range of abilities develops (and usually increases as students progress through school) is the relationship between *learning to read* and *reading to learn*. According to de Beaugrande:

> Learning to read *subsumes all settings in which written texts are processed with the dominant (though not exclusive) goal of rehearsing, improving, or organizing the processes themselves.* Reading to learn, *on the other hand, subsumes all settings in which texts are processed with the dominant (though not exclusive) goal of acquiring knowledge about the topic domain underlying the text in use.*[5]

In other words *learning to read* refers to *learning the process* of reading and mastering and developing control over the strategies that are needed in school and throughout life. *Reading to learn* refers to *applying the process*, using those strategies for the primary purpose of gaining information and understanding the message conveyed in the text.

It is important to note that *learning to read* is sometimes defined too narrowly as "the capacity to interpret the written symbols for the oral language that [children] have been hearing since birth."[6] This narrow definition leads to criticism of the *learning-to-read/reading-to-learn* dichotomy by people who believe that instruction in reading to learn can and should begin as soon as possible in the primary grades. Much of the heat of this criticism is dissipated, however, if one accepts de Beaugrande's definitions. He emphasizes that *learning to read* and *reading to learn* are not mutually exclusive and therefore can be developed concurrently from the outset.

Whichever of these perspectives one embraces, there is a consensus supported by research that a strong reading foundation needs to be established in kindergarten through grade three. When students enter grade four, teacher expectations and curriculum demands rise. From grade four, students are increasingly assigned tasks such as reading a chapter in a textbook and answering questions about the content. They are expected to apply their knowledge about the reading process more frequently and more independently to materials such as social studies books, math word problems, and science experiments.

Teacher expectations and curriculum demands continue to increase as students progress from one grade level to the next. Unfortunately, when students have not developed their *learning-to-read* foundation in kindergarten through grade three, they will in all likelihood be unable to fulfill these *reading-to-learn* expectations in grades four through twelve.[7] Two actions must take place to address this problem and provide students with appropriate instructional support:

- First, students' levels of reading achievement must be identified (*at or above grade level, below grade level*, and *beginning reader*) because students in each group have different capabilities and thus would benefit from different types of instruction.
- Second, a conceptual framework for literacy development must be in place

so that educators can understand the areas in which readers develop strengths and weaknesses as they progress along the *learning-to-read/reading-to-learn* continuum.

Levels of Reading Achievement

Students reading at or above grade level are capable of reading most instructional materials independently, but they will still need and benefit from instructional support from the teacher. Even though students in this group have learned to read and are capable of applying their *reading-to-learn* skills, sometimes the tasks they are asked to complete or the materials they are asked to read present new or unexpected challenges. Teachers must be sensitive to these challenges and be careful not to overlook the needs of these students even though they are not as severe as those of the other groups. Therefore, *students reading at or above grade level* will benefit from:

- Support and reinforcement in their reading-to-learn skills to ensure their ongoing success and independent capabilities
- Abundant opportunities for reading and writing in various genres (i.e., types of writing)

Students in the other two groups— those reading below and those reading significantly below grade level—need support in two areas. First, they need help in understanding the more complex concepts required of students at their grade level. Second, they need to develop a stronger reading foundation so they can function more independently. However, because a significant difference exists between these groups' levels of reading achievement, the type of instruction required to help each group differs.

The needs of the group that is reading below grade level—but has mastered the fundamental principles of decoding—can often be met by effective *reading-to-learn* instruction. That is, in classes across the curriculum, a student who is reading below grade level can be guided to an understanding of concepts and the application of reading skills by teachers using appropriate instructional strategies. Coupled with effective language arts instruction delivered by a teacher in a self-contained, intermediate-grade classroom or by a language arts teacher in middle school or high school, such strategies can help students in the second group to reach their grade level in reading. Additionally, some students in that group may need a reading intervention (i.e., carefully designed instruction in reading). In summary, *students whose reading abilities are below grade level* will benefit from:

- Strategic instruction across the curriculum

- Abundant reading at their independent and instructional levels (See step 10 on page 49 for guidelines.)

- Abundant writing experiences in various genres

- A reading intervention promoting comprehension and vocabulary development tailored to students' needs

Students in the third group—those beginning readers reading significantly below grade level—need more direct instruction and modeling of the reading process than can typically be given in an academic class. Those students need intensive reading intervention directed at the *learning-to-read* base that ideally should have been established in the primary grades. In addition, they require an integrated *reading-to-learn* component that provides the opportunity for teacher modeling, guided practice, and contextualized transfer of these components to content area materials. Thus, *beginning readers who are still mastering decoding* need systemically integrated approaches that include:

- An intensive reading intervention involving a combination of fluent decoding, vocabulary, and comprehension based on an in-depth assessment of students' needs

- Integrated strategic instruction in all content areas and appropriate instructional materials

- Plentiful reading experiences in various genres, supported as needed, to ensure success at students' independent and instructional reading levels (See step 10 on page 49 for guidelines.)

- Plentiful writing experiences in various genres

See the *Reading/Language Arts Framework* (pages 96–100) for more detailed recommendations pertaining to both (1) strategic interventions for students learning to read; and (2) possible supports for students reading to learn in self-contained classrooms and content areas.

An additional challenge that some schools and districts face is having teachers who are unwilling to accept responsibility for supporting literacy development. Too often middle school and high school teachers from departments *other* than English–language arts believe they should not have to assume any responsibility for reading instruction. "That's the English teacher's job" is an all-too-common refrain; in reality, secondary English teachers receive no more formal preparation to teach reading than do teachers of any other subject area.

Nonetheless, well-trained and highly motivated subject area teachers *can* deliver the necessary *reading-to-learn* instruction for group one (students reading at or above grade level) and group two (below-grade-level readers). Furthermore, they can deliver it within the context of their classes without abandoning their primary responsibility, which is teaching the concepts and processes of the core curriculum. Although group three (beginning readers) will benefit from the *reading-to-learn* instruction delivered by these teachers (primarily by gaining greater access to concepts and processes), these students will not receive enough direct reading instruction in their academic classes alone to read independently in academic settings. For teachers to better

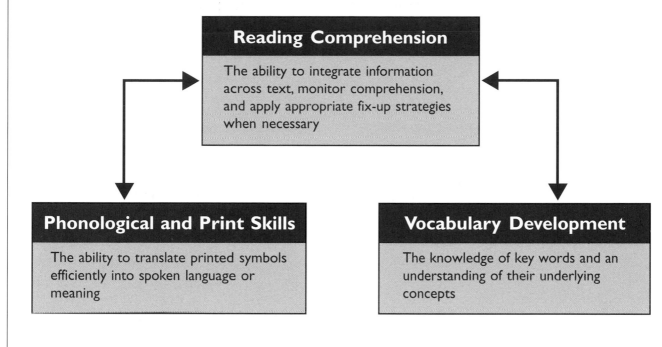

Conceptual Framework for Literacy Development

Reading Comprehension

The ability to integrate information across text, monitor comprehension, and apply appropriate fix-up strategies when necessary

Phonological and Print Skills

The ability to translate printed symbols efficiently into spoken language or meaning

Vocabulary Development

The knowledge of key words and an understanding of their underlying concepts

Figure 3

Source: Rebecca Barr, Marilyn W. Sadow, and Camille L. Z. Blachowicz, *Reading Diagnosis for Teachers: An Instructional Approach.* Copyright 1990. Adapted by permission of Addison-Wesley Educational Publishers Inc.

understand why, they must consider the components of reading.

Conceptual Framework for Literacy Development

The "Conceptual Framework for Literacy Development" (figure 3), adapted from a book by Barr and others, depicts three components of reading ability: phonological and print skills, vocabulary development, and reading comprehension.[8] *Phonological and print skills* refers to the ability to translate printed symbols efficiently into spoken language or meaning. This component, as defined by Barr and others, includes distinguishing phonemes within words, decoding, analyzing word structure, using context clues, being fluent, and being able to instantly recognize high-frequency words. *Vocabulary development* is the knowledge of key words and their underlying con-

cepts; *reading comprehension* refers to the ability to integrate information across one or more texts, monitor comprehension, and apply appropriate strategies when necessary. According to these authors, this framework "is applicable to all levels of skill, from initial reading acquisition to mature reading proficiency. That is, it is useful for understanding the strengths and weaknesses of a beginning reader as well as of a college student."[9] Thus, decisions on reading instruction for all student groups should be based on assessments of students' abilities in each of the components of reading.

Summary

Given the specialized nature of the reading components and the curriculum demands of the various subject areas, even well-trained and highly motivated teachers of academic subjects will be limited in what they can achieve with students reading significantly below grade level. Consequently, it is easy to understand why establishing reading classes or programs is becoming a high priority of middle school and high school administrators. At the same time acknowledging these limitations does not absolve teachers of their dual responsibility to provide content and literacy instruction for those students who may benefit from this approach. Instead, this reality underscores the need for resources (such as this book) for teachers working in grades four through twelve.

Notes

1. J. Campbell and others, *NAEP 1994 Reading Report Card for the Nation and the States.* Washington, D.C.: U.S. Department of Education, 1996.

2. *Learning to Read, Reading to Learn: Resource Guide.* Washington, D.C.: American Federation of Teachers, 1996.

3. Roger Farr and Robert Pritchard, "Assessment in the Content Areas: Solving the Assessment Puzzle," in *Content Area Reading and Learning: Instructional Strategies.* Edited by Diane Lapp, James Flood, and Nancy Farnan. Boston: Allyn and Bacon, 1994.

4. Campbell and others, *NAEP 1994 Reading Report Card.*

5. Robert de Beaugrande, "Learning to Read Versus Reading to Learn: A Discourse-Processing Approach," in *Learning and Comprehension of Text.* Edited by Heinz Mandl, Nancy L. Stein, and Tom Trabasso. Hillside, N.J.: Erlbaum, 1984, 159–91.

6. *Learning to Read, Reading to Learn.*

7. *Reading/Language Arts Framework for California Public Schools, Kindergarten Through Grade Twelve.* Sacramento: California Department of Education, 1999.

8. Rebecca Barr, Marilyn W. Sadow, and Camille L. Z. Blachowicz, *Reading Diagnosis for Teachers: An Instructional Approach* (Second edition). New York: Longman, 1990.

9. Ibid., p. 9.

INSTRUCTIONAL STRATEGIES

ART II PRESENTS 55 INSTRUCTIONAL STRATEGIES. SOME ARE TEACHER-constructed study guides, such as the anticipation guides; some are student-centered activities, such as the writing-reading workshop; others are long-term interventions, such as collaborative strategy instruction.

Organization

The strategies are organized into the following subsections: reading comprehension, vocabulary development, and phonological and print skills. Each strategy is defined and is presented in the following format:

- Goals
- Teacher preparation
- Instructional procedures
- Relevant *English–Language Arts Content Standards*
- Further resources

Embedded in the discussion of each strategy is a strategy index, which indicates the particular focus of the strategy in relation to the following categories:

- *Student Audience*: The three groups of reading levels discussed in detail in the subsection "Delivering Strategic Instruction" are *beginning readers* who are significantly below grade level, students reading *below grade level*, and students reading *at or above grade level*. Although many strategies can be adapted for use with all three audiences, some are best suited for one. For example, most of the print skill strategies are designed to be used with beginning readers, who demonstrate a specific need in a particular area such as phonemic awareness, and would not be appropriate for students in the other two groups.

- *Text Type*: Many strategies can be used with either literary or informational text. However, some were originally developed for use with a particular genre or type of text. The text type is indicated in the index.

- *Special Features*: This category refers to the particular emphasis of a strategy or to the various ways in which the strategy can engage students in learning. These ways include automaticity with print; prior knowledge and interest; discussion about texts; collaborative learning; writing emphasis; graphic representation; student control of reading process; and student ownership of strategy. Most of the strategies address more than one special feature.

Part II references each strategy to the *English–Language Arts Content Standards for California Public Schools* in two places. First, the broad *strand(s)* that each strategy addresses is shown on the strategy list at the beginning of each subsection (Reading Comprehension, page 23; Vocabulary Development, page 113; and Phonological and Print Skills, page 137).

Second, the description of each strategy identifies the strands and specific standards addressed in the content standards. For example, in the LINK strategy (page 118) the following *strand* is addressed:

Grades One Through Twelve: Reading Comprehension

2.0   Students read and understand grade-level-appropriate material.

The specific *standard* that the LINK strategy addresses is as follows:

Grade Four: Reading Comprehension

2.3   [Students] make and confirm predictions about text by using prior knowledge and ideas presented in text itself.

The strands (identified as 1.0, 2.0, and 3.0) are more general than the specific standards (identified as 1.1, 1.2, etc.) and typically cover more than one grade level.

Strategy Selection

The information in Part II about each strategy helps teachers to select the most appropriate one or a combination of strategies for use with the material they will be teaching. As described in *Strategic Teaching and Learning: Cognitive Instruction in the Content Areas* (1987),[1] this process should begin with a review of the content to be taught and proceed in the following manner:

- Establish content priorities in relation to students' prior knowledge of content.
- Consider organizational patterns in the text and students' experience in using organizational strategies.
- Decide the expected outcomes and tasks in light of larger instructional goals, standards, and assessments.
- Plan instructional strategies to activate prior knowledge.
- Check the vocabulary and text features.
- Plan the sequence of instruction.
- Evaluate student work to determine progress toward mastery of standards and reflect on ways to promote higher achievement.

Ultimately, each strategy must be viewed in context and adjusted to the particular needs of students. This process is particularly crucial for struggling readers representing a broad range of reading levels, as discussed in Part I.

In considering the strategies that may be useful to support beginning and below-grade-level readers, educators should take care not to think narrowly about the menu of offerings for those students. Some students will need strategies, such as those described under "Phonological and Print Skills" to help them decode fluently. Those same students also need the scaffolding, rich interactive discussions, practice with graphic organizers, and writing opportunities contained in the "Reading Comprehension" and "Vocabulary Development" sections. For some students the ideal may be a more comprehensive approach, such as tutoring as a high-impact intervention, collaborative strategy instruction, writing-reading workshop, or community-based reading and writing in which skills are developed in a supportive and integrated context. Teachers at the school should select strategies on the basis of ongoing assessments and close observations of student work.

Schoolwide Literacy Model

To make optimal use of this book, schools should establish a literacy team that will assume leadership by adopting a schoolwide literacy model. Leaders at a school site may wish to incorporate key ideas from Part I and select strategies from Part II in designing their own research- and standards-based models. A schoolwide model may encompass the following components:

- A content literacy focus incorporating the use of a core set of strategies from this book for reinforcement across the curriculum
- A standards-based English–language arts core (as illustrated in the *Reading/Language Arts Framework*)
- Appropriate interventions for beginning and below-grade-level readers
- Time for independent reading (The *English–Language Arts Content Standards* recommends students read one million words annually on their own by grade eight, two million words annually by grade twelve.)
- A well-stocked and staffed library-media center and collaboration with the library-media teacher

- Real-world uses of literacy in school, service-learning, environmental education, civic settings, community service, and the workplace
- Home/school/community partnerships in which student-owned strategies from this book are shared with parents and community tutors
- Professional development, coaching, and collegial study groups—especially critical for the more complex strategies in this book such as reciprocal teaching, reading-writing workshop, and tutoring as a high-impact intervention
- Evaluation of progress in light of the data on student performance

This book is intended to be a useful resource for educators endeavoring to ensure literacy for every student. For further discussion of schoolwide responsibilities and support for proficiency in the language arts, see Chapter 8 of the *Reading/Language Arts Framework.*

Notes

1. *Strategic Teaching and Learning: Cognitive Instruction in the Content Areas.* Edited by Beau Fly Jones, Anne Marie Palincsar, Donna Sederburg Ogle, and Eileen Glynn Carr. Alexandria, Va.: Association for Supervision and Curriculum Development, 1987.

Strategy List

Strategy	Strand		Page
Anticipation Guide	R 2.0		24
Character Quotations	R 3.0		26
Collaborative Strategy Instruction	R 1.0, 2.0		29
Community-Based Reading and Writing	R 3.0	W 1.0, 2.0	32
Directed Reading-Thinking Activity	R 2.0		35
Focused Dialectical and Interactive Journals	R 2.0, 3.0	W 2.0	36
Graphic Outlining	R 2.0		40
Guided Imagery	R 1.0, 2.0		43
Guided Reading	R 2.0, 3.0		45
"Just Right" Book Selection	R 2.0		48
KWL Plus	R 2.0	W 1.0	51
Learning Log	R 3.0	W 1.0	56
Literature Circles and Discussion Groups	R 2.0, 3.0		58
Paragraph Frames	R 2.0	W 1.0	61
PLAN	R 2.0	W 2.0	64
Problematic Situations	R 2.0		70
Proposition/Support Outlines	R 2.0	W 1.0	72
Question-Answer Relationships	R 2.0		74
Questioning the Author	R 2.0, 3.0		77
RAFT	R 2.0	W 1.0	81
Reading from Different Perspectives	R 2.0	W 1.0	84
Reciprocal Teaching	R 2.0		87
The Research Process	R 2.0	W 1.0, 2.0	89
Structured Discussions	R 2.0		91
Text Sets	R 2.0, 3.0		96
Think Aloud	R 2.0		97
Think Sheets	R 2.0	W 1.0, 2.0	99
Tutoring as a High-Impact Intervention	R 1.0, 2.0		102
Working Through Reading Stances	R 3.0	W 2.0	105
Writing-Reading Workshop	R 1.0, 2.0	W 2.0	108

Strands in the English–Language Arts Content Standards

Reading

1.0—Word Analysis, Fluency, and Systematic Vocabulary Development
2.0—Reading Comprehension (Focus on Informational Materials)
3.0—Literary Response and Analysis

Writing

1.0—Writing Strategies
2.0—Writing Applications (Genres and Their Characteristics)

Anticipation Guide

An anticipation guide is a series of teacher-generated statements about a topic that students respond to before reading about that topic. A prereading discussion of student responses to the statements elicits preconceived ideas that students have about the topic and encourages students to consider those ideas in relation to the information presented in the reading.

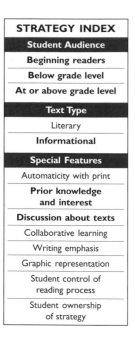

STRATEGY INDEX

Student Audience

Beginning readers

Below grade level

At or above grade level

Text Type

Literary

Informational

Special Features

Automaticity with print

Prior knowledge and interest

Discussion about texts

Collaborative learning

Writing emphasis

Graphic representation

Student control of reading process

Student ownership of strategy

Goals

1. Promote active, in-depth engagement with the reading selection by activating prior knowledge, establishing purposes for reading, and arousing student interest.

2. Encourage students to think critically about the concepts presented in the reading selection.

Teacher Preparation

1. Identify the major concepts that you want students to focus on in the selection.

2. Consider whether the major concepts are likely to support or challenge students' preconceived ideas.

3. Develop statements that may challenge students' thinking about the topic. The statements should also convey a sense of the major concepts students will encounter, activate and draw on students' prior knowledge, and be general rather than specific.

4. Arrange the statements in a format that requires students to respond either positively or negatively to each one.

Instructional Procedures

1. Distribute the anticipation guide to students prior to the reading.

2. Direct students to complete the guide individually and then discuss their responses in small groups.

3. Have students read the text material after sharing their responses.

4. Ask students to respond to the statements again, after reading, to determine whether their beliefs about the topic have changed.

Relevant English–Language Arts Content Standards

Grade Four: Reading Comprehension

2.3   Make and confirm predictions about text by using prior knowledge and ideas presented in the text itself.

2.4   Evaluate new information and hypotheses by testing them against known information.

Grade Five: Reading Comprehension

2.4   Draw inferences, conclusions, or generalizations about text and support them with textual evidence and prior knowledge.

Grade Six: Reading Comprehension

2.6   Determine the adequacy and appropriateness of the evidence for an author's conclusions.

Further Resources

Duffelmeyer, F. A. "Effective Anticipation Guide Statements for Learning from Expository Prose," *Journal of Reading*, Vol. 37 (March 1994), 452–57.

Anticipation Guide

Directions: Before reading the passage about weather, check the following statements that you think are true. Discuss your choices with your classmates and be ready to support your decisions. After reading the passage, validate your correct choices and check any others the author reports to be true.

YOU	AUTHOR	
T	T	Weather may be defined as cold or hot, dry or wet, stormy or calm, and cloudy or clear atmospheric conditions.
T	F	The combination of air, pressure, and water determines the weather.
T	T	The range in temperatures on the earth is caused by the tilt of the earth.
T	T	Heat on the earth is supplied by the sun.
F	F	Air rises when it is cooled and sinks when it is heated.
F	T	Wind blows away from ground level when a high-pressure area moves toward and pushes under a low-pressure area.
T	T	A nephoscope is used to measure the speed and direction of clouds; therefore, it also indicates the direction of the wind high above the earth.

Character Quotations

Character quotations is a strategy that uses representative quotations by a person as a means of developing greater insight into that person. It can be used to introduce characters in fictional literature or spark discussions about real individuals.

Goals

1. Introduce several important facets of a character's or individual's personality before students begin reading.
2. Involve students in predicting some of the major themes and issues of a story or selection.

Teacher Preparation

1. Preview the story, novel, or other reading selection to identify several quotations by a character that illustrate different traits of his or her personality. Select quotations that will encourage students to develop varying descriptions of what kind of person this character might be.
2. Write each quotation on a separate slip of paper or index card.

Instructional Procedures

1. Organize students into groups of about three to four individuals. Give each group a different quotation to consider. Each group is responsible for generating as many words or phrases as possible based on the quotation that might describe this character.
2. After each group has had sufficient time to generate descriptors, ask a member of each group to (1) read his or her quotation to the entire class; and (2) share the list of character qualities and traits that he or she associates with that character. At this time inform the students that all the quotations were uttered by the same individual. Write these qualities and

traits on the chalkboard or overhead transparency as presented by each group.

3. Involve the students in making some generalizations about the character or individual. The students work again in their cooperative groups to write a preliminary personality profile of this character by using the qualities and traits generated by the entire class. The summary should contain four or five statements that mention the qualities on the list.

4. The students are now ready to begin reading the story, novel, or other text assignment. After completing their reading, they can return to their personality profiles to discuss new qualities or traits they might add and possible changes to the profile to make it better match their understanding of the character. Students may select further quotations that provide new information about their character, or they could identify representative quotations that lead to understanding a second character or individual. In addition, students could explore character qualities in their journal writing and in further literary response-and-analysis activities.

Variation

1. Have students select a famous person from a particular historical period (e.g., Albert Einstein, Sojourner Truth, or Franklin Roosevelt).

2. Students research the person selected, focusing on the conditions under which he or she labored. Emphasize the importance of relevant background information, especially primary-source material such as speeches, letters, diaries, or quotations revealing character traits.

3. Students meet in groups and brainstorm questions to ask the character who will sit that day in the "seat of honor." If the character is a scientist, encourage students to bring relevant,

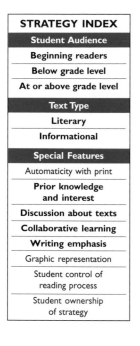

STRATEGY INDEX
Student Audience
Beginning readers
Below grade level
At or above grade level
Text Type
Literary
Informational
Special Features
Automaticity with print
Prior knowledge and interest
Discussion about texts
Collaborative learning
Writing emphasis
Graphic representation
Student control of reading process
Student ownership of strategy

scientific issues of interest into the questioning.

4. A student assumes the persona of the character and starts with a conversation about his or her life, reflecting what life was like for the person and the person's family.

5. As the selected character, the student answers questions from students in the class. Questions may focus on why a character did something or how he or she felt about an event.

6. The process continues until all students have taken a turn.

Relevant English–Language Arts Content Standards

Grade Three: Literary Response and Analysis

3.3 Determine what characters are like by what they say or do and by how the author or illustrator portrays them.

Note: Determining what characters are like by what they say is also central to the following standards in Literary Response and Analysis: grade four, 3.3; grade five, 3.3; grade six, 3.2; grade seven, 3.3; grade eight, 3.3; grades nine and ten, 3.3; grades eleven and twelve, 3.7.

Further Resources

Buehl, Doug. *Classroom Strategies for Interactive Learning.* Schofield: Wisconsin State Reading Association, 1995.

Character Quotations

The following quotations are spoken by a character in *The True Confessions of Charlotte Doyle,* by Avi:

"A sailor chooses the wind that takes the ship from a safe port. Ah, yes, but once you're aboard, as you have seen, winds have a mind of their own. Be careful, Charlotte, careful of the wind you choose."

Student-generated traits: Fatherly, wise, and worldly

"Charlotte, what I first told you when you come aboard? That you, a girl, and I, an old . . . man, were unique to the sea?"

Student-generated traits: Unique, insightful, and instructive

---

One-minute brainstorm: Zachariah is a sailor who befriends a girl named Charlotte. He is intelligent and has experienced many things in his lifetime. Zachariah is extremely brave and unique in his time.

Collaborative Strategy Instruction

Collaborative strategy instruction is an approach in which a teacher and students collaborate by discussing and evaluating strategies they use for understanding prose. It highlights collaboration, strategy combining, and reading as problem solving. This method was developed for adolescents in grades six through ten who were reading below a grade four level and was used successfully twice a week for three months (approximately 24 sessions of 40 minutes each).

Goals

1. Encourage active reading for improved understanding by helping students evaluate their existing strategies for understanding informational texts.
2. Change attitudes of poor readers who believe that any difficulty in reading reflects gross incompetence, and help them develop positive attitudes toward reading.

Teacher Preparation

1. Identify numerous and varied (more than 100) informational texts on a variety of subjects. If possible, select texts from sources that are used in real life, such as nonfiction magazines or workplace documents. Try to include topics that are interesting and familiar to students but also provide new information. Use somewhat challenging texts so that problems they encounter can be discussed during reading.
2. Plan to provide instruction in small groups of delayed readers (two to ten). Include students with a variety of reading problems and strengths.

Instructional Procedures

1. Open a conversation with students by defining the learning goal: to become a more active reader in order to understand the text better. Explain that the focus is on revealing and treating problems as objects of inquiry to be discussed and resolved by the group. Explain that the group will be reading aloud to make reading performance easier to analyze and make solutions to problems more obvious to the group. And point out that research shows that oral reading seems to increase reading comprehension for students reading difficult material.

2. Review with students the following format for a typical session:

   a. After receiving the text, students discuss what they already know about the topic.

   b. Students skim the text to get an idea of what it might be about and to look for potential problems.

   c. Students decide to discuss some difficult aspect of the text and save other aspects for discussion during reading.

   d. Students discuss what they might want to find out from reading the text.

   e. Students volunteer to read parts of the text while detecting difficulties in the text and generating strategies to understand it. Breaks in reading are recovered by periodic reviewing to ensure coherence and comprehension.

   f. After reading, students return to the ideas they expressed earlier on what they thought the text was about and what they wanted to find out. These ideas are compared with the information students discovered during reading.

   g. Students discuss new learning on the content of the text.

STRATEGY INDEX
Student Audience
Beginning readers
Below grade level
At or above grade level
Text Type
Literary
Informational
Special Features
Automaticity with print
Prior knowledge and interest
Discussion about texts
Collaborative learning
Writing emphasis
Graphic representation
Student control of reading process
Student ownership of strategy

h. Students discuss the problems they had and the strategies they tried. The focus is on what worked, what did not, and why. Students discuss what they learned about reading during the session that would help them to read other texts.

As instruction proceeds according to the format, build in the following processes flexibly, spontaneously, and repeatedly. Work through steps 3 and 4 first before starting intensive collaboration around reading strategies.

3. Inform students that recognizing and dealing with reading problems are characteristics of good readers rather than poor ones. Reveal a reading problem of your own and model the use of strategies to solve it. Continue this process until students begin to treat their problems openly as objects of inquiry to be discussed and resolved strategically and collaboratively by the group.

Example

T: We've got some big words in here! Are big words going to be a problem?

S1: No.

T: We've got to figure out some big words. We might have some difficulty. Should we give up because there are big words in here? Some of those words are longer than any I've ever seen.

S2: No.

T: Have we had any practice dealing with that? What do we do when we come to big words?

S3: We sound them out or we find some little words inside the big words. Then we put them together.

T: So it's not hopeless, is it? When we come to big words, we say, "Let's try to work it out."

S1: I had trouble understanding this part. There were too many ideas.

T: You had trouble understanding. It's good that you told us that. Which particular bit did you have trouble with? Maybe we can help you.

S1: The end, the last sentence: "The East Coast may be more dangerous than the West."

S2: I could read it back to him.

T: Good. How else could we help?

S3: You could try and give him a hint.

S4: Or you could explain it in other words.

4. Demonstrate cognitive empathy. Observe students' reactions carefully by looking for signs of thinking (furrowed brows, pauses, puzzled looks, etc.). Catch students in a moment of thinking about text and encourage students to make thoughts public by asking them questions; for example, "What's on your mind? You seem to be thinking about something—what are you trying to figure out? How are you going about it? How can we help?" Continue this process until students express cognitive empathy to each other; then the discussion about strategies can begin in earnest.

5. Draw out existing strategies used by students and help students judge the effectiveness of their strategies in light of the problems and texts at hand. Encourage students to explain what they are doing in their own words and inform them of more formal reading terminology, such as understanding importance, predicting, summarizing, and self-monitoring.

6. Encourage group members to reveal their strategies to each other so that alternatives can be considered.

Example

T: What are some of the strategies you can use to find out words that are a problem for you?

S1: Read to the end of the sentence.

T: All right. Read to the end of the sentence. What's another strategy?

S2: Break it up into little words.

T: Good. Anything else?

S3: Sound it out. And keep reading the entire sentence over again.

7. Model ways of solving reading problems by explaining what good readers would do to understand the text. For example, students faltered on the word "colonists" in the title of a text. Show them how to skim through a bit of text to see how many times the word appears as one way to gauge the importance of the word.

8. Model the abilities of good readers to combine strategies. For example, model the use of context in combination with rereading when encountering a difficult word. Provide students with easier alternatives for generating strategies as well. For example, if a student cannot summarize a passage to check understanding, suggest skimming back over the text to get the gist.

9. Encourage students to ask the kinds of questions that people might actually ask each other about text: What is it about? What do you find interesting? What is important about it?

Note: Principles for fostering active reading are as follows:

- Treat difficulties in reading openly as objects of inquiry among members of the group.
- Stress aspects and strategies of learning how to read (learning goals) throughout instruction rather than a mere understanding of the content of a particular text (task goals).
- Place emphasis on new learning rather than on what the students already know.
- Keep students informed of purposes, problems, and progress.

- Emphasize the process rather than the product—learning how to do something rather than simply getting the answers right.
- Try to maximize the ability of students to carry out all parts of the reading process independently. The reading that students should become competent in handling includes the mental activities that precede and follow reading as well as all the thinking and questioning that go on during active reading.

Relevant English–Language Arts Content Standards

Grades Four Through Six: Word Analysis, Fluency, and Systematic Vocabulary Development

1.1 [Students] read narrative and expository text aloud with grade-appropriate fluency and accuracy and with appropriate pacing, intonation, and expression.

Grades One Through Three: Reading Comprehension

2.0 Students read and understand grade-level-appropriate material. They draw upon a variety of comprehension strategies as needed (e.g., generating and responding to essential questions, making predictions, comparing information from several sources).

Grades Five Through Twelve: Reading Comprehension

2.0 Students read and understand grade-level-appropriate material.

Further Resources

Anderson, Valerie, and Marsha Roit. "Planning and Implementing Collaborative Strategy Instruction for Delayed Readers in Grades 6–10," *The Elementary School Journal*, Vol. 94 (November 1993), 121–37.

Teaching Reading: A Balanced, Comprehensive Approach to Teaching Reading in Prekindergarten Through Grade Three. Sacramento: California Department of Education, 1996.

Community-Based Reading and Writing

In this activity students are involved in writing a book for future students to use—a book that could be placed in their classrooms and school and community libraries. The stories grow from the students' own lives. Students collect, tell, tape-record, and eventually write stories they have heard or told, "stories from home." The book might include written versions of each story in more than one language, but first the students learn to tell the stories as skillfully as they might be told at home or on television. Literacy activities involve speaking, writing, and reading in English and students' home languages and polishing the prose into a form appropriate for publication.

Goals

1. Involve students in an extended literacy activity that calls upon their strengths—knowledge of their own culture, literature, and home language—and engages them in meaningful productions through which students gain higher literacy. (Avoid the all-too-common practice of providing English learners with a steady diet of short passages and fill-in exercises before providing them with contexts that permit them to use those skills in interesting and meaningful ways.)

2. Provide practice, encouragement, and support to students in using literacy strategies in their own reading and writing and in responding to others over extended periods, and show how these strategies make a difference in creating the kind of book they would want.

Teacher Preparation

1. Think of some folktales and stories shared by your own family members to tell students.

2. Locate tape recorders for student use, and plan small work groups.

3. Plan ways to provide access to folktales, stories, anthologies, and books that are appropriate to the cultural backgrounds of your students and that will accommodate their range of reading abilities.

4. Create handouts or posters of guidelines for students to use in reviewing their own stories and in editing other students' work (see "Guidelines for Reviewing Your Own and Others' Stories" on page 34).

Instructional Procedures

1. Teachers tell students folktales and stories from their own experiences.

2. Students are given the following instructions: Learn a story. Discuss favorite stories with people at home. They can be ones your grandmother or mother told when you were young or ones you have shared with friends. If you cannot find a story, make one up. If possible, practice the story with someone who told it or knows it to make sure you have "got it right."

   a. Tape-record the story for self-review.

   b. When you are ready, tell it to your group for feedback.

   c. Revise and retell it until you and others feel it sounds right.

   d. When you are ready, write it in the language of your choice.

   e. Get feedback from your group. Revise the story and get feedback as often as needed.

   f. Translate the story into another language if the opportunity exists.

   g. Polish both versions for publication.

STRATEGY INDEX
Student Audience
Beginning readers
Below grade level
At or above grade level
Text Type
Literary
Informational
Special Features
Automaticity with print
Prior knowledge and interest
Discussion about texts
Collaborative learning
Writing emphasis
Graphic representation
Student control of reading process
Student ownership of strategy

At each step remind students to do all they can on their own and to continually seek help and feedback when they think it might be useful. Over time, students work and rework their stories. Some may be revised as many as five times.

The ongoing writing activity is interspersed with reading selections, books, and stories from multiple sources and anthologies. Through this process students "live through" the literature, share their responses, take on multiple perspectives, and discuss their interpretations. They also distance themselves and reflect as critics, just as they do in their writing groups. Once final drafts are completed in both languages, photographs of each student are taken, and each student writes a brief biographical sketch for the book.

3. The activity culminates in a schoolwide fair for parents. Students display their stories and illustrations and tell the stories to passersby.

4. The stories are then published in a book or compiled in a final collection for use as literature and models for future classes.

For guidelines on educating English learners, see the guiding principles in *Educating English Learners for the Twenty-First Century* (1999).

Relevant English–Language Arts Content Standards

Grades One Through Twelve: Writing Strategies

1.0 Students progress through the stages of the writing process as needed.

Grades Five Through Twelve: Writing Applications

2.0 Student writing demonstrates a command of standard American English and the research, organizational, and drafting strategies outlined in Writing Standard 1.0.

Grades Four Through Twelve: Literary Response and Analysis

3.0 Students read and respond to historically or culturally significant works of literature that reflect and enhance their studies of history and social science.

Further Resources

Educating English Learners for the Twenty-First Century: The Report of the Proposition 227 Task Force. Sacramento: California Department of Education, 1999.

Langer, Judith A. "Literacy Acquisition through Literature," *Journal of Adolescent and Adult Literacy,* Vol. 40 (May 1997), 606–14.

Guidelines for Reviewing Your Own and Others' Stories

Content

1. Is there anything missing that needs to be added?

2. Is there anything confusing that needs to be made clear?

3. Is there anything said more than once that needs to be deleted?

4. Is there anything that needs to be developed more in order to understand it better?

5. What could be added to this story to make it more interesting?

Genre

1. What type of story is this? What could be changed or added to make it more like that kind of story? What needs to be changed to make it more like a *cuento de hadas* (fairy tale)? More like a *fábula* (fable)?

2. Are there any special ways to begin a piece of this kind? If you heard the story on the radio or read it in a book, what would be different?

3. What can you change to make it resemble the way your original source (e.g., your grandmother) would have told it? Does anything need to be changed in the beginning, middle, or end? In the words you use? In the feeling or mood?

Presentation

1. What changes can be made in the words, sentences, or organization of the story to help a reader follow and understand it better?

2. What do you think needs to be checked before your story is ready for publication? Look at the spelling, punctuation, and layout. Make the changes you can, and mark anything you are unsure about so you can ask someone else.

Directed Reading-Thinking Activity

The directed reading-thinking activity (DRTA) is a framework for instruction that parallels the active reading process by providing a scaffold of how proficient readers ask questions of a text and predict what will happen next.

Goals

1. Encourage students to read actively by predicting, reading to gather information, and reconsidering their original predictions.
2. Connect prior knowledge with new information by providing a reader-generated bridge between previously learned and new information.

Teacher Preparation

1. Select a passage that will encourage students to make predictions. Texts on topics familiar to the students but that they have not read allow students to make predictions without becoming frustrated. DRTA is most commonly used with literary texts, although informational texts can be used when the content and structure lend themselves to making predictions.
2. Read the text prior to teaching the lesson to identify the best stopping points for reconsidering previous predictions and making new ones.

Instructional Procedures

1. Present the topic or title to the students and ask them to make predictions about what they expect to find in the passage.
2. Read the passage while the students follow their own copies, or have the students read the text silently. Stop at the predetermined points and ask students to summarize what has been read. This step reinforces comprehension and helps students generate more meaningful predictions.
3. Ask students to consider previous predictions and make new ones.
4. Ask students to provide reasons for each decision, citing supporting evidence from the text when appropriate.
5. Check for comprehension after the reading and predicting have been completed. A follow-up writing activity in which students are asked to prepare a visual map to pull together and organize what they remember is one alternative.

Relevant English–Language Arts Content Standards

Grade Four: Reading Comprehension

2.3. Make and confirm predictions about text by using prior knowledge and ideas presented in the text itself, including illustrations, titles, topic sentences, important words, and foreshadowing clues.

Grade Five: Reading Comprehension

2.4. Draw inferences, conclusions, or generalizations about text and support them with textual evidence and prior knowledge.

Further Resources

Manzo, Anthony V., and Ula C. Manzo, *Content Area Literacy: Interactive Teaching for Active Learning* (Second edition). Columbus, Ohio: Merrill, 1997.

Stauffer, Russell. *Directing Reading Maturity as a Cognitive Process.* New York: Harper & Row, 1968.

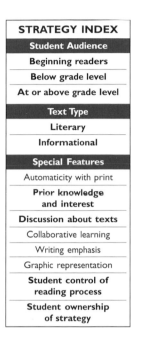

STRATEGY INDEX
Student Audience
Beginning readers
Below grade level
At or above grade level
Text Type
Literary
Informational
Special Features
Automaticity with print
Prior knowledge and interest
Discussion about texts
Collaborative learning
Writing emphasis
Graphic representation
Student control of reading process
Student ownership of strategy

Focused Dialectical and Interactive Journals

The focused dialectical journal is a way for students to become meaningfully engaged with literature as they critically examine the text. In this process students generate a dialogue with themselves, the characters, and even the author of the text by asking questions, making observations, forming associations, seeing patterns, and creating hypotheses about situations, events, and characters. It also enables students to acquire the language of literary criticism and to develop their own thesis statements for their written compositions in response to the literary selection.

Interactive journal writing is a strategy that encourages students to take notes primarily on informational texts or lectures and to add their own reflections in response to prompts.

Goal of Focused Dialectical Journals

Help students develop a sense of voice when writing about literature; gain understanding of the structural features of literature; and acquire the language of literary analysis.

Goal of Interactive Journals

Help students explore ideas, note their responses, and take risks in giving opinions about their reading as they comprehend and learn new information.

Teacher Preparation

1. For focused dialectical journals, select a novel, short story, poem, or play for students to read, identifying key elements for instruction in literary analysis.
2. For interactive journal writing, identify the reading selection(s) for students to read and the format for writing that best matches the targeted instructional objectives.

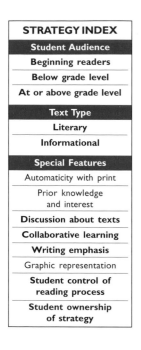

STRATEGY INDEX

Student Audience
Beginning readers
Below grade level
At or above grade level

Text Type
Literary
Informational

Special Features
Automaticity with print
Prior knowledge and interest
Discussion about texts
Collaborative learning
Writing emphasis
Graphic representation
Student control of reading process
Student ownership of strategy

Instructional Procedures

1. As students read, they keep a double-column or split-page journal. On the left-hand side, they write down particular words, passages, lines, quotations—anything from the text that they find interesting. These may be passages that they question, find particularly beautiful or distressing, or wonder about. The passages may be ones in which students note a relationship between the passage and some other passage or text they have read or just relate to their own background experiences.

   On the left-hand side of a page, students also note the exact locations of the passage (e.g., page numbers, line numbers, act and scene). Longer passages need only be referred to by the first few words. Noting the location of the passage will help others locate it during the discussion phase and correctly quote the passage later on in their papers. Initially, the teacher models the process for the class and maintains an ongoing dialectical journal with the students.

2. On the right-hand side of the page, students react to each passage by giving an initial response or reason for selecting that particular passage. A response may be an emotional or intellectual reaction, a question or hypothesis, a possible interpretation, an insight, a judgment, a connection to something else they have read or experienced, or any form of personal interaction with the text. Their responses become a dialogue with the text. Students need to be encouraged to stretch their interaction with the text by including as many of the suggested forms of reaction as possible.

3. In groups of three or four, each student reads his or her passages and comments. Sometimes, students will disagree with one another about a certain passage, but this dialogue

leads to some critical literary thinking and always draws the students back to the text. The group as a whole must then agree on only one passage that the members think is the most important, most critical, or most enlightening of all those discussed in their group. They must be prepared to tell why that particular passage was chosen. Throughout this process students should be encouraged to make notes as they make new connections.

4. A spokesperson from each group discusses with the class that group's selection and the rationale for its selection. This step allows students to gather even more ideas and perspectives from their peers.

5. By now students have worked through a text by themselves, with a small group of peers, and with the class. Time is allotted for students to review their journals and notes. This reflective time is necessary for them to be able to discover their point of interest or thesis of choice for their paper. By this time students should be prepared to write essays in response to the literary selection.

6. After students have mastered the dialectical approach, the teacher focuses their attention on specific elements of text and directs students to include entries in their journals that exemplify particular literary elements. In this way students practice the elements of literary analysis in language that they can use later when they write in-class essays.

Note: Dialectical journals can also be structured to foster thinking and prewriting for other genres and contexts.

Variations

Double-entry journal. The student takes notes and adds personal reflections while reading informational text. Divide the paper into two columns. On the left, the student identifies a particular passage or quotation of significance in the reading. He or she records anything that is enlightening, enigmatic, stimulating, or disturbing. On the right, he or she responds, questions, elaborates, makes personal connections, evaluates, reflects, analyzes, or interprets.

Metacognition journal. Students analyze their own thought processes. Students divide the paper into two columns: one titled "What I Learned" and the other, "How I Came to Learn It." They record their thoughts in the columns.

Learning journal. Students interact with the reading selection by writing responses in the left-hand column, "Write to Learn," or in the right-hand column, "Write to Think." Entries in the left-hand column may be research notes, lecture notes, or vocabulary terms. Entries in the right-hand column are the student's response, interpretation, questions, or analysis of entries in the left-hand column.

Problem-solution journal. The student identifies a problem and suggests and explores possible solutions. Divide the paper into two columns: "Problems" and "Consequences of Failing to Resolve the Problem." Through writing, the student identifies a problem, brainstorms possible alternatives, chooses a probable solution, anticipates the obstacles, and proposes arguments.

Speculation about effects/prediction journal. Students examine events and speculate about the possible long-term effects of these events, the "What if." Students divide their papers into two columns: "What Happened" and "What Might/Should Happen as a Result."

Synthesis journal. The student reflects on a project, paper, or performance in light of background experiences and plans for personal application. Students divide the paper into three columns: "What I Did," "What I Learned," and "How I Can Use It."

Relevant English–Language Arts Content Standards

Grades Four Through Twelve: Reading Comprehension

2.0 Students read and understand grade-level-appropriate material.

Grades Five Through Eight: Literary Response and Analysis

3.0 Students read and respond to historically or culturally significant works of literature that reflect and enhance their studies of history and social science. They clarify the ideas and connect them to other literary works. The selections in *Recommended Readings in Literature, Kindergarten Through Grade Eight* illustrate the quality and complexity of the materials to be read by students.

Grades Five Through Eight: Writing Applications

2.0 Students write narrative, expository, persuasive, and descriptive texts of at least 500 to 700 words in each genre. Student writing demonstrates a command of standard American English and the research, organizational, and drafting strategies outlined in Writing Standard 1.0.

Grades Nine Through Twelve: Writing Applications

2.0 Students combine the rhetorical strategies of narration, exposition, persuasion, and description to produce texts of at least 1,500 words each. Student writing demonstrates a command of standard American English and the research, organizational, and drafting strategies outlined in Writing Standard 1.0.

Grades Nine Through Twelve: Literary Response and Analysis

3.0 Students read and respond to historically or culturally significant works of literature that reflect and enhance their studies of history and social science. They conduct in-depth analyses of recurrent patterns and themes. The selections in *Recommended Readings in Literature, Grades Nine Through Twelve* illustrate the quality and complexity of the materials to be read by students.

Further Resources

Berthoff, Ann E. *Forming, Thinking, Writing: The Composing Imagination*. Montclair, N.J.: Boynton Cook, 1982.

Farnan, Nancy, and Patricia R. Kelly. "Response-based Instruction at the Middle Level: When Student Engagement Is the Goal," *Middle School Journal* (September 1993), 46–49.

Kelly, Patricia K., and Nancy Farnan. "Promoting Critical Thinking Through Response Logs: A Reader-Response Approach with Fourth Graders." Edited by Jerry Zutell and Sandra McCormick. *Fortieth Yearbook of the National Reading Conference*. N.p., National Reading Conference, Inc., 1991.

Ollman, Hilda E. "Creating Higher Level Thinking with Reading Response," *Journal of Adolescent and Adult Literacy* (April 1996), 576–81.

Sonnenburg, Edie. "The Dialectical Journal and the Art of Literary Analysis," *California English* (September/October 1989), 8–9, 29.

Focused Dialectical Journal

King Richard II by William Shakespeare

BOLING: My body shall make good upon this earth or my divine soul answer it in heaven. Thou art a traitor and a miscreant.

MOWBRAY: Call him a slanderous coward and a villain.

BOLING: Mowbray hath received eight thousand nobles in name of lendings for our highness' soldiers. The which he hath detained for land employments.

MOWBRAY: Through the false passage of thy throat, thou liest.

KING RICHARD: Forget, forgive; conclude and be agreed; our doctors say this is no month to bleed.

MOWBRAY: O dark dishonor's use thou shalt not have. I am disgraced, impeached and baffled here. Mine honor is my life.

BOLING: The slavish motive of recanting fear and spit it bleeding in his high disgrace, where shame doth harbor, even in Mowbray's face.

KING RICHARD: Since we cannot do to make you friends, be ready as your lives shall answer it.

I understand that Shakespeare is writing in the English of his age; however, when I read it over again it becomes easy to understand. Shakespeare is showing the discontent between Boling and Mowbray. Boling makes a religious proclamation of his truth as he accuses Mowbray.

Shakespeare shows that both characters are at odds and that their differences will not be easily resolved.

Shakespeare shows that King Richard has no stomach for the fight and wants a peaceful resolution.

Both Mowbray and Boling speak about being disgraced by each other's words and the king's inability to take a hard stand. They both decide that only through violence will victory triumph. Shakespeare shows the strength and commonality of the characters through conflict.

Graphic Outlining

Graphic outlining is a method of representing information from a text so that the organizational pattern of the text is highlighted. It helps students understand what they read by leading them to predict and organize information they encounter.

Goals

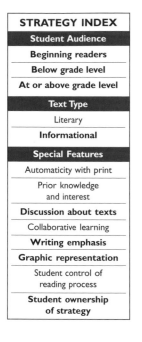

1. Guide the student's comprehension process by creating graphic representations of the text (e.g., clusters or concept maps, such as a flow chart).

2. Help students recognize and use the organizational patterns inherent in informational texts (e.g., description, sequence, comparison, cause and effect, problem-solution).

Teacher Preparation

1. Introduce to the students the five organizational patterns of informational text.

2. Identify a section of text that clearly follows one of the five organizational patterns.

Instructional Procedures

1. Have students survey the text passage by examining the title and headings, looking for clues to the organizational pattern used by the author.

2. Ask questions that focus on the differences between the different patterns. For instance, does the author describe a cause-and-effect relationship? Are two or more concepts being compared?

3. Guide students to make predictions about the text's basic structure. When they think they have begun to develop a relatively clear sense of the pattern being used, ask them to make a graphic representation of the pattern.

4. Direct students to check their graphic outline as they continue reading to see whether it picks up the important ideas in the text selection and shows the relationship among those ideas. Students should also be looking for ideas that are not yet represented in their outline. Add subtopics to the outline as needed.

5. Model the process for completing the graphic outlines, and provide students with samples of the various patterns.

6. Guide students through the process of using their outlines to write a summary of the selection.

Variations

Bubble map. The map may be useful for stimulating students' ideas about a given topic. When asked to describe a topic or idea studied, students jot down associated words and draw a bubble around words, clustering them in some kind of order. Students may use the map for a prewrite, generate ideas before writing in journals, or review for a test.

Double bubble map. The map may be used for drawing comparisons. Students note the qualities that are unique in the outer parts of two overlapping circles. Attributes common to both things are listed in the middle. This technique helps students to distinguish common qualities from unique qualities before writing about or discussing a topic.

Flow chart. The chart is useful for helping students organize a series of items or thoughts in a logical order. Students write major stages of the sequence in large rectangles and substages in smaller rectangles under the larger rectangles.

Cause-and-effect chart. The chart is an aid for students to learn cause-effect reasoning. In the center of a sheet of paper, write the topic (the focus of the lesson). On the left-hand side, write the apparent causes of the topic. On the right-hand side, write the apparent effects of the topic.

STRATEGY INDEX
Student Audience
Beginning readers
Below grade level
At or above grade level
Text Type
Literary
Informational
Special Features
Automaticity with print
Prior knowledge and interest
Discussion about texts
Collaborative learning
Writing emphasis
Graphic representation
Student control of reading process
Student ownership of strategy

Supporting idea chart. The chart helps students become aware of the relationship between a whole thing (structure) and its parts. Write the idea on a single line to the left. On the next set of lines to the right, write the major parts of the idea. Finally, fill in the subparts on lines that branch off the major parts of the idea.

Relevant English–Language Arts Content Standards

Grade Four: Reading Comprehension

2.1   [Students] identify structural patterns found in informational text (e.g., compare and contrast, cause and effect, sequential or chronological order, proposition and support) to strengthen comprehension.

Grades Five Through Eight: Reading Comprehension

2.0   Students read and understand grade-level-appropriate material. They describe and connect the essential ideas, arguments, and perspectives of text by using their knowledge of text structure, organization, and purpose.

Grade Six: Reading Comprehension

2.4   [Students] clarify an understanding of texts by creating outlines, logical notes, summaries, or reports.

Further Resources

Cook, Doris. *Strategic Learning in the Content Areas.* Madison: Wisconsin Department of Public Instruction, 1989.

Example of Graphic Outlining

Descriptive

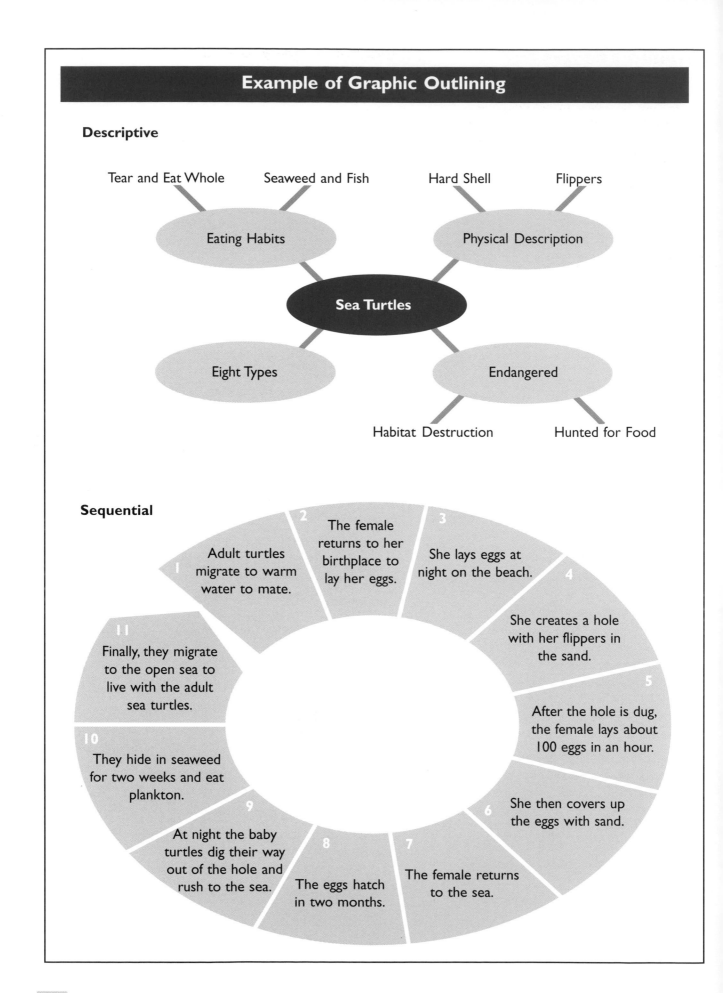

Tear and Eat Whole   Seaweed and Fish   Hard Shell   Flippers

Eating Habits   Physical Description

Sea Turtles

Eight Types   Endangered

Habitat Destruction   Hunted for Food

Sequential

1. Adult turtles migrate to warm water to mate.
2. The female returns to her birthplace to lay her eggs.
3. She lays eggs at night on the beach.
4. She creates a hole with her flippers in the sand.
5. After the hole is dug, the female lays about 100 eggs in an hour.
6. She then covers up the eggs with sand.
7. The female returns to the sea.
8. The eggs hatch in two months.
9. At night the baby turtles dig their way out of the hole and rush to the sea.
10. They hide in seaweed for two weeks and eat plankton.
11. Finally, they migrate to the open sea to live with the adult sea turtles.

Guided Imagery

Guided imagery is a technique that helps students create mental images in response to what they read or hear. Guided imagery may be teacher-directed or self-directed, depending on the extent to which students require teacher modeling and prompting to trigger visualization.

Goals

1. Encourage students to generate images of ideas and concepts while reading.
2. Increase student engagement with the reading material.

Teacher Preparation

1. Identify an important concept or understanding that you want students to learn.
2. Develop an analogy that depicts the concept if it is appropriate to the content. For example, the behavior of ants may be compared to that of people in a city.
3. Develop a script that appeals to the five senses and uses the analogy. Multisensory statements increase the vividness of the experience for students by evoking a variety of senses. For example, suppose you have been turned into a worker ant and have entered a colony of ants. The script continues and helps students create mental images of ant behavior.
4. Determine whether the script would be best used as a *prereading* or *postreading* activity. A *prereading* script is most appropriate for reading selections in which a concept or experience that is familiar to the students is described; a *postreading* script works best when the students must read a passage to acquire some background knowledge about the experience or concept before they can successfully visualize something about it.
5. Preview the text and assess the accuracy and visual effectiveness of the illustrations.

Instructional Procedures

1. Prepare students for the guided imagery activity by asking them to describe what they visualize in response to a series of familiar, concrete concepts (such as a food, an animal, or a storm). Sharing what they have visualized with a partner will increase the willingness and ability of some students to become actively engaged in the activity.
2. Use an additional technique to facilitate the visualization process by asking students to preview the reading selection. By seeing the pictures and other visual elements contained in the reading, students are prompted to imagine what the text is about.
3. Ask students to close their eyes, relax as much as possible, and listen to you while you read your script. Suggest the image one sentence at a time. Repeating words and phrases and pausing periodically allow students the opportunity to develop and expand the images they are creating.
4. When you have finished your script, ask students to describe and explain their images. Ask students to tell what they see, hear, and feel. Focus on the similarities and differences between their images and the content of the reading selection.
5. Discuss and reinforce the ways in which creating these images can facilitate comprehension and retention of the concepts in the reading selection.

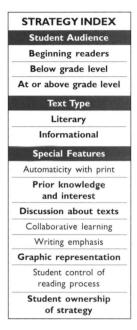

STRATEGY INDEX
Student Audience
Beginning readers
Below grade level
At or above grade level
Text Type
Literary
Informational
Special Features
Automaticity with print
Prior knowledge and interest
Discussion about texts
Collaborative learning
Writing emphasis
Graphic representation
Student control of reading process
Student ownership of strategy

Variation

1. Explain that a good way to improve understanding of what you read is to look carefully at the pictures in a story and then to make mental pictures about the things that you read.

2. If good illustrations accompany the text, direct students to look carefully at them before reading.

3. Tell students to visualize or make mental pictures as they read silently.

4. Have students talk about and then draw or write about the images, pictures, or other graphics they visualized during reading.

Relevant English–Language Arts Content Standards

Grade One: Reading Comprehension

2.6 [Students] relate prior knowledge to textual information.

Grade Four: Reading Comprehension

2.3 [Students] make and confirm predictions about text by using prior knowledge and ideas presented in the text itself, including illustrations, title, topic sentences, key words, and foreshadowing clues.

Grade Eight: Word Analysis, Fluency, and Systematic Vocabulary Development

1.1 [Students] analyze idioms, analogies, metaphors, and similes to infer the literal and figurative meanings of phrases.

Further Resources

Claggett, Fran, and Joan Brown. *Drawing Your Own Conclusions: Graphic Strategies for Reading, Writing, and Thinking.* Portsmouth, N.H.: Heinemann, 1992.

Gambrell, L. B., and P. B. Jawitz. "Mental Imagery, Text Illustrations, and Children's Story Comprehension and Recall," *Reading Research Quarterly* (July/August/September 1993), 264–76.

Rakes, Glenda C.; Thomas A. Rakes; and Lana J. Smith. "Using Visuals to Enhance Secondary Students' Reading Comprehension of Expository Texts," *Journal of Adolescent and Adult Literacy,* Vol. 39 (September 1995), 46.

Example of Guided Imagery Technique

You watch your mother wipe her dripping hands on her crisp white apron that hangs from her collar to the floor. You are going on a picnic and your mother has spent the morning baking. *Your mouth waters with the smell of baked ham and apple pie that fills the air.*

You take your best carriage to the hillside and join the crowds of *people that have formed a giant patchwork quilt with their blankets laid out.* The air is still; your shirt is damp and clings to your skin. Voices are filled with excitement. You have come to watch the defeat of the rebel South.

The valley below rings out in deafening gunfire as the smoke rises and burns your eyes. You strain to see through the smoke and try to breathe without coughing. You feel your stomach wrench and sour when the cries and moans of the wounded fill your ears. *Through the haze of clearing smoke, you see that General Jackson and his rebel soldiers have formed a human wall.* Fear and despair shake your being; you know that Bull Run will not be the last battlefield.

Guided Reading

Guided reading is a technique to guide students to deeper levels of thought by considering aspects of the author's craft, the relevance of the information, or the meaning of the text. It is a flexible approach that needs to be carefully adjusted to the reading competencies of students. It should be used intuitively and spontaneously to help students read beyond the superficial level and to assume control for considering, evaluating, and assimilating what they read.

Goals

1. Help students know how to apply the cognitive strategies of predicting, sampling, and confirming text and to regain control when meaning is lost.

2. Make students aware of how they can use the strategies noted above to cope with more complex challenges in the content and structure of the text.

3. Stimulate readers to ask more questions of themselves or of the text.

Teacher Preparation

1. Identify texts that will yield complex challenges, such as math, science, social studies texts, and many of the books students choose to read for their own pleasure and study. Guided reading works best, however, when students are asked to read materials at their instructional reading level (see step 10 on page 49 for definitions of reading levels).

2. Think of key questions to ask before, during, and after guided reading that show students how to go beyond the superficial and how to assume control for considering, evaluating, and assimilating what they read.

Instructional Procedures

1. When introducing a reading, ask questions that require students to consider aspects of the author's craft, the relevance of the information or its meaning, such as the following:

   a. How do you think the author will treat this topic (or theme)?

   b. Think about what you already know about the topic. What extra information are you seeking?

   c. What other books have you read by the same author? What comments do you have about the author's writing style or choice of topic? Do you expect this book to follow the author's usual style?

   d. What other books have you read about a similar topic? How does this one differ? Does the blurb or cover give any clues about how this book treats the topic? What about the table of contents or chapter headings? Did you get any clues from your first skimming of the text?

   e. What genre is this? What do you know about works of this kind?

   f. What kind of a book do you expect from looking at the cover?

   g. The title (or subtitle or blurb) indicates that this work is *(writing form)* text. Think about the way you expect the ideas or information to be presented. What are some of the conventions you expect to find?

2. While the reading is in progress, pose questions to help students clarify, amend, and confirm their purpose for the reading and their expectations of the text. The questions may engender some discussion about different understandings or viewpoints, but this should not cause students to lose sight of the meaning or diminish their interest in the text. Have the students do the following:

   a. Read until a change occurs in the plot.

   b. Read to the end of the episode. How did the ending add to your understanding?

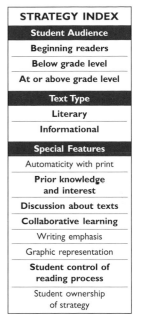

STRATEGY INDEX
Student Audience
Beginning readers
Below grade level
At or above grade level
Text Type
Literary
Informational
Special Features
Automaticity with print
Prior knowledge and interest
Discussion about texts
Collaborative learning
Writing emphasis
Graphic representation
Student control of reading process
Student ownership of strategy

c. Read until _____. Is this how you expected the story line to unfold (or the information to be presented)?

d. How did the text confirm, add to, or change what you already know about _____?

3. After this first reading, encourage students with further questions or prompts to reread the text and show them how to read with a more specific or different purpose in mind. For example, prompt students as follows:

   a. Read as though you were planning notes for an illustrator.

   b. Which character do you think you know the best? Why? Read the text again to see what else you can find out about that character.

   c. As you reread, consider which incident had the most impact on the story line.

   d. As you reread, think about the techniques the author uses to create a mood or tension; portray characters; and set the scene and the pace without long explanations.

   e. What do you think was the significance of _____?

   f. Reread the introduction and survey the glossary. Consider how much information you were given before you began reading. How did this influence your purpose for reading or the way you read?

4. After the reading, offer additional questions to encourage deeper levels of thought. Some questions should encourage further discussion about different perspectives or views; others should provoke further thought or reflection.

5. During a guided reading lesson, your role is to act as a group member by taking the following actions:

   a. Listen to the students' discussion to gain insight into how they perceive their world and themselves as both readers and users of language.

   b. Judge the most appropriate moments to intervene.

   c. Observe each student's contribution to the reading and to the discussion.

   d. Provide students an opportunity to assist and guide each other so that you can gain more insight into each student's competencies as a reader and as a group member.

   e. Involve students in responding to the contributions of their peers by highlighting either complementary or divergent points of view.

6. The focus should be on guiding students toward making informed decisions about the most appropriate paths to take through and beyond the text. When students seem unable to draw upon the appropriate resources within themselves or within the text, try to hint at some of the options and favor only one option above others when danger zones (being unable to maintain or regain meaning) are imminent.

Relevant English–Language Arts Content Standards

Grades One Through Twelve: Reading Comprehension

2.0   Students read and understand grade-level-appropriate material.

Grades One Through Four: Reading Comprehension

2.0   [Students] draw upon a variety of comprehension strategies as needed (e.g., generating and responding to essential questions, making predictions, comparing information from several sources).

Grade Six: Literary Response and Analysis

3.1   [Students] identify the forms of fiction and describe the major characteristics of each form.

Grade Seven: Reading Comprehension

2.1   [Students] understand and analyze the differences in structure and purpose between various categories of informational materials (e.g., textbooks, newspapers, instructional manuals, signs).

Further Resources

Mooney, Margaret. "Guided Reading Beyond the Primary Grades," *Teaching K–8* (September 1995), 75–77.

"Just Right" Book Selection

"Just right" book selection is a strategy for teaching students to become responsible for choosing books that achieve students' reading purposes and meet their needs for independent reading in and outside class. The approach involves discussion, modeling, guidelines for judging books, documentation, and conferencing.

Goals

1. Foster ownership of the reading process; build responsibility for making sound reading choices that enhance their own skills, knowledge, and reading enjoyment; and motivate students to enjoy books.

2. Enhance learning and growth in reading proficiency by ensuring there is a good match between the difficulty level of materials and individual student reading abilities.

3. Help faltering readers understand that even proficient readers encounter reading difficulty, and remove the stigma of reading easy books when they are needed for fluency practice.

Teacher Preparation

1. Schedule regular classroom time for independent reading and make decisions regarding independent reading as homework. Provide students with access to the school library or a changing classroom library with a rich diversity of books and materials.

2. Select books that are too easy, just right, and too hard for discussion and modeling. Prepare handouts or posters containing guidelines for choosing books (see "How to Choose Books").

Instructional Procedures

1. Introduce the concept that some books are too hard (challenge), some most appropriate (just right), and some too easy (vacation).

2. Identify each category of books by modeling with your own, such as saying:

    "A *too hard* book is one you'd really like to read—perhaps your older brother or sister has read it, or I have read it aloud to the class. But you know it's too difficult for you right now. That's okay. You can pull it out every once in a while to see if it's getting easier. If it is getting easier, what's happening to you? Right! You're getting to be a better reader! Sometimes it might be just a few months before you'll be able to read it better; but sometimes it might be years!"

3. Show students a book such as James Joyce's *Ulysses* (1934), explaining that it is a book many people read in college. Explain that the book is very difficult for you because there are many unfamiliar words and some very long sentences, and it is written in a unique style. Read aloud one page to show how difficult it is.

4. Explain *just right* books:

    "These are also books you want to read. A *just right* book is one that isn't too difficult—one or two words per page that you don't know. You can use this book to help you learn to read by practicing the strategies you've been learning. After you've learned to read it really well, then maybe you'll think of it as a *too easy* book."

5. Share a current *just right* book you are reading. Give a short summary, adding things you have learned by discussing the book with others. Read a short, interesting selection fluently and with obvious enjoyment.

6. Present *too easy* books:

   "*Too easy* books are old favorites. They're books you like to read for fun and for independent reading times. They're ones you might decide to pick up and read when you need a break from hard books, when you're feeling kind of low, or when you just need a 'good read.' Often it's a book you've read before or one you've practiced reading lots of times. It doesn't always have to be a story book; it can be a magazine, newspaper, joke book, comic book, or nonfiction book."

7. Display a favorite picture book and explain that you always have fun reading the book even though it is an easy one for you to read.

8. Teach students how to determine whether a book would be too difficult in terms of word identification by taking a sample of three or four pages of a book and counting the words you do not know. Together decide how to classify the book. Generally, a book is likely to be too difficult if there are more than five unknown words out of 50.

9. Help students determine whether a book would be too difficult. Tell them to ask themselves, "Do I *really* understand what is happening in this book?" Model reading a book with frustration and retelling the story with obvious confusion, showing that all readers can encounter difficulty.

10. Develop a set of guidelines based on careful observations of students' reading to help students judge the difficulty of a book. A book is said to be at a reader's *independent* level if 95 to 100 percent of the words can be read correctly; *instructional* level if 90 to 94 percent can be read correctly; and *frustration* level if 89 percent or below can be read correctly. Comprehension of different genres, author styles, text formats, and other strategies may be the key

for the three proficiency levels of readers in the upper grades for whom decoding is no longer an issue.

11. Encourage students to spend some time with books representing all three levels and most of their time with *just right* books.

12. Have students keep a form to record their selections, thus enabling you to monitor their ability to choose wisely. The form may include the date, level of difficulty of the book, title of the book/story, author, date of the book review submitted or book talk (talk about a book), and so on. The information may be used in student-teacher conferences to determine individual successes, difficulties, needs, and goals.

The guidelines below are intended for teachers to post on their bulletin boards.

How to Choose Books

Vacation Books

Ask yourself these questions. If all your answers are yes, this book is probably too easy for you. Have fun reading it!

1. Have you read it many times before?
2. Do you understand the story (text) very well?
3. Can you understand almost every word?
4. Can you read it smoothly?

Just Right Books

Ask yourself these questions. If all your answers are yes, this book is probably just right for you. Go ahead and learn from it!

1. Is this book new to you?
2. Do you understand some of the book?
3. Are there just a few words per page that you do not know?
4. Is your reading smooth in some places and choppy in others?
5. Can someone help you with this book? Who?

Challenge Books

Ask yourself these questions. If all your answers are yes, this book is probably too hard for you. Spend a little time with it now. Give it another try later (perhaps in a couple of months).

1. Are there more than a few words on a page you do not know?
2. Are you confused about what is happening in most of this book?
3. Does your reading sound quite choppy?

Relevant English–Language Arts Content Standards

Grades Five Through Twelve: Reading Comprehension

2.0 Students read and understand grade-level-appropriate material. . . . The selections in *Recommended Readings in Literature,* *Kindergarten Through Grade Eight* illustrate the quality and complexity of the materials to be read by students. In addition, . . . students read one million words annually on their own [and] by grade twelve, two million words annually on their own, including a wide variety of classic and contemporary literature, magazines, newspapers, and online information.

Further Resources

Ohlhausen, Marilyn M., and Mary Jepsen. "Lessons from Goldilocks: 'Somebody's Been Choosing My Books But I Can Make My Own Choices Now!'" *The New Advocate*, Vol. 5 (Winter 1992), 31–46.

Teaching Reading: A Balanced, Comprehensive Approach to Teaching Reading in Prekindergarten Through Grade Three. Sacramento: California Department of Education, 1996.

KWL Plus

KWL Plus is based on three principal components of KWL, a reading-thinking strategy that activates and builds on the student's prior knowledge and natural curiosity to learn more. KWL requires a reader to identify what is *known* about a particular subject *(K)*, what the reader *wants* to know *(W)*, and what is *learned* as a result of reading the text *(L)*. KWL Plus adds mapping (see page 54) and summarization to the original KWL strategy; these two tasks incorporate the powerful tools of restructuring of text and rewriting to help students process information. After learning KWL Plus under teacher direction, students implement it on their own while receiving corrective feedback until they can complete the task independently.

Goals

1. Engage students in an active reading process that demonstrates that reading means asking questions and thinking about ideas while reading.

2. Enhance students' proficiency in setting purposes for reading, gleaning information from texts, organizing that information into graphic outlines, and writing summaries based on those graphic outlines.

Teacher Preparation

1. Select an informational passage or article appropriate to the grade level and reading ability of your students. Note manageable segments within the text.

2. Prepare copies of the KWL work sheet for the class, and write the KWL grid on an overhead transparency or chalkboard.

Instructional Procedures

1. After listing the main topic of the selection at the top of the KWL grid, activate background knowledge through brainstorming what students know about the topic. Students note on their KWL work sheets what they think they know about the topic under *K* (what is known). They create a column titled "Categories of Information We Expect to Use."

2. Guide students in categorizing the information they have generated and anticipate categories of information they may find in the article. By awaking students' expectation at the outset, KWL enhances awareness of content and how it may be structured. Model the categorization process by thinking aloud while identifying categories and combining and classifying information.

3. Guide students in generating questions they want answered as they read. These questions become the basis for *W* (what students want to learn). Questions may be developed from information gleaned in the preceding discussion and from thinking of the major categories of anticipated information. This process helps students to define independently their purpose(s) for reading.

4. After a manageable segment (one or two paragraphs for struggling readers), have students interrupt their reading and pause to monitor their comprehension by checking for answers to questions listed in column *W*. This should help students become aware of what they have learned and what they have not comprehended. As students read and encounter new information, additional questions can be added to the *W* column.

5. As they read, students should note new information in the *L* portion of the work sheet. This helps them select important information from each paragraph, and it provides a basis for future reference and review.

6. After reading, students discuss what they learned from the passage. Questions developed before and

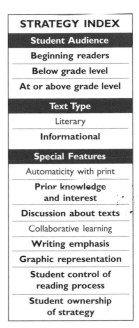

STRATEGY INDEX

Student Audience
Beginning readers
Below grade level
At or above grade level

Text Type
Literary
Informational

Special Features
Automaticity with print
Prior knowledge and interest
Discussion about texts
Collaborative learning
Writing emphasis
Graphic representation
Student control of reading process
Student ownership of strategy

during the reading should be reviewed to determine how they were resolved. If some questions have not been answered, students can be guided to seek further information in appropriate materials.

7. To produce a map or graphic outline of the text, students categorize the information listed under *L*. To do so, students ask themselves what each statement describes. Through listing and categorizing, the students accomplish the most difficult tasks of constructing a map: selecting and relating important information from the text. (See page 54, "Example of a Concept Map.")

   Students use the article title or topic as the center of their map. The categories on the KWL work sheet become the map's major concepts; explanatory details are supplied underneath. Lines show the relationship of the main topic to the categories.

8. Guide students in writing a summary of the material. The most difficult part of summarizing—selecting information and organizing it—has already been completed. Instruct students to use the map as an outline for their summary. Because the map depicts the organization of the information, a summary is comparatively easy to construct. The map's center will probably be the title of the summary. Then students should number the categories on the map as they see fit. Each category becomes the topic for a new paragraph. Finally, supporting details in each category are used to expand the paragraph or explain the main idea.

Relevant English–Language Arts Content Standards

Grade Six: Reading Comprehension

2.4 [Students] clarify an understanding of texts by creating outlines, logical notes, summaries, or reports.

Grades Five Through Eight: Writing Strategies

1.0 Students write clear, coherent, and focused essays.

Further Resources

Bryan, Jan. "K-W-W-L: Questioning the Known," *The Reading Teacher,* Vol. 7 (April 1998), 618–20.

Carr, E., and D. Ogle. "K-W-L Plus: A Strategy for Comprehension and Summarization," *Journal of Reading* (April 1987), 626–31.

Hanf, Marilyn B. "Mapping: A Technique in Translating Reading into Thinking," *Journal of Reading,* Vol. 14 (January 1971), 225–30, 270.

Ogle, Donna. "K-W-L: A Teaching Model That Develops Active Reading of Expository Text," *The Reading Teacher,* Vol. 39 (February 1986), 564–70.

Winograd, P. "Strategic Difficulties in Summarizing Texts," *Reading Research Quarterly,* Vol. 19 (Summer 1984), 404–25.

Blank KWL Chart

K What We Know	W What We Want to Learn	L What We Learned

Sample KWL Chart on Colonial America

K What We Know	W What We Want to Learn	L What We Learned
Earliest settlers came from Europe.	Why did they come?	They burned oil and candles for light. (T)
Slaves came from Africa.	What jobs did people do?	They were laborers in cities and shipyards. (O)
Most were farmers.	How did they light their homes?	Some came for religious and political freedoms. (R)
Livestock were used for transportation.	How did people heat their homes?	Some came as indentured servants. (R)
There was no electricity.	How did people cook?	Ships took tobacco back to Europe. (C)
Immigration started in the early 1600s.	What did settlers export?	Some people were specialized merchants, such as bankers, tailors, and barbers. (O)
People arrived by ship.	What connections did they have to the Old World?	They burned wood for cooking and heating. (T)
People did manual work.	Did people ever go back?	Sometimes people returned to Europe. (C)

Categories of Information We Expect to Use:

Level of Technology (T)

Reasons for Coming (R)

Occupations (O)

Connections to Old World (C)

Example of a Concept Map

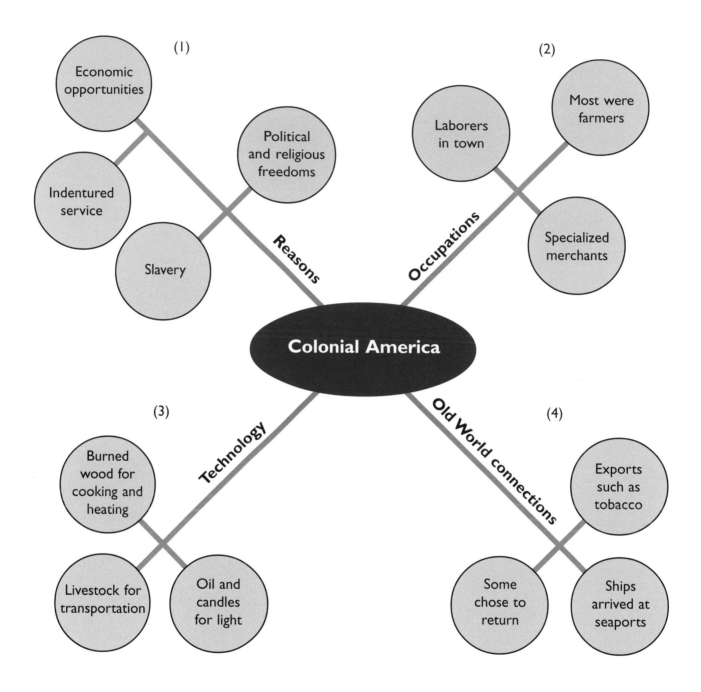

Example of Summary

Colonial America was settled by immigrants from Europe. Immigration started in the early 1600s. The earliest settlers included nobles and indentured servants from Europe and people brought as slaves from Africa. Some came for economic opportunities. Others came for political and religious freedoms. Indentured servants were contracted in service to others until they gained their freedom. The Africans were captured and forced into slavery and sent to America against their will.

Many people during this time were self-employed as farmers. In the northern colonies there were growing cities and shipbuilders who employed different kinds of laborers. There were also specialized merchants, such as bankers, tailors, and barbers, and many other tradesmen in towns and cities.

The level of technology in Colonial America was primitive compared with modern technology. Colonists used wood as fuel for cooking and heating their homes. They used livestock for transportation and plowing their fields. Candles and oil were used to light their homes because there was no electricity. Men and women worked with their hands to create products for everyday life.

There were connections between Colonial America and Europe, known as the Old World. Ships bringing goods and people to America landed at seaports along the coast. Some colonial exports, such as tobacco, were new to Europeans. Sometimes people returned to their life in Europe because life in the colonies was too rough. Slaves, people brought to America against their will, were not given the choice to leave; life was hardest for them.

Learning Log

A learning log is a written record of students' perceptions of how and what they are learning as well as a record of student growth and learning over time.

Goals

1. Increase students' awareness of their own learning process and progress.
2. Identify gaps in student learning.
3. Help students explore relationships between what they are learning and their past experiences.
4. Promote fluency and flexibility in student writing that can be transferred to other written assignments.
5. Provide a vehicle for student reflection and metacognition (learning about one's own learning).

Teacher Preparation

1. Decide whether it is necessary to provide specific prompts to students. Often, teachers need to offer suggestions when learning logs are first assigned; for example, what did (or didn't) I understand about the work we did in class today? At what point did I get confused? What did I do about it? How does what we studied relate to experiences I have had in the past?
2. Use an alternative to specific prompts by having students focus on either "process" entries or "reaction" entries. The former records *how* they have been learning, and the latter records *what* they have been learning. Students will need to record both types of entries.

Instructional Procedures

1. Explain the rationale for keeping a learning log. This activity will be particularly important in classes in which writing, especially reflective

writing, is not a regular part of the curriculum.
2. Allocate a specific amount of time for writing in the logs (suggestions range from five to 15 minutes per day) and, if possible, schedule it consistently. Many teachers find that the practice works best and comes most logically at the end of class. Others prefer to begin class with this activity when there is a quiet, reflective atmosphere.
3. Develop a system for responding to student entries. Quick, impressionistic responses are usually sufficient and need to be given regularly. Teachers should respond at least once a week.
4. Consider encouraging students to share their entries periodically in small groups. Such sharing may lead to discussions about the material and comparisons of different points of view.

Relevant English–Language Arts Content Standards

Grades Five Through Eight: Literary Response and Analysis

3.0   Students read and respond to historically or culturally significant works of literature that reflect and enhance their studies of history and social sciences. They clarify the ideas and connect them to other literary works. The selections in *Recommended Readings in Literature, Kindergarten Through Grade Eight* illustrate the quality and complexity of the materials to be read by students.

Grades One to Four: Writing Strategies

1.0   Students write clear and coherent sentences and paragraphs that develop a central idea.

Further Resources

Alvermann, Donna E., and Stephen F. Phelps. *Content Reading and Literacy: Succeeding in Today's Diverse Classrooms.* Needham Heights, Mass.: Allyn and Bacon, 1998.

Commander, Nannette E., and Brenda D. Smith. "Learning Logs: A Tool for Cognitive Monitoring," *Journal of Adolescent and Adult Literacy,* Vol. 39 (March 1996), 446–53.

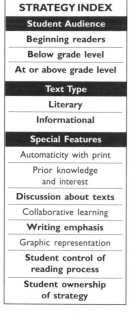

STRATEGY INDEX

Student Audience
Beginning readers
Below grade level
At or above grade level

Text Type
Literary
Informational

Special Features
Automaticity with print
Prior knowledge and interest
Discussion about texts
Collaborative learning
Writing emphasis
Graphic representation
Student control of reading process
Student ownership of strategy

Sample Learning Log

What I Did	How I Worked and Learned	What I Learned
I watched and listened to the history of tessellations and looked at some of M. C. Escher's artwork.	I wanted to try and create some tessellating artwork.	I have to learn some geometric basics in order to make the artwork.
I went on a walk with the class around the campus to look for tessellations. We made patterns out of leaves we found.	It was interesting to see tessellations in ordinary things like leaves.	I learned that tessellations are all around me in places I never thought of before and that not all patterns are tessellations.
We took notes on the definition and properties of a polygon. We made tessellations with pattern blocks and then on dot paper.	I enjoyed making tessellations with the pattern blocks and then making a tessellation on dot paper.	I learned that the word *polygon* means "many angles." I also found out that the corners are vertices and that polygons are named according to the number of sides they have. I also learned the Greek prefixes for the names.
I measured the angles of several different triangles and different polygons using tangram pieces and then together we discovered the formula for the sum of angles.	At first I was confused because I didn't understand how to use the tangrams to measure angles, but once I understood how to do it, it was interesting.	I learned that to find the sum of angles means to add up all the angles of the polygon. The sum of a triangle always adds up to 180 degrees; for a quadrilateral, the sum adds up to 360 degrees. The formula for finding the sum of angles is (n - 2) 180. To find the sum of angles of a hexagon, take the number of sides (6) and subtract 2, then multiply it by 180, which equals 720.
Today, we ripped the corners off many different triangles and placed them around a point. We measured the degrees that they filled around the point. Then we all made our own triangles and tessellated them.	I really liked this activity because I was amazed that all the triangle tessellations really worked. I thought that some triangles would not tessellate.	After all the different triangle tessellations were displayed, I noticed they all tessellated. I think they tessellated because one triangle's sum is 180 degrees, which fills up halfway around the point. Two triangles completely fill the space around the point with no gaps or overlaps, which would be 360 degrees. If they could all meet evenly around a point, then all triangles would tessellate.

Literature Circles and Discussion Groups

A literature circle emphasizes reading, discussing a topic in depth, and writing about unabridged, unexcerpted children's or adolescent literature. The approach emphasizes the importance of reading complete books, talking about books, giving students some choice in what they read, providing plenty of time to read, and ensuring that students read a great deal of high-quality literature throughout the school year.

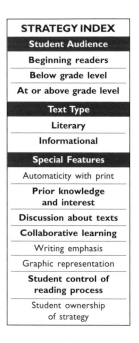

STRATEGY INDEX

Student Audience
Beginning readers
Below grade level
At or above grade level

Text Type
Literary
Informational

Special Features
Automaticity with print
Prior knowledge and interest
Discussion about texts
Collaborative learning
Writing emphasis
Graphic representation
Student control of reading process
Student ownership of strategy

Goals

1. Develop confident, engaged, and knowledgeable readers who read enthusiastically and with a critical stance.

2. Help students develop an appreciation for language and deeper understanding of the craft of writing.

Teacher Preparation

1. Every week (or as appropriate) make available six to eight copies of four or five books that will interest your students and generate discussion. Try to find unabridged, unexcerpted children's or adolescent literature.

2. Plan follow-up assignments related to each book that extend your students' understanding of the craft of writing and help them reflect seriously on ideas, issues, and themes suggested by each book.

Instructional Procedures

1. Every week, give a book talk and enthusiastically describe each of four or five books that will interest your students and generate discussion.

2. Tell students to select a book. If too many students want the same title, use a lottery system to decide who gets the book. Titles are usually available on more than one occasion; if students do not get the book of their choice for literature circles, they may always read it as outside reading.

3. Students are given large blocks of time in class to read (20 minutes at first, then up to one hour as they become comfortable reading for longer periods).

4. After a few days of independent reading, meet with each group for a 20- to 30-minute discussion so that the group can share its initial reactions to the book. The discussion may generate an assignment to extend students' understanding of the craft of writing. For example, after a discussion of Theodore Taylor's *The Cay* (1969), the group may be challenged to investigate how the author revealed changes in the young boy's character. Another assignment may ask the following question: "What does the author do to make you feel as though you're at the scene? Find clues to back up your answer."

5. Each student works on the assignment before returning to the literature circle for a second discussion session one or two days later. Although the first session is often devoted to personal, aesthetic responses to the literature, the second and sometimes subsequent sessions focus more on an analysis of literary elements, such as plot development, character development, or the role of the narrator. All members of the circle come with evidence to support their views. Differences are respected, but views must be supported. The role of the teacher is to skillfully guide the discussion and encourage students to talk with each other as well. (For ideas about extended activities and written assignments, see the Literary Response and Analysis strands for grades five through twelve in the *English–Language Arts Content Standards.*)

6. At the end of each discussion, the group briefly reflects on how the session proceeded. Then students evaluate their own and each other's contributions to the discussion. While one group is meeting with the teacher, the rest of the students are reading quietly, writing in their literature logs, or doing the assignment for a follow-up session. When books are finished, new groups form around new reading choices.

Variations

Variations of discussion groups, a strategy applicable to informational text, are as follows:

Think-pair-share. This simple technique promotes active learning. Students are encouraged to first write their ideas or thoughts about a topic, illustration, or text and then discuss them with a partner. Finally, the teacher asks students to share their responses with the class.

Write-draw-discuss. This technique encourages participation, allowing students to assimilate new information creatively. Students first write to clarify ideas and then create an illustration or drawing. Students share responses and drawings with a partner after several minutes. Finally, the teacher asks students to share responses and displays a few examples.

Fishbowl. This technique helps students understand basic discussion techniques, such as active listening, generating discussion from others' comments, and asking one another questions for clarification. A small group in an inner circle carries on a discussion while the students in the outer circle observe. During the discussion, ask the outside circle of observers to note how the group participants manage to keep the discussion going, get everyone involved, and build on one another's thinking. After the discussion, reverse the roles of students in the inner and outer circles and continue the discussion. Use this procedure frequently until students have mastered basic

processes and can conduct independent discussions for at least 15 to 20 minutes.

Jigsaw. This highly structured approach promotes learning by giving students the task of teaching. After students have finished reading a text, divide participants into home groups. Assign each person in each home group an "expert" number (for example, 1 through 5) and explain that these numbers correspond to important sections of material they have just read. Students meet in the "expert" groups (that correspond to the number they were assigned) to reread, discuss, and master a section of text and determine how best to teach the material to their home groups. Experts return to home groups, and each home group member teaches the content she or he learned in the expert group.

Relevant English–Language Arts Content Standards

Grades Four Through Twelve: Reading Comprehension

2.0 Students read and understand grade-level-appropriate material.

Grades Five Through Eight: Literary Response and Analysis

3.0 [Students] read and respond to historically or culturally significant works of literature that reflect and enhance their studies of history and social science. They clarify the ideas and connect them to other literary works. The selections in *Recommended Readings in Literature, Kindergarten Through Grade Eight* illustrate the quality and complexity of the materials to be read by students.

Grades Nine Through Twelve: Literary Response and Analysis

3.0 [Students] read and respond to historically or culturally significant works of literature that reflect and enhance their studies of history and social science. They conduct in-depth analyses of recurrent themes. The selections in *Recommended Literature, Grades Nine Through Twelve* illustrate the quality and complexity of the materials to be read by students.

Further Resources

Cornett, Claudia E. "Beyond Retelling the Plot: Student-led Discussions," *Teaching Reading,* Vol. 6 (March 1997), 527–28.

Daniels, Harvey. *Literature Circles: Voice and Choice in the Student-Centered Classroom.* York, Maine: Stenhouse Publishers, 1994.

Hill, Bonnie Campbell; Nancy J. Johnson; and Katherine L. Schlick Noe. *Literature Circles and Response.* Norwood, Mass.: Christopher-Gordon Publishers, 1995.

McMahon, Susan I., and others. *The Book Club Connection.* New York: Teachers College Press, Columbia University, 1997.

Samway, Katharine D., and others. "Reading the Skeleton, the Heart, and the Brain of a Book: Students' Perspectives on Literature Study Circles," *The Reading Teacher,* Vol. 45 (November 1991), 196–205.

The following is an example of an entry in a student log after a literature circle discussion:

Sample Student Activity

The author reveals the character of Sorry in "The Bomb," by Theodore Taylor, in several ways. First, the author's description of Sorry's family members and how they relate to him helped me develop an understanding of how he grew up and what role he must play in his family. Second, the author describes what Sorry plans on doing if the soldiers threaten his sister. His plan would be against the wishes of the village elders; however, he believes his role as the family patriarch is more important than following council wishes. Finally, as Sorry engages in dialogue with family members, the author shows me that Sorry's world and everything that is important to him is on Bikini Atoll. Sorry's beliefs as revealed through his conversations with others show me that he would do anything to protect his way of life.

Paragraph Frames

The use of paragraph frames helps students write more effectively about informational texts by providing a structure to help them put into their own words what they are reading and restructure that information into an appropriate written form.

Goals

1. Ease the transition from narrative to content area reading and writing and offer opportunities for students to write about the knowledge learned in content area reading.

2. Provide a structure that helps students write about their background knowledge and prompts them to go beyond merely copying what they have read, a common problem that typically occurs as a result of students' comprehension difficulties and limited background knowledge.

Teacher Preparation

1. Provide students with access to a school, public, or classroom library where they can read materials appropriate to their reading abilities and take notes about a given thematic curriculum unit.

2. Prepare a demonstration "Prior Knowledge + Revision Frame" and a "Prior Knowledge + Reaction Frame" (see page 63) on two pages of a flip chart and on overhead transparencies.

Instructional Procedures

1. Explain that all writing comes from a writer writing with a purpose in an appropriate form for an audience. Students should have a clear purpose in mind for both their reading and their written communication.

2. Have students collect pages of copied notes in their learning logs during their course of study. Invite them to talk about one thing that they found particularly interesting or that made them think in a new way.

3. Display on an overhead transparency the "Prior Knowledge + Revision Frame" and the "Prior Knowledge + Reaction Frame." Using the flip chart or transparency, show students how their information could be organized and written.

4. Teach them the words that signal connections and transitions between paragraphs. Ask students to select one of these frames to guide their own writing. Explain that the frames will help them put information in their own words.

5. Build students' confidence about adding to the frames, continuing the same pattern of connectives and phrases. Once this happens the frames may be used as prompts to encourage students to make independent decisions about their own learning.

6. Note that struggling writers may need several sessions during which the teacher writes their dictated sentences before students attempt their own writing. Begin with the "Prior Knowledge + Reaction Frame" to make them active users of the frames.

7. Use the frames over time to guide students in creating multiple-paragraph compositions.

Relevant English–Language Arts Content Standards

Grade Four: Writing Strategies

1.1 [Students] select a focus, an organizational structure, and a point of view based upon purpose, audience, length, and format requirements.

Grades Five Through Eight: Reading Comprehension

2.0 Students read and understand grade-level-appropriate material. They describe and connect the essential ideas, arguments, and perspectives of the text by using their knowledge of text structure, organization, and purpose.

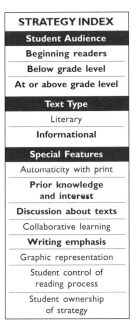

STRATEGY INDEX
Student Audience
Beginning readers
Below grade level
At or above grade level
Text Type
Literary
Informational
Special Features
Automaticity with print
Prior knowledge and interest
Discussion about texts
Collaborative learning
Writing emphasis
Graphic representation
Student control of reading process
Student ownership of strategy

Grades Five Through Eight: Writing Strategies

1.0 Students write clear, coherent, and focused essays. The writing exhibits students' awareness of the audience and purpose. Essays contain formal introductions, supporting evidence, and conclusions. Students progress through the stages of the writing process as needed.

Grade Six: Reading Comprehension

2.4 [Students] clarify an understanding of texts by creating outlines, logical notes, summaries, or reports.

Further Resources

Caerney, T. H. *Teaching Reading Comprehension*. N.p.: Open University Press, 1990.

Christensen, Francis, and Bonnie Jean Christensen. *Notes Toward a New Rhetoric: Nine Essays for Teachers* (Second edition). New York: Harper and Row, 1978.

Gray, James, and Robert Benson. *Sentence and Paragraph Modeling.* Berkeley: Bay Area Writing Project Publications, 1982.

Lewis, Maureen; David Wray; and Patricia Rospigliosi. ". . . And I want it in your own words," *The Reading Teacher,* Vol. 47 (April 1994), 528–36.

Sample

Prior Knowledge + Revision Frame

Before I began this topic I thought that the earthquake that struck San Francisco destroyed the city; however, I now know that the fires and broken water lines added to the destruction of the city.

I also learned that the magnitude of the earthquake measured more than 8 on the Richter scale and that the ground rolled like waves with upheavals that split streets open. The earthquake lasted only 50 seconds and occurred around 5:00 a.m.

Second, I learned that the city burned for three days and three nights and that the earthquake cracked gas pipes and split electric wires that added to the fires. The spread of the fires slowed with the change in wind direction, a condition that enabled the firefighters to pump water from the bay.

Finally, I learned that many people survived the earthquake but lost their homes and most of their belongings. They slept in tents in the park and went to relief stations for food and clothes. The President and people throughout the nation sent relief aid to San Francisco.

Sample

Prior Knowledge + Reaction Frame

Although I already knew that the earthquake caused fires, I now know that it also caused power outages that made the fire alarms ineffective. This problem added to the destruction.

I have learned some new facts. I learned that streets split open up to six feet wide and then closed again during the earthquake. At 5:02 a.m., the only people out on the streets were the police and the milk and fruit vendors.

I also learned that the military came into the city to help stop looters, locate and rescue people, and fight the fires. The Navy and Marines brought the long hoses needed to pump the water from the bay.

Other facts I learned were that people put up signs to tell family members that they had moved to refugee camps and the newspapers published names of found persons and their new locations.

However, the most interesting thing I learned was that people made up funny songs and signs during this disastrous time to make themselves and others feel better. They had lost everything, but they realized they still had the most precious thing—their lives.

PLAN

PLAN is a study-reading strategy consisting of four steps that students are taught to use before, during, and after reading: *Predict, Locate, Add,* and *Note.* Direct instruction and practice of PLAN will probably take up to 12 weeks or longer for younger (upper elementary) students.

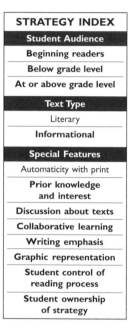

STRATEGY INDEX
Student Audience
Beginning readers
Below grade level
At or above grade level
Text Type
Literary
Informational
Special Features
Automaticity with print
Prior knowledge and interest
Discussion about texts
Collaborative learning
Writing emphasis
Graphic representation
Student control of reading process
Student ownership of strategy

Goals

1. Help students, especially those with reading difficulties, to become aware of reading as an active process and, ultimately, develop the ability to select an effective reading strategy for a particular study-reading task.

2. Help students learn to engage prior knowledge, recognize the structure of the text, monitor comprehension, and elaborate on text information through writing.

Teacher Preparation

1. Select, for the strategy awareness assessment, a chapter or passage representative of the more challenging material your students are expected to read and study in a content area at their grade level. The exact content, level of difficulty, and length will depend on the grade level and reading abilities of your students.

2. Preview the four PLAN strategies and select two one-page articles: one for teacher modeling and the other for the students' first practice. The article for modeling should be well-organized, with explicitly stated main ideas and helpful visual features. The article for student practice in small collaborative groups may be one that is more poorly organized, with implicit main ideas and misleading or no visual cues.

Instructional Procedures

1. Explain that there are two fundamental kinds of text: narrative and informational. Ask students to identify the strategies they already use for reading narrative text. Call attention to what they know about reading; compare and relate the informational text strategies they will be learning to what they already know about reading; and stimulate their thinking about their own reading and learning processes.

2. Ask students to read a chapter or passage for a test and to list the study and reading strategies they would probably use with this text. After the test, ask students to assess the effectiveness of those strategies.

3. Explain that PLAN is a study-reading strategy consisting of four steps to use before, during, and after reading: *Predict, Locate, Add,* and *Note.*

4. Guide students through the first step, which is to *Predict* the content and structure of the text prior to reading:

   - Engage students' prior knowledge through prompted journal writing and guided discussion.

   - Use a one-page article of well-organized text and model for students a method of creating a probable map or diagram of the author's ideas that shows the chapter title at the center and the subtitles, highlighted words, and information from the graphics as major and minor branches. (See "Example of Student's Map with the Predict Step.")

   - Have students work in small collaborative groups to create their own prediction maps based on a different one-page text and report back to the large group their success with the guided application.

- Instruct students to independently write a second journal entry describing their current understanding of the step.
- Have students apply the *Predict* step first to a practice text and then to a textbook.

5. Explain the second step of PLAN, which is to *Locate* known and unknown information on the map by placing check marks (✓) next to familiar concepts and question marks (?) by unfamiliar concepts. This step enables students to assess their prior knowledge related to the author's ideas while they preview the material.
   - Prompt students, through journal writing and guided discussion, to activate their own background knowledge.
   - Model the *Locate* step for students.
   - Have students work in small collaborative groups to locate known and unknown information on the map and report back to the large group their success with the guided application.
   - Instruct students to independently write a second journal entry describing their current understanding of the step.
   - Have students first apply the *Locate* step to a practice text and then to a textbook.

   Note: The *Locate* step also enables students to choose the speed and depth of their reading to accomplish the task. (See "Example of Student's Map with the Locate Step" on page 67.)

6. Explain the third step, *Add*, and demonstrate it as students read:
   - Engage students' understanding of fix-up strategies (such as rereading the section, using a dictionary or glossary, or dismissing the point on the prediction map as not important to the text's central message)

through prompted journal writing and guided discussion.
- Model step 3 by adding words to your map to explain concepts marked with question marks and to extend known concepts indicated with check marks.
- Have students work in small collaborative groups to add words or short phrases to their maps, clarifying and extending concepts.
- Instruct students to independently write a second journal entry describing their current understanding of the step.
- Have students apply the *Add* step first to a practice text and then to a textbook. (See "Example of Student's Map with the Add Step on page 68.")

7. Instruct students to *note* their new understanding after reading the text and use it to complete their task. Using a well-organized text, explain and model for students *Note*, the fourth and final step:
   - Use prompted journal writing and guided discussion to engage students' understanding of how they can improve their reading through writing.
   - Have students work in small collaborative groups to create a written product from the one-page text.
   - Instruct students to independently write a second journal entry describing their current understanding of the step.
   - Have students apply the *Note* step first to a practice text and then to an authentic textbook.

Initially, students may need to reconstruct their map if their predictions for the text pattern do not reflect the pattern of organization they found in the text. For example, if they had predicted a pattern of categorization, and the text is structured in a comparison/contrast pattern, students may change their map to a comparison/contrast chart or a Venn diagram.

Students may reproduce the map from memory if the task is to prepare for a recognition test, or they may write a summary if the task is to recall information for an essay test. Students may engage in a discussion or write an extended journal entry to extend their understanding. (See "Example of Student's Revised Map and Summary for the Note Step" on page 69.)

Later, as students come to understand the study-reading process in the PLAN strategy, they adapt to the text and to the assigned task. Although they still engage prior knowledge, recognize text structure, monitor comprehension, and elaborate on text information, they learn to plan for their study-reading, instead of mechanically performing the four steps.

Relevant English–Language Arts Content Standards

Grade Four: Reading Comprehension

2.1 Identify structural patterns found in informational text (e.g., compare and contrast, cause and effect, sequential or chronological order, proposition and support) to strengthen comprehension.

2.2 Use appropriate strategies when reading for different purposes (e.g., full comprehension, location of information, personal enjoyment).

2.3 Make and confirm predictions about text by using prior knowledge and ideas presented in the text itself, including illustrations, titles, topic sentences, important words, and foreshadowing clues.

PLAN strategies (engaging prior knowledge, recognizing text structure, monitoring comprehension, and elaborating on text information through writing) also directly address the following standards in the strand Reading Comprehension: grade five: 2.1, 2.2, 2.3, and 2.4; grade six: 2.2, 2.3, and 2.4; grade seven: 2.2, 2.3, and 2.4; grade eight: 2.2, 2.4, and 2.7; grades nine and ten: 2.1, 2.3, and 2.7; grades eleven and twelve: 2.2.

Grade Seven: Writing Applications

2.5 Write summaries of reading materials.

Further Resources

Caverly, David; Thomas F. Mandeville; and Sheila A. Nicholson. "PLAN: A Study-Reading Strategy for Informational Text," *Journal of Adolescent and Adult Literacy,* Vol. 39 (November 1995), 190–99.

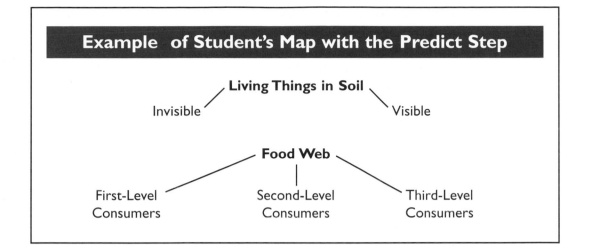

Example of Student's Map with the Predict Step

Living Things in Soil

Invisible   Visible

Food Web

First-Level   Second-Level   Third-Level
Consumers   Consumers   Consumers

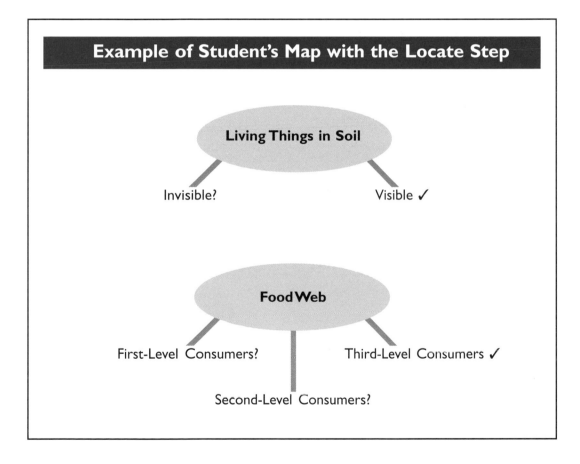

Example of Student's Map with the Locate Step

Living Things in Soil

Invisible?   Visible ✓

Food Web

First-Level Consumers?   Third-Level Consumers ✓

Second-Level Consumers?

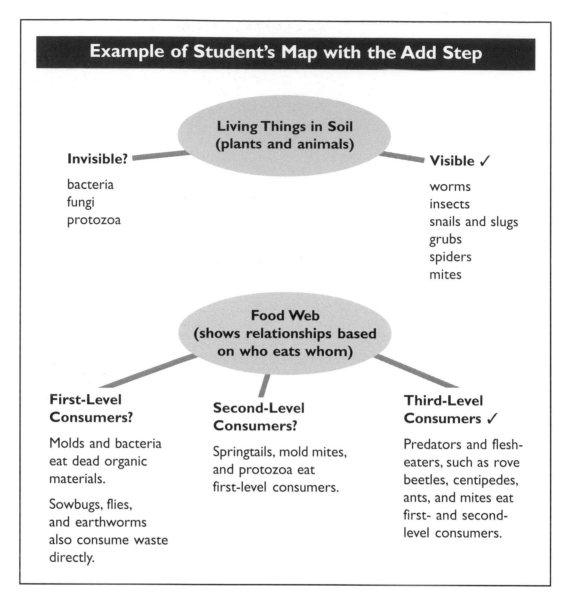

Example of Student's Map with the Add Step

Living Things in Soil (plants and animals)

Invisible?

bacteria
fungi
protozoa

Visible ✓

worms
insects
snails and slugs
grubs
spiders
mites

Food Web (shows relationships based on who eats whom)

First-Level Consumers?

Molds and bacteria eat dead organic materials.

Sowbugs, flies, and earthworms also consume waste directly.

Second-Level Consumers?

Springtails, mold mites, and protozoa eat first-level consumers.

Third-Level Consumers ✓

Predators and flesh-eaters, such as rove beetles, centipedes, ants, and mites eat first- and second-level consumers.

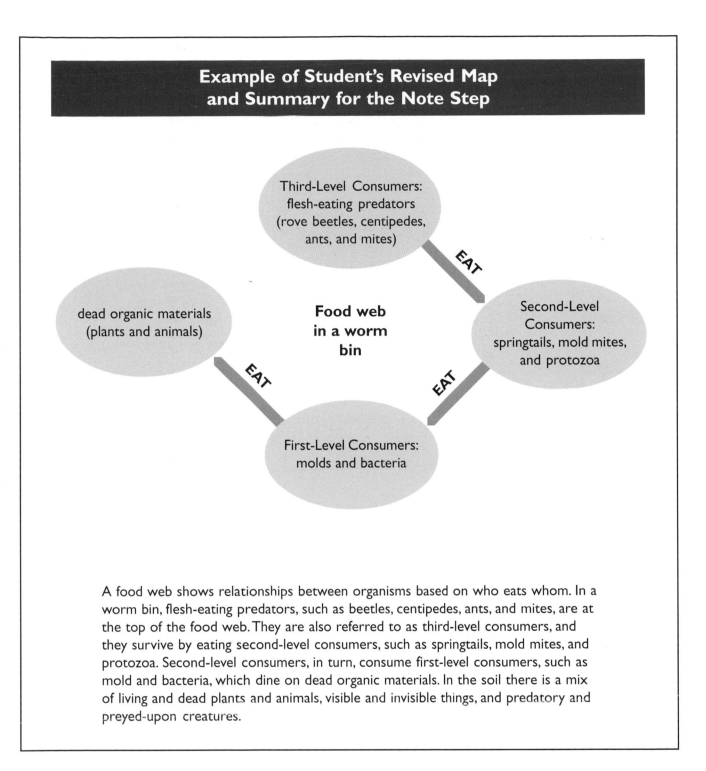

A food web shows relationships between organisms based on who eats whom. In a worm bin, flesh-eating predators, such as beetles, centipedes, ants, and mites, are at the top of the food web. They are also referred to as third-level consumers, and they survive by eating second-level consumers, such as springtails, mold mites, and protozoa. Second-level consumers, in turn, consume first-level consumers, such as mold and bacteria, which dine on dead organic materials. In the soil there is a mix of living and dead plants and animals, visible and invisible things, and predatory and preyed-upon creatures.

Problematic Situations

Problematic situations is a strategy that engages students in the process of considering possible solutions to a difficult situation that emerges in a reading selection.

Goals

1. Engage students in the reading selection by exciting their curiosity and increasing their motivation.
2. Activate prior knowledge students have about the situation or the factors that cause it.
3. Focus student attention on important elements of the reading selection.

Teacher Preparation

1. Examine the reading selection to see whether a problematic situation will logically emerge as students read the text.
2. After identifying a problematic situation, determine the background information about the situation that should be provided to the students.
3. Consider the way in which the context of the situation may be clearly defined for the students.

Instructional Procedures

1. Present the problematic situation to students in small groups and have them hypothesize about possible solutions and results.

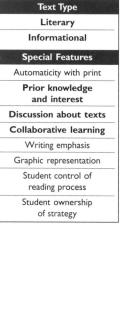

STRATEGY INDEX
Student Audience
Beginning readers
Below grade level
At or above grade level
Text Type
Literary
Informational
Special Features
Automaticity with print
Prior knowledge and interest
Discussion about texts
Collaborative learning
Writing emphasis
Graphic representation
Student control of reading process
Student ownership of strategy

2. List on a chalkboard each group's hypothesis if it is appropriate to the situation, and have each group rank all the possible solutions.
3. Have students read the selection to confirm or reject their original hypothesis. As students read, encourage them to revise or change their solutions as necessary.
4. Discuss the nature of and rationale for any modifications students make to their original solution.
5. Discuss whether some of the student options might be better solutions than those presented by the author.

Relevant English–Language Arts Content Standards

Grade Four: Reading Comprehension

2.3   Make and confirm predictions about text by using prior knowledge and ideas presented in the text itself, including illustrations, titles, topic sentences, important words, and foreshadowing clues.

2.4   Evaluate new information and hypotheses by testing them against known information and ideas.

Grade Six: Reading Comprehension

2.7   Make reasonable assertions about a text through accurate supporting citations.

Further Resources

Vacca, R., and J. Vacca. *Content Area Reading* (Fourth edition). New York: HarperCollins College Publishers, 1993.

Sample Problematic Situation

Although many communities have a recycling program in place, the number of people who make a conscious effort to recycle all possible recyclable products is minimal.

Possible Solutions and Consequences	Ranking
We will run out of containers and resources for products.	7
Some products that are rare will become very expensive.	6
The cost of trash pick-up will double or triple because landfill space will become limited.	3
Pollution will remain high or increase because of the amount of possible recyclable products that are being thrown away.	5
People should have to pay a fine if they are throwing away more than they are recycling.	2
Manufacturers should be required to minimize the amount of packaging they use for their products.	4
Manufacturers should receive governmental rewards for supporting recycling.	1

Proposition/Support Outlines

Proposition/support (or opinion/proof) outlining is an organizational system that teaches students how to support an argument with evidence. Students find this format useful for organizing information in reading assignments and for prewriting activities. Students may use proposition/support outlining before, during, or after reading.

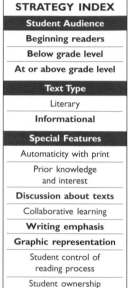
Goals

1. Provide students with a structure that helps them organize their thinking, writing, and classroom discussions.

2. Help students develop and use higher level thinking skills as appropriate in all content areas.

Teacher Preparation

1. Identify an appropriate reading selection for teaching the use of proposition/support outlines.

2. Decide whether students develop their own opinion and find evidence for support or whether you intend to give the student a statement to prove.

Instructional Procedures

1. Direct the students to divide their paper into two columns and label the columns "Proposition" and "Support" or "Opinion" and "Proof." Do the same on an overhead transparency or the chalkboard.

2. Have students read the assigned selection.

3. Model the strategy for students by developing a proposition or opinion statement based on the selection.

4. Show students how to support this statement with details from the selection. Add these details to the "Support" column on the overhead transparency or chalkboard.

5. Direct the students to develop their own proposition or opinion from the selection and find evidence in the selection to support it. Guide them on using the outlines as a framework.

6. Guide the students as they construct a summary paragraph based on the proposition statement and the details that support it. Eventually students may use their outlines to write longer position papers.

7. Guide the students in analyzing their summaries by using a checklist.

Relevant English–Language Arts Content Standards

Grades Five Through Twelve: Writing Strategies

1.0 Write clear, coherent, and focused essays. The writing exhibits the students' awareness of the audience and purpose. Essays contain formal introductions, supporting evidence, and conclusions. Students progress through the stages of the writing process as needed.

Grade Six: Reading Comprehension

2.6 Determine the adequacy and appropriateness of the evidence for an author's conclusions.

2.7 Make reasonable assertions about a text through accurate, supportive citations.

Grade Seven: Reading Comprehension

2.6 Assess the adequacy, accuracy, and appropriateness of the author's evidence to support claims and assertions, noting instances of bias and stereotyping.

Grade Eight: Reading Comprehension

2.7 Evaluate the unity, coherence, logic, internal consistency, and structural patterns of text.

Grades Nine and Ten: Reading Comprehension

2.8 Evaluate the credibility of an author's argument or defense of a claim.

Grades Eleven and Twelve: Reading Comprehension

2.6 Critique the power, validity, and truthfulness of arguments set forth in public documents; their appeal to both friendly and hostile audiences; and the extent to which the arguments anticipate and address reader concerns and counterclaims (e.g., appeal to reason, to authority, to pathos and emotion).

Further Resources

Buehl, Doug. *Classroom Strategies for Interactive Learning*. Schofield: Wisconsin State Reading Association, 1995.

Cook, Doris. *Strategic Learning in the Content Areas*. Madison: Wisconsin Department of Public Instruction, 1989.

Santa, Carol M. *Content Reading Including Secondary Systems*. Dubuque, Iowa: Kendall Hunt, 1988.

Sample Proposition/Support Outline

Proposition: Orcas, like Keiko, should be returned to the sea from captivity.

Support:

1. Facts about orcas
   - Killer whales, also called orcas, travel together in family groups.
   - Orcas live in all the oceans of the world.
   - They can eat 300 pounds of fish in one day.
   - Killer whales have a complex communication system.
   - Orcas can swim up to 40 miles per hour and cover large distances.

2. Statistics about Keiko
   - Keiko, an orca, was captured at age two in the North Atlantic.
   - Keiko has spent most of his life performing tricks for people.
   - He spent 11 years in a pool that was too small and too warm.
   - Keiko's pool should have been kept at 45 degrees to ensure health.

3. Reasons for returning orcas to the sea
   - Keiko's skin broke out in sores from his captivity in Mexico.
   - His dorsal fin flopped to one side instead of pointing straight up.
   - Keiko lost weight during his time in captivity.
   - A concrete pool is an unnatural habitat for orcas and can cause harm to them.

4. Expert authority
   - Marine biologists believed Keiko would survive the move.
   - They hope that Keiko may be able to hunt or communicate as do other killer whales.
   - The Free Willy Keiko Foundation has moved him to a natural pen in the North Atlantic near his birthplace.
   - Experts are working on providing him with the proper water temperature, food, and habitat.

5. Logic and reasoning
   - Keiko has been returned to the area where he was born; therefore, he may recognize the language of other orcas.
   - Each pod has its own system of noises and sounds; therefore, Keiko's family may recognize him.
   - Caretakers will continue to feed him as he learns the ways of wild whales.
   - The Free Willy Keiko Foundation is committed to caring for the orca as long as it takes to ensure his safe return to the sea.

Question-Answer Relationships

The question-answer relationship (QAR) strategy is based on a four-part system for classifying questions: *right there, think and search, author and you,* and *on your own*. Students learn to classify questions and locate answers, recognizing in the process that reading is influenced by the characteristics of the reader, the text, and the context.

Goals

1. Develop students' ability to recognize the relationship between a question and the location or source of possible answer locations (i.e., readers' background knowledge as well as information presented in a text).

2. Enhance students' performance in answering questions about content area materials.

Teacher Preparation

1. Select or prepare three passages based on familiar topics. Keep in mind the grade level and reading ability of your students when selecting passages.

2. Prepare at least one question for each passage from each of the four QAR categories.

Instructional Procedures

1. Introduce the concept of QAR categories, in reference to the first passage, by discussing with the class the questions, answers, categories, and reasons why the categories are appropriate.

2. Provide the students with the second passage and set of questions. They answer the questions while working in small groups, indicate the QAR categories, and justify their selections. Provide each group with immediate feedback on the accuracy and completeness of its explanations.

3. Give students the third passage and have them work in groups to prepare questions representing each QAR category. Groups then exchange questions, answer them, and evaluate the appropriateness of the questions in relation to the QAR categories they are supposed to represent.

4. Allow students to practice the QAR approach on progressively longer passages while increasing the number of questions asked.

Relevant English–Language Arts Contents Standards

Grade Four: Reading Comprehension

2.2 Use appropriate strategies when reading for different purposes (e.g., full comprehension, locating information, and personal enjoyment).

2.4 Evaluate new information and hypotheses by testing them against known information.

Further Resources

McIntosh, Margaret E., and Roni Jo Draper. "Applying the Question-Answer Relationship Strategy in Mathematics," *Journal of Adolescent and Adult Literacy,* Vol. 39 (October 1995), 120–31.

Raphael, T. E., and C. Wonnacott. "Heightening Fourth-Grade Students' Comprehension: Sources of Information for Answering Comprehension Questions," *Reading Research Quarterly,* Vol. 20 (Spring 1985), 282–96.

STRATEGY INDEX

Student Audience
Beginning readers
Below grade level
At or above grade level

Text Type
Literary
Informational

Special Features
Automaticity with print
Prior knowledge and interest
Discussion about texts
Collaborative learning
Writing emphasis
Graphic representation
Student control of reading process
Student ownership of strategy

Right There

The answer is explicitly stated in the text. The question asks for details that are *right there*.

Think and Search

The answer will require integrating information from different areas in the text. The question asks the reader to *think and search* for related information in more than one paragraph.

Author and You

The answer is a combination of information that the reader already knows and what the author states in the text. The question asks for information from the *author and you*.

On Your Own

The answer will come from the reader's own personal knowledge and experience. The question asks for an opinion or information from the reader.

Electricity

All matter is made up of atoms. Within each atom there is a nucleus, and this nucleus has tiny particles called electrons orbiting around it. Atoms with different atomic numbers have different numbers of electrons. When electrons break from their orbit and become free-flying, they form electricity. Rubbing objects against each other, also known as friction, is one way to free electrons.

The term *electricity* dates back to ancient Greece and the experiments of a man named Thales. Thales took an amber stone and rubbed it between his fingers. He noticed that the stone attracted threads from his clothes. In Greek the word *amber* is called *electron*.

1. Where are the charged particles called electrons found?

   Right There _____

   Think and Search _____

   Author and You _____

   On Your Own _____

2. What happened to the electrons in the amber stone that Thales used?

   Right There _____

   Think and Search _____

   Author and You _____

   On Your Own _____

3. Why does static electricity occur in newly carpeted rooms?

   Right There _____

   Think and Search _____

   Author and You _____

   On Your Own _____

4. Should Thales have taken more time and thought when he named this new energy source? Why?

   Right There _____

   Think and Search _____

   Author and You _____

   On Your Own _____

Questioning the Author

Questioning the author is an approach designed to engage students in the ideas of the text and build understanding.

Goals

1. Provide a concrete way for students to experience the key to successful comprehension: transforming an author's ideas into a reader's ideas.

2. Encourage students to judge the author's success in making ideas clear and admit to finding difficulties in the text without viewing themselves as failures.

3. Overcome students' tendency to resist grappling with text that does not come easily by stimulating young readers to become engaged with the text and consider ideas deeply.

Teacher Preparation

1. Identify a text to use for modeling the questioning-the-author strategy or prepare a copy of the sample text provided. The text should be representative of the content area textbooks students are expected to read and contain some vague or confusing language so that questioning the author can be modeled.

2. Prepare several passages from content area texts on a variety of topics to use for further applications of the questioning-the-author strategy.

Instructional Procedures

1. Remind students of the presence of an author of a textbook; tell them that textbooks are just someone's ideas written down. Explain that different people write things in different ways and that sometimes textbooks are not written as well or as clearly as they should be because what someone has in their mind to say does not always come through clearly in their writing. Because written text is the product of a fallible author, students may need to work to figure out what the ideas are behind an author's words.

2. Demonstrate an application of the questioning-the-author strategy to text. Ask your students to follow along as you read a brief text and model your interaction with it. An example follows:

A Russian Traveler

The day is Friday, October 4. The year is 1957. People in many parts of the earth turned on radios and heard strange news. "Russia has used rockets to put a new moon in the sky," said one station.

At this point in the text, express puzzlement over putting "a new moon in the sky." Read the next segment:

The tiny new moon is a metal ball. It has a radio in it. The radio goes "Beep! Beep! Beep!" as the moon travels along.

Express confusion over how a metal ball with a radio in it can be a moon. Continue reading:

The new moon is named Sputnik.

Explain that now you understand, because you remember that the first Russian satellite was named *Sputnik.* Mention that the author could have said that in a clearer way. Then read:

The ship is just big enough to carry a little dog. The ship sends out signals about the dog.

Say: "Oh! There is a dog on the spaceship! I thought they just meant that's what size it was—big enough for a dog!" Read on:

Everywhere people became interested in rockets and spaceships.

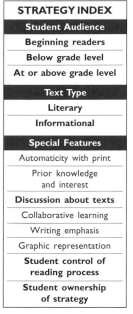

STRATEGY INDEX
Student Audience
Beginning readers
Below grade level
At or above grade level
Text Type
Literary
Informational
Special Features
Automaticity with print
Prior knowledge and interest
Discussion about texts
Collaborative learning
Writing emphasis
Graphic representation
Student control of reading process
Student ownership of strategy

Say: "That seems like a big jump from talking about the dog. I guess maybe the author is trying to connect the sentence with the beginning about people all over the world turning on their radios."

Culminate the discussion by making clear the analogy in a revised version of the text, as follows:

Russia has used rockets to put a satellite into space. The tiny satellite is shaped like a metal ball.

After introducing students to the strategy, proceed with several sessions presenting passages from content area texts on a variety of topics. The teacher's role is to guide the student through the text, making sense of the author's words by using prompts. A general procedure for continuing sessions follows in steps 3, 4, and 5.

3. Ask students to read the text and talk about the ideas the author is trying to get across and to judge whether the author has made those ideas clear. As students read, prompts are offered to keep the focus on seeking out and putting together the author's ideas:

   • What is the author trying to tell you?

   • Why is the author telling you that?

   • Is the message stated clearly?

   Examples of further queries developed to guide questioning-the-author discussions are provided on the following pages.

4. As students discover confusing problems in the text, prompt them to recast those ideas in clearer language:

   • How could the author have stated the ideas in a clearer way?

   • What would you want to say instead?

5. Keep the interaction going by reacting conversationally to the students, sometimes recapping what the students have said or reinforcing a student's point, saying, "You're right; that's not very clear, is it?" or "I think you've got something there." Foster interaction among students by asking a student to elaborate on another student's comment.

Relevant English–Language Arts Contents Standards

Grade Four: Reading Comprehension

2.4   Evaluate new information and hypotheses by testing them against known information and ideas.

Grade Five: Reading Comprehension

2.3   Discern main ideas and concepts presented in texts, identifying and assessing evidence that supports those ideas.

2.4   Draw inferences, conclusions, or generalizations about text and support them with textual evidence and prior knowledge

The questioning-the-author approach, if skillfully extended, would also address the Literary Response and Analysis standards (grades four through twelve) and the standards under Expository Critique (grades five through twelve).

Further Resources

Beck, Isabel L., and others. "Questioning the Author: A Yearlong Classroom Implementation to Engage Students with Text," *The Elementary School Journal,* Vol. 96 (March 1996), 4.

Beck, Isabel L., and others. *Questioning the Author.* Newark, Del.: International Reading Association, 1997.

McKeown, Margaret G.; Isabel L. Beck; and M. Jo Worthy. "Grappling with Text Ideas: Questioning the Author," *The Reading Teacher,* Vol. 46 (April 1993), 7.

Sample 1
Questioning the Author

Focusing Queries Developed for Informational Text

Goal	Queries
Initiate discussion.	What is the author trying to say?
	What is the author's message?
	What is the author talking about?
Help students focus on the author's message.	That's what the author says, but what does it mean?
Help students link information.	How does that connect with what the author already told us?
	What information has the author added here that connects to or fits in with _____?
Identify difficulties with the way the author has presented information or ideas.	Does that make sense?
	Is that said in a clear way?
	Did the author explain that clearly? Why or why not? What's missing? What do we need to figure out or find out?
Encourage students to refer to the text either to show them they have misinterpreted a text statement or to help them recognize that they have made an inference.	Did the author tell us that?
	Did the author give us the answer to that?

Sample 2
Questioning the Author

Focusing Queries Developed for Narrative Text

Goal	Queries
Encourage students to recognize plot development.	What do you think the author is getting at here? What's going on? What's happening? What has the author told us now?
Motivate students to consider how problems are addressed or resolved.	How did the author settle that? How did the author work that out?
Help students recognize the author's technique.	How has the author let you know that something has changed in the story? How is the author painting a picture here? How did the author let you see, feel, or smell something? What is the author doing here? How did the author create humor, suspense, sadness, and so on? Why do you suppose the author used foreshadowing or flashback, and so on?
Prompt students to consider characters' thoughts or actions.	How do things look for (character's name) now? What is the author trying to tell us about (character's name)?
Prompt students to predict what a character might do.	Given what the author has already told us, how do you think (character's name) will handle this situation?

RAFT

The RAFT technique is an engaging way to incorporate writing into content area reading. RAFT is an acronym whose letters stand for four things to consider before writing: _role of the writer, audience, format_, and _topic beginning with a strong verb_.

Goals

1. Provide students with practice in writing on a well-focused topic in a given format, for a specific purpose, to an audience different from the teacher, and in a voice different from that of the student.

2. Offer opportunities for students to write about knowledge learned in content area reading.

Teacher Preparation

1. Select informational, narrative, or other text that is appropriate to the reading abilities of your students and contains important and interesting information.

2. Analyze the important ideas or information that you want students to learn from their reading. Consider how a writing assignment would help students to consolidate this learning or require them to think about it from another perspective.

Instructional Procedures

1. Explain that all writers need to consider the following in every composition: the role of the writer, the audience, the format, and the topic.

2. Brainstorm ideas about a topic related to the reading that your students have just completed. Select several topics from those mentioned.

3. Write RAFT on the board, and list possible roles, audiences, and formats that are appropriate for each topic.

4. Ask students to choose one of the examples to write about or, after discussing a topic, have students create their own RAFT writing assignment.

Relevant English–Language Arts Content Standards

Grade Five: Reading Comprehension

2.3 [Students] discern main ideas and concepts presented in texts, identifying and assessing evidence that supports those ideas.

Grades Five Through Eight: Writing Strategies

1.0 Students write clear, coherent, and focused essays. The writing exhibits students' awareness of the audience and purpose.

Further Resources

Buehl, Doug. _Classroom Strategies for Interactive Learning_. Schofield: Wisconsin State Reading Association, 1995.

Cook, Doris. _Strategic Learning in the Content Areas_. Madison: Wisconsin Department of Public Instruction, 1989.

Santa, C. M. _Content Reading Including Secondary Systems_. Dubuque, Iowa: Kendall Hunt, 1988.

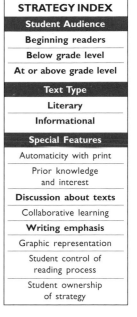

STRATEGY INDEX
Student Audience
Beginning readers
Below grade level
At or above grade level
Text Type
Literary
Informational
Special Features
Automaticity with print
Prior knowledge and interest
Discussion about texts
Collaborative learning
Writing emphasis
Graphic representation
Student control of reading process
Student ownership of strategy

Applications of the RAFT Technique

Role	Audience	Format	Strong Verb and Topic
Character in literature	Mourners	Eulogy	Describe the contributions of a person's life as it related to others.
Travel guide	Vacationers	Travel brochure	Show the benefits of travel to other locations.
Environmentalist	Legislative body	Letter	Warn of the dangers of not recycling everyday materials.
Meteorologist	World Science Council	Speech	Explain the destructive force of changing weather patterns.
Retailer	Consumers	Commercial	Persuade others to purchase the retailer's goods or services.
Search engine developer	Internet users	Instruction sheets	Describe the most effective ways to use a search engine.
Employer	Employee	Evaluation	Describe the characteristics of a good and bad employee.
Body's cells	Digestive system	Schedule	Explain the duration of cellular absorption of food after it enters the body.

Example of the RAFT Technique

Role: A coordinate (5)

Audience: A point

Format: Letter of introduction

Topic: Explain the relationship between a point and its coordinate(s)

Dear Point Man,

   I would like to introduce myself to you, my dear friend. You may not know it, but you and I have a special relationship.

   As a point, you are a location having no dimensions—no height, length, or width. Since you have no dimensions, you need someone to help identify you. That's where I come in. As your coordinate, I am a set of numbers or a single number that locates you on a line, a plane, or in space. If you are known to be on a given line, I need only to be one number to locate you. If you are on a given plane, I consist of two numbers. If you are out there in space, I am three numbers long. Thanks for being on line and making life easy for me.

   Many members of Euclid's Coordinates Club charge a fee for their services, but I am happy to announce that I will continue to serve as your locater free of charge.

Your coordinate,

Five

Reading from Different Perspectives

Perspective and background knowledge of a topic significantly influence a reader's understanding and interpretation of the text. Reading from different perspectives is a strategy that guides students through repeated readings of a selection and helps them discover alternative ways to interpret a particular reading. For example, after reading an article on acid rain, students may reread the selection from one of the following perspectives: a fish, a fisherman, the lake, a resort owner, or the president of an electric utility company.

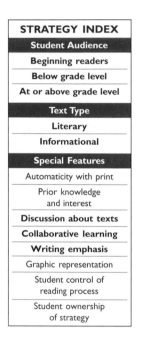

STRATEGY INDEX

Student Audience
Beginning readers
Below grade level
At or above grade level

Text Type
Literary
Informational

Special Features
Automaticity with print
Prior knowledge and interest
Discussion about texts
Collaborative learning
Writing emphasis
Graphic representation
Student control of reading process
Student ownership of strategy

Goals

1. Help students develop critical reading skills and gain new insights into concepts as they go beyond narrow interpretations and become aware of multiple interpretations of a reading.
2. Provide students with meaningful and interesting reasons to reread a selection.

Teacher Preparation

1. Select one story, article, or book for a reading.
2. Identify some perspectives on important concepts and ideas in the reading. Selections may be reread from various perspectives: father, mother, sister, doctor, labor union member, or governor, for example; or reread from different ideological positions: Marxist, Freudian, environmentalist, Republican, Libertarian.
3. See "Your Perspective on Reintroduction of Wolves into the United States" on page 86 for an example of how to use the technique.

Instructional Procedures

1. Have students first read the selection to get the gist of the material.

2. List a number of perspectives on the chalkboard or an overhead transparency. Model how a person from one of these perspectives would react to the materials the students have just read. You may wish to demonstrate how a person with a given perspective would respond to a variety of situations.

3. Divide the class into small groups and assign each group a perspective to assume as they reread the selection.

4. Guide each group as it defines the concerns and needs of that perspective. Assist students as they complete their perspective guide by listing the most important concerns and needs for their assigned perspective.

5. Have students identify statements from the text that are most important to their assigned perspective as they reread the passage. Guide students in listing these statements and noting their reactions based on their perspectives.

6. Guide students as they determine whether there is any information missing from the selection that would be important to them.

7. Discuss with the entire class the insights that students gained through their rereading from different perspectives. Direct students to write a summary position statement on both the text information and the different perspectives. Such summaries serve as the basis for further student writing in different genres, such as dialogues, essays, and arguments.

Relevant English–Language Arts Contents Standards

Grades Five Through Eight: Reading Comprehension

2.0 Students read and understand grade-level-appropriate material. They describe and connect the essential ideas, arguments, and perspectives of the text by using their knowledge of text structure, organization, and purpose.

Grade Six: Reading Comprehension

2.4 [Students] clarify an understanding of texts by creating outlines, logical notes, summaries, or reports.

Grades Nine Through Twelve: Reading Comprehension

2.0 [Students] analyze the organization patterns, arguments, and positions advanced.

Grades Five Through Twelve: Writing Strategies

1.0 Students write clear, coherent, and focused essays. The writing exhibits students' awareness of the audience and purpose. . . . Students progress through the stages of the writing process as needed.

Further Resources

Cook, Doris. *Strategic Learning in the Content Areas*. Madison: Wisconsin Department of Public Instruction, 1989.

McNeil, John D. *Reading Comprehension: New Directions for Classroom Practice*. Glenview, Ill.: Scott, Foresman, 1984.

Your Perspective on
Reintroduction of Wolves into the United States
(Farmer, Hunter, National Park Visitor, Environmentalist)

Role: Farmer

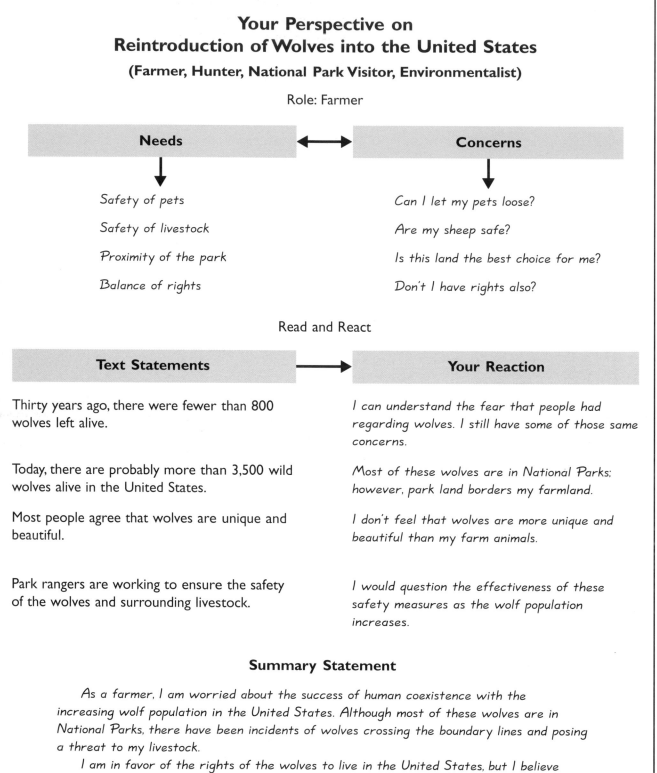

Needs	↔	**Concerns**

Safety of pets	Can I let my pets loose?
Safety of livestock	Are my sheep safe?
Proximity of the park	Is this land the best choice for me?
Balance of rights	Don't I have rights also?

Read and React

Text Statements →	**Your Reaction**
Thirty years ago, there were fewer than 800 wolves left alive.	I can understand the fear that people had regarding wolves. I still have some of those same concerns.
Today, there are probably more than 3,500 wild wolves alive in the United States.	Most of these wolves are in National Parks; however, park land borders my farmland.
Most people agree that wolves are unique and beautiful.	I don't feel that wolves are more unique and beautiful than my farm animals.
Park rangers are working to ensure the safety of the wolves and surrounding livestock.	I would question the effectiveness of these safety measures as the wolf population increases.

Summary Statement

As a farmer, I am worried about the success of human coexistence with the increasing wolf population in the United States. Although most of these wolves are in National Parks, there have been incidents of wolves crossing the boundary lines and posing a threat to my livestock.

I am in favor of the rights of the wolves to live in the United States, but I believe that as a person trying to earn a living, I have rights also. Does the environmentalist value the rights of the wolves over the rights of the farmer? I am a person, and a wolf is an animal.

As the population of these animals increases, I will be working toward a balance of rights for wolves and farmers.

Reciprocal Teaching

Reciprocal teaching is an instructional approach characterized by an interactive dialogue between the teacher and students in response to segments of a reading selection. The dialogue is based on four processes: questioning, summarizing, clarifying, and predicting.

Goals

1. Help students develop the ability to construct meaning from text and monitor their reading comprehension to ensure that they are in fact understanding what they read.

2. Provide modeling, role-playing practice, and feedback of effective strategies that good readers use to facilitate their comprehension.

3. Help students become actively engaged in their reading as they gradually assume the role of discussion leader and develop the ability to conduct the dialogues with little or no assistance from the teacher.

Teacher Preparation

1. Select materials that are sufficiently challenging and representative of the types of materials that students read in class.

2. Review the first few paragraphs of the reading selection and plan how to model the flexible and independent use of all four processes.

Instructional Procedures

1. Introduce questioning, summarizing, clarifying, and predicting as helpful processes that good readers use.

2. Work with a small group of readers (four to six). Use the four processes to model leading a dialogue about a short segment (typically one to two paragraphs) of a textbook.

Question: After students read the selection, ask a student to answer an important question about the reading.

Summarize: Restate what you have read in your own words.

Clarify: Focus on what makes the reading difficult by discussing any confusing aspects of the selection.

Predict: Speculate about what is likely to occur next.

3. Be sure students are comfortable with the four processes, then repeat the procedure with the next segment of text and a student in the role of discussion leader.

4. Provide guidance and feedback on the use of the four processes while students take turns leading the group through the steps in the succeeding segments.

Variation

Reciprocal teaching may be taught and practiced with videos as a warm-up exercise before students use the technique on written texts.

1. Divide the class in pairs. One person is designated "A" and the other, "B."

2. Introduce the video to the class, telling students what they will be viewing and what to examine.

3. Start the video and stop it every ten minutes.

4. When the video is stopped the first time, partner A will lead a dialogue by asking partner B questions that involve summarizing, questioning, clarifying, and predicting based on the content in the video.

5. Restart the video after approximately three minutes.

6. Continue the procedure, alternating the leadership role in the dialogue between partners A and B.

7. Discuss the video with the entire class, calling on students randomly.

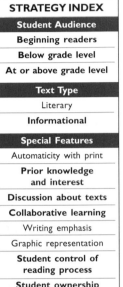

STRATEGY INDEX		
Student Audience		
Beginning readers		
Below grade level		
At or above grade level		
Text Type		
Literary		
Informational		
Special Features		
Automaticity with print		
Prior knowledge and interest		
Discussion about texts		
Collaborative learning		
Writing emphasis		
Graphic representation		
Student control of reading process		
Student ownership of strategy		

Relevant English–Language Arts Content Standards

Grade Two: Reading Comprehension

2.4 [Students] ask clarifying questions about essential textual elements of exposition (e.g., *why, what if, how*).

2.5 [Students] restate facts and details in the text to clarify and organize ideas.

Grades Five Through Eight: Reading Comprehension

2.0 They describe and connect the essential ideas, arguments, and perspectives of the text by using their knowledge of text structure, organization, and purpose.

Grade Five: Reading Comprehension

2.3 [Students] discern main ideas and concepts presented in texts, identifying, and assessing evidence that supports those ideas.

2.4 [Students] draw inferences, conclusions, or generalizations about text and support them with textual evidence and prior knowledge.

Grade Six: Reading Comprehension

2.7 [Students] make reasonable assertions about text through accurate supportive citations.

Further Resources

Palinscar, A. M., and A. L. Brown. "Reciprocal Teaching of Comprehension-Fostering and Comprehension-Monitoring Activities," *Cognition and Instruction,* Vol. 1 (1984), 117–75.

Rosenshine, Barak, and Carla Meister. "Reciprocal Teaching: A Review of the Research," *Review of Educational Research,* Vol. 64 (Winter 1994), 479.

Example of Reciprocal Teaching Technique

Present students with a sample passage, such as the following:

> A light bulb consists of several components: a filament, an inert gas, electrical contacts, and a glass container called a bulb. Light is produced when an electric current passes through the filament, a threadlike conductor. The electric current heats the filament to a temperature that is high enough to produce white light.

The student leader directs a dialogue about the passage as follows:

Question: What are the components of a light bulb? What has to occur for light to be produced?

Summarize: Retell in your own words the steps needed to produce light, or draw a diagram.

Clarify: What exactly is a filament and how does the current react to it?

Predict: What will the author explain next?

The Research Process

The research process is a library research inquiry process that begins when a student first identifies a need for information and continues to access, evaluate, and use the information. Information literacy is achieved when the student finally analyzes and evaluates the results of the process and internalizes it for future application. The collaborative expertise of a library-media teacher will be valuable in carrying out the research process.

Goals

1. Help students become creative and critical thinkers and effective users of ideas and information.

2. Help students develop the ability to access, evaluate, and use information from a variety of sources.

Teacher Preparation

1. Plan the scope of the assignment and the most essential skill-building activities.

2. Plan the resources to be made available to students, including the help of a library-media teacher, if possible.

Instructional Procedures

1. Explain to students a problem or an assignment, including how the research process and the results will be evaluated, allowing students to generate questions or find topics of personal interest.

2. Have students identify general types of questions or other information needs. Generate ideas by using individual and group brainstorming, discussions, and prompted writing. Use cluster and map techniques (see page 130) to organize brainstorming notes.

3. Explain that the first step of the quest involves formulating a preliminary central question or thesis statement.

4. Have students record prior knowledge relating to the central question through prompted writing, brainstorming, noting key words, and organizing important ideas into a graphic organizer or outline (see page 42). If their prior knowledge is limited, use general sources of information (e.g., a knowledgeable person, encyclopedia, video) to focus on key terms, and encourage students to restate information in their own words.

5. Identify potential resources, which may include personal interviews, firsthand observations, newspapers and magazines, maps, online searches, web sites, video and laserdisc programs, museums, and print or online subject-specific reference sources.

6. Help students determine the components of the central question of the search and phrase these as subquestions, which will become a plan for the search. Encourage students to distinguish between more important and less important questions and to reanalyze search strategies as success or failure is experienced.

7. Support students as they locate and explore previously identified resources. This involves locating a citation or reference to a source, gaining access to the source itself, and using initial sources as a lead to other sources. Students revise or redefine the central question by narrowing or broadening it as necessary.

8. Encourage students to select the most useful resources by evaluating the strengths and weaknesses of the resources in light of the central research question.

9. Help students extract the relevant and useful information from the appropriate resources after skimming to locate relevant material. Teach students to interpret, paraphrase, and summarize

STRATEGY INDEX	
Student Audience	
Beginning readers	
Below grade level	
At or above grade level	
Text Type	
Literary	
Informational	
Special Features	
Automaticity with print	
Prior knowledge and interest	
Discussion about texts	
Collaborative learning	
Writing emphasis	
Graphic representation	
Student control of reading process	
Student ownership of strategy	

as they take notes and to organize their paraphrased notes according to their search questions. In some cases drawing diagrams, making audio recordings, or collecting artifacts may serve the purpose instead of writing notes.

10. Have students evaluate their information for objectivity, consistency, and usefulness in addressing the central question; consider whether it is up-to-date; and decide whether the source is an authority on the subject. Remind students of the distinctions between fact, opinion, and propaganda throughout this process. Direct students to organize their notes and ideas by developing an outline or graphic organizer.

11. Direct students to integrate the fragments of information into a comprehensible whole in preparation for presentation. Students may present papers, dramatizations, panel discussions, multimedia presentations, models, demonstrations, or schoolwide projects.

12. Conclude by having students evaluate in writing both the project and the search process. The student evaluation should include (1) the steps in the search, resources used, problems encountered, and breakthroughs; (2) what was learned; (3) what it means to the student; and (4) how the student has grown as a researcher.

Relevant English–Language Arts Content Standards

Grade Five: Reading Comprehension

2.1   Understand how text features (e.g., format, graphics, sequence, diagrams, illustrations, charts, maps) make information accessible and usable.

Grades Five Through Eight: Writing Applications

2.3   Write research reports.

Grades Nine and Ten: Writing Applications

2.3   Write expository compositions, including analytical essays and research reports.

Grades Eleven and Twelve: Writing Applications

2.4   Write historical investigation reports.

2.6   Deliver multimedia presentations.

Grade Eight: Writing Strategies

1.4   Plan and conduct multiple-step information searches by using computer networks and modems.

Grade Four: Speaking Applications

2.2c Make informational presentations that incorporate more than one source of information (e.g., speakers, books, newspapers, television or radio reports).

Grade Seven: Speaking Applications

2.3c Deliver research presentations that include evidence generated through the formal research process (e.g., use of a card catalog, *Reader's Guide to Periodical Literature*, computer databases, magazines, newspapers, dictionaries).

Grades Eleven and Twelve: Speaking Applications

2.4a Deliver multimedia presentations that combine text, images, and sound by incorporating information from a wide range of media, including films, newspapers, magazines, CD-ROMS, online information, television, videos, and electronic media-generated images.

Further Resources

From Library Skills to Information Literacy. Prepared by the California School Library Association. San Jose, Calif.: Hi Willow Research and Publishing, 1997.

Structured Discussions

Structured discussions involve students in interactive talk, high-quality questioning, substantiated reasoning, and critical and creative thinking about ideas, issues, and information. Variations of this strategy include *Re Quest,* inner-outer circles, Socratic seminars, four-corner debates, and scored discussions. Once students achieve mastery of the thinking and discussion techniques, the structures ultimately become unnecessary.

Goals

1. Promote comprehension, questioning, and higher level thinking that uses evidence in reasoning, views ideas from multiple perspectives, and is able to change viewpoints in the face of evidence.

2. Provide all students opportunities to assume increased responsibility for producing high-quality discussions while using reading, writing, speaking, and listening in learning content.

Teacher Preparation

1. Identify a reading selection that is likely to engage student interest, provoke questioning and critical thinking, and whose content lends itself to multiple viewpoints.

2. For Re Quest, identify a reading selection and prepare some high-quality questions as models.

3. For the inner-outer circle discussion, identify a topic that will lend itself to the development of many thought-provoking, student-generated questions.

4. For the Socratic seminar, create a question that has no single right answer and will engage students in thoughtful reflection about significant content.

5. For the four-corner debate, create signs for four corners of the room as

follows: Strongly Agree, Somewhat Agree, Strongly Disagree, and Somewhat Disagree. Make a controversial statement.

6. For scored discussions, create one or more discussion agendas, a discussion score sheet, a plan for organizing students into small groups, and an expanded discussion score sheet with room for the names of the group members listed under each discussion behavior.

Instructional Procedures for Re Quest

1. Explain to students that Re Quest will help them learn to ask their own high-quality questions about content material, help them establish a purpose for their reading and listening, develop their comprehension abilities, and give them practice predicting and hypothesizing.

2. The students and the teacher silently read or listen to part of a text selection, such as the Gettysburg Address. (The portion may range from one sentence to several paragraphs.)

3. The teacher stops, and students ask questions about the material.

4. The teacher questions the students about the material, modeling good questioning behavior.

5. The next segment of text is read or listened to, and steps 3 and 4 are repeated.

6. The exchange of questions stops when students have processed enough information to make predictions about the remainder of the material.

7. Students read or listen to the rest of the material to verify their predictions.

8. The teacher facilitates follow-up discussion of the material by having students compare their predictions with the text.

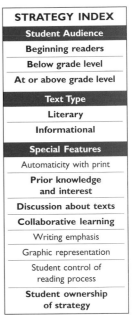

STRATEGY INDEX

Student Audience
Beginning readers
Below grade level
At or above grade level

Text Type
Literary
Informational

Special Features
Automaticity with print
Prior knowledge and interest
Discussion about texts
Collaborative learning
Writing emphasis
Graphic representation
Student control of reading process
Student ownership of strategy

Instructional Procedures for the Inner-Outer Circle Discussion

1. Identify a topic for discussion, and explain that students will work in small groups to develop several types of questions, such as eliciting background knowledge and experience related to the topic, cause and effect, problem solution, comparison/contrast, and evaluation. For example, in a unit on the use of government power to maintain order and stability, the topic for discussion is the British use of power prior to the American Revolution and in Northern Ireland today. One group may be asked to design compare-and-contrast questions.

2. Divide students into small groups to formulate questions.

3. Once the questions on the topic are completed, the students form two circles.

4. Explain that the students in the outer circle ask questions and those in the inner circle answer questions; the roles of questioning and responding will be reversed later in the period or at a later date. Talking is to occur only in the question-answer format.

5. Have a volunteer from the outer circle ask a question, then the discussion begins.

   Students in the inner circle may clarify what has been said, add information, or disagree politely.

   If outer circle students wish to make a follow-up comment, they must do so in the form of a question.

6. At an appropriate point, reverse the roles so that the students in the inner circle ask questions that have not yet come up for discussion.

Instructional Procedures for the Socratic Seminar

1. Tell students that the reading assignment will be followed by a Socratic seminar.

2. Review and post the following rules for the discussion:
   - Listen carefully.
   - Participate openly.
   - Value others' opinions, but refer to the reading selection to defend your position.

3. Review and post the following procedures for the seminar:
   - Respond to the seminar's opening question.
   - Examine the reading selection to support your answer.
   - I agree with . . . but would like to add . . .
   - I disagree with . . . because . . .
   - I am confused by . . .

4. Begin the Socratic discussion with an opening question that has no single right answer, such as the following:
   - What is meant by . . . ?
   - What is the title, theme, and tone of the reading?
   - What is your own interpretation of the reading?

   Example

   What scientific knowledge should be gathered and what problem-solving process employed to transform the degraded habitat described in the scenario into an environment that might sustain both plant and animal life? What actions would need to be taken and what values addressed?

5. Keep students focused:
   - Ask students to clarify or restate a viewpoint.
   - Ask them about the implications.
   - Encourage students to paraphrase other students' responses: "Nicole, what did you understand Carmen to say?"

6. Conduct a debriefing:
   - Have students write a reflection or discuss the seminar.

- Ask students: If you have changed your mind about a particular point or issue, what made you change it?

Instructional Procedures for the Four-Corner Debate

1. Present a thought-provoking, controversial statement related to what students have read, such as the following: "Acid rain must be controlled regardless of the economic consequences to people."

2. Have students respond in writing to the statement.

3. Have students select a position on the statement and go to the corner with the sign that identifies their position (i.e., Strongly Agree, Strongly Disagree, Somewhat Agree, or Somewhat Disagree).

4. Instruct students as follows:
   - Discuss your opinion about the statement with your group.
   - Share information from your background knowledge and reading.
   - Prepare a position statement to present to the entire class.
   - Select a spokesperson to report the opinions of the group.

5. Instruct each group to present the arguments for its position in an attempt to win members from the opposing corners.

6. Open the floor for debate.

7. Provide students the opportunity to reevaluate their initial choices by staying where they are or moving to another corner.

Instructional Procedures for Scored Discussions

1. Divide the class into discussion groups consisting of approximately four to seven students. Make an expanded copy of the discussion score sheet (see page 95) with the names of the discussion group members in the space below each type of discussion behavior.

2. In the study of a topic, provide students with a discussion agenda for their use or to serve as a model for student-produced discussion agendas. The agenda provides structure to the research process and the discussion itself. For example, an agenda for a 20-minute scored discussion of "Miners of the Old West" might look like this:

   I. Introduction of discussion topic
   II. Discovery of gold
      A. Who, when, where, how
      B. Effects on local communities
      C. Effects of "gold fever" on the rest of the country
      D. Getting to the gold fields
   III. Miners' lives
      A. Mining techniques
      B. Daily life
      C. Stories of success and failure
   IV. End of the gold mining era
      A. How it ended
      B. Lessons for history
      C. Personal lessons or insights derived from studying gold mining
   V. Conclusion of discussion topic

   Shorter periods (eight to 12 minutes) are effective for students to discuss current event topics drawn from local, state, national, and international news. The structure of the discussion may be based on who, what, when, where, and why questions and may solicit students' reaction.

3. The agenda provides guidance for student research, a structure for organizing research notes, and a process for conducting the actual scored discussion. Students are allowed, encouraged, or required to use notes depending on the

instructional focus of the lesson. Each student in the small group must be prepared to discuss every item on the agenda. The agenda is not to be divided and turned into a series of individual oral reports.

4. Encourage students to take notes based on their discussion agenda and to carefully label and categorize their information as if they were writing a standard research paper.

5. Explain that the most useful aspect of the agenda is to help students keep track of their scored discussions and engage in high-quality discussions. For example, a student who realizes the group's need to follow the agenda may suggest the following: "We've been discussing mining techniques for a while, and I think we should move on to the daily lives of miners. Does anyone have any last comments on mining techniques?"

6. Organize students into a "fishbowl" arrangement with one group of participants in the middle of the classroom and the remaining students and teacher watching from a large outer circle. One student begins the discussion, and others contribute in like fashion for no more than five to 15 seconds each.

7. Assign scores to the group members' contributions while students listen to the discussion. Discussions last from eight to 20 minutes, depending on the topic and grade level; the group members keep the discussion on track with the help of a discussion agenda.

8. Students in a scored discussion receive points or deductions each time they participate in the discussion. These points are shown on the sample score sheet; however, reallocate point counts if necessary for particular emphases.

    Award points for the following behaviors:

    • Taking a position on a question

    • Making a relevant comment

• Using evidence to support a position or presenting factual information

• Drawing another person into the discussion

• Asking a clarifying question or moving the discussion along

• Drawing an analogy

• Recognizing contradictions

• Recognizing irrelevant comments

    Deduct points for the following behaviors:

• Not paying attention or distracting others

• Interrupting

• Making irrelevant comments

• Monopolizing the discussion

• Making personal attacks

    Points are usually awarded for a single activity, such as presenting factual material or stating a position. However, if Arturo presents his information and then adds, "Lee, what can you add to this part of the discussion?" another point will be awarded to Arturo. Students may also receive points for clarifying questions and moving the discussion along.

    Students can earn points by carefully listening and politely noting when a speaker:

• States a contradiction

• Contributes irrelevant information

9. To evaluate the discussion, place tally marks by a student's name each time he or she exhibits a particular behavior.

10. Conclude with a written assignment requiring students to use the information presented by each of the groups in a scored discussion. For example, in a unit on U.S. foreign policy in Central America, there may be four scored discussion groups representing views on U.S. involvement in Panama, Cuba, El Salvador, and Nicaragua. As a culminating assignment, students would be asked to

propose a comprehensive U.S. foreign policy for Central America based on prior U.S. involvement in these nations during the twentieth century.

Relevant English–Language Arts Content Standards

Grade Four: Reading Comprehension

2.3   Make and confirm predictions about text by using prior knowledge and ideas presented in the text itself. . . .

Grade Four: Listening and Speaking Strategies

1.1   Ask thoughtful questions and respond to relevant questions with appropriate elaboration in oral settings.

Grade Five: Listening and Speaking Strategies

1.1   Ask questions that seek information not already discussed.

Grade Six: Listening and Speaking Strategies

1.5   Emphasize salient points to assist the listener in following the main idea and concepts.

1.6   Support opinions with detailed evidence. . . .

Grade Seven: Listening and Speaking Strategies

1.1   Ask probing questions to elicit information, including evidence to support the speaker's claims and conclusions.

1.2   Respond to persuasive messages with questions, challenges, or affirmations.

Grades Nine and Ten: Listening and Speaking Strategies

1.1   Formulate judgments about the ideas under discussion and support those judgments with convincing evidence.

Further Resources

Manzo, Tony V. "The Re Quest Procedure," *Journal of Reading* (November 1969), 123–26.

Kagan, S. *Cooperative Learning: Resources for Teachers*. San Juan Capistrano: Resources for Teachers, 1989.

Zola, John. "Scored Discussions," *Social Education* (February 1992), 121–25.

Discussion Score Sheet

Points

(2)   Taking a position on a question

(1)   Making a relevant comment

(2)   Using evidence to support a position or presenting factual information

(1)   Drawing another person into the discussion

(1)   Asking a clarifying question or moving the discussion along

(2)   Drawing an analogy

(2)   Recognizing contradictions

(2)   Recognizing irrelevant comments

Deductions

(–2)   Not paying attention or distracting others

(–2)   Interrupting others

(–1)   Making irrelevant comments

(–3)   Monopolizing the discussion

(–3)   Making personal attacks

Text Sets

A text set is a group of books or other reading materials that are related in some way. They may be written by the same author; be examples of the same genre; illustrate the same setting or theme; or provide a different perspective on the same person, event, or concept. The use of text sets is an approach that extends and broadens student understanding.

Goals

1. Encourage students to think about and share what they already know about a topic, an author, or the theme of the text set.
2. Establish understandings that can carry over into independent reading of additional items related to the focus.
3. Provide students with supplementary reading materials with a wide range of difficulty levels to increase student access to concepts.

Teacher Preparation

1. Identify the focus of the text set (e.g., same author, same concept).
2. Provide multiple copies of reading material related to the focus. The materials should represent a variety of genres and include fiction, nonfiction, trade books, and magazines. The materials should be at a range of difficulty levels sufficiently broad to allow all students in the class access to at least one item of the set that they can read independently.
3. Prepare a book talk for each item in the text set to introduce them to the students. As an alternative to the book talks, provide time for students to preview independently the items in the text set.

Instructional Procedures

1. Introduce the focus of the text set or the topic that the text set is being used to supplement.
2. Have students select and read an item from the text set to learn more about the focus or topic.
3. Have students meet in cooperative groups after completing their reading to discuss the items they read. Encourage students to use one another's ideas and insights to collaboratively establish more complex links among texts by focusing on broad connections within and comparisons across the text set.

As students read and discuss additional items from the text set, their understanding of the focus and their awareness of diverse perspectives on similar topics should increase.

Relevant English–Language Arts Content Standards

Grades Four Through Twelve: Reading Comprehension

2.0 Students read and understand grade-level-appropriate material.

Grades Six Through Twelve: Literary Response and Analysis

3.0 Students read and respond to historically or culturally significant works of literature that reflect and enhance their studies of history and social science.

Further Resources

Harste, Jerome C.; Kathy G. Short; and Carolyn Burke. *Creating Classrooms for Authors*. Portsmouth, N.H.: Heinemann, 1988.

Jacobson, Jeanne M. *Content Area Reading: Integration with Language Arts*. San Francisco: Delmar Publishers, 1996.

Tompkins, Gail E. *Literacy for the 21st Century: A Balanced Approach*. Columbus, Ohio: Merrill, 1997.

STRATEGY INDEX

Student Audience
Beginning readers
Below grade level
At or above grade level

Text Type
Literary
Informational

Special Features
Automaticity with print
Prior knowledge and interest
Discussion about texts
Collaborative learning
Writing emphasis
Graphic representation
Student control of reading process
Student ownership of strategy

Think Aloud

The think-aloud strategy is an approach in which teachers verbalize their own thought processes while reading orally to students. In this way teachers model for students the cognitive and metacognitive[1] processes that good readers use to construct meaning and monitor comprehension.

Goals

1. Give students the opportunity to see the kinds of strategies a skilled reader uses to construct meaning and cope with comprehension problems.
2. Develop students' ability to monitor their reading and take corrective action when needed.
3. Provide an opportunity for students to experience effective reading and problem solving and to transfer these strategies to their independent reading.

Teacher Preparation

1. Select a passage that contains points of difficulty, ambiguities, or unknown words in preparation for oral reading.
2. Preview the passage and imagine that you are reading it for the first time as one of your good readers would.
3. Use a copy of the passage to make note of the comments and questions to model for students.

Instructional Procedures

1. Read the passage aloud, telling students to follow along silently and listen to how you construct meaning and think through trouble spots. The following are examples of the thought processes you might model for your students:
   - Make predictions. (Show how to develop hypotheses.)
   - Describe any pictures forming in your head while you read. (Show how to develop images during reading.)
   - Share an analogy. (Show how to link prior knowledge with new information in the reading selection.)
   - Verbalize a confusing point. (Show how you monitor your ongoing comprehension and become aware of problems.)
   - Demonstrate fix-up strategies. (Show how you address comprehension problems by using fix-up strategies.)
2. Select a logical stopping point, and have students use some of those strategies during a silent reading of the passage.
3. Model several experiences, then have students work with partners to practice "think alouds" by taking turns in reading orally and sharing thoughts. For struggling readers, move from carefully developed materials with obvious problems to school materials of various types and lengths.

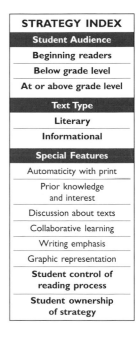

STRATEGY INDEX
Student Audience
Beginning readers
Below grade level
At or above grade level
Text Type
Literary
Informational
Special Features
Automaticity with print
Prior knowledge and interest
Discussion about texts
Collaborative learning
Writing emphasis
Graphic representation
Student control of reading process
Student ownership of strategy

Relevant English–Language Arts Content Standards

Grades Two Through Four: Reading Comprehension

2.0 Students read and understand grade-level-appropriate material. They draw upon a variety of comprehension strategies as needed, including generating and responding to essential questions, making predictions, and comparing information from several sources.

Grade Four: Reading Comprehension

2.2 [Students] use appropriate strategies when reading for different purposes (e.g., full comprehension, locating information, personal enjoyment).

Further Resources

Davey, B. "Think Aloud—Modeling the Cognitive Process of Reading Comprehension," *Journal of Reading* (October 1983), 44–47.

---

[1]Metacognition means awareness of one's own processing behaviors.

Example of Think Aloud

The following material is an example of a passage and the thoughts that a teacher might express aloud during the oral reading:

Passage

Salaam frantically searched for the address listed on his clipboard; he had six more packages to deliver before his shift ended. The building he had entered had eight floors, and he hoped that number 456 Lakeside was an apartment on the fourth floor of this old, dilapidated building.

Teacher Thinking Aloud

I predict that Salaam, who is a delivery man for a shipping company, will not find the address because the author described the building as being run-down.

I see the building as being one of many apartment buildings on a busy street in a big city. I imagine that there could be paint peeling off the walls and bars on the windows.

I can compare this situation to the time I was in my hometown, and I had driven into an area that looked like what the author is describing. I was afraid and wanted to leave.

Passage Continued

Salaam climbed the stairs to the fourth floor. As he walked from door to door checking numbers, he felt the floor vibrate. He felt invisible hands push him from side to side. The whole building started to rumble. Hanging on to the package, Salaam reached for the bannister on the stairwell as it gave way.

Teacher Thinking Aloud

I don't understand how invisible hands could be pushing him. I'm not sure what is happening to Salaam and where the story is going.

I'm going to keep reading and hope my level of understanding will increase. If it doesn't, then I will reread the passage or ask someone.

Think Sheets

Through the use of think sheets, students are taught to approach their reading as writers. Students learn the strategies used by authors of informational text, apply the strategies in their own writing, and through participation in the writing process learn to read critically and monitor the clarity of the text they are reading whether or not they themselves are the authors.

Goals

1. Help both good and poor readers improve their ability to compose and comprehend informational text.

2. Simulate strategy use for planning and gathering of information, writing a rough draft, revising ideas, and editing.

3. Help students work through specific problems in using their reading for writing reports.

Teacher Preparation

1. Make available reference materials appropriate to the thematic unit and the range of reading levels in the classroom.

2. Create think sheets appropriate to the targeted text structures, including prewriting, organizing, first draft, edit, peer editor, and revision.

Instructional Procedures

1. An initial stage in introducing students to the different structures is to have them write different types of papers on their own experiences. For example, students may begin with explanations based on something they know how to do well (e.g., making a certain kind of sandwich, building a model, playing a game) by using think sheets tailored to a sequence or process. They write a comparison/contrast paper by considering two people, places, or things they know a lot about. They similarly write problem/solution and narrative papers about familiar topics. During this initial writing step, make explicit the questions each type of text is designed to answer and make students aware of the key words and phrases that suggest the text structure used.

Making Connections to Reading

2. Students learn to identify the text structure elements by analyzing samples of students' writing displayed on overhead transparencies. Example of illustrative dialogue:

T: Think about the different papers you wrote over the last several weeks. In some papers you told how two people or places were alike and how they were different. In still others you told about a problem and how it was solved. I'm going to read the paper that is on the overhead transparency while you read along with me. As we read, decide what kind of paper this is. . . . Well, what do you think?

S1: Explanation.

T: How do you know?

S1: It tells "how."

S2: You can tell it's not about problems or comparing.

S1: In one place it says "how to" and there are steps for making the airplane.

T: These are all ways that you can tell the text is an explanation. This explanation is particularly good because it gives us a lot of clues about the kind of paper it is. For example, just as in your science books authors explain how to do experiments, this paper tells us how to do something. It answers certain questions because it is an explanation. Think about the questions you answered when you wrote

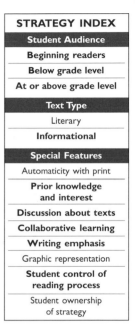

STRATEGY INDEX		
Student Audience		
Beginning readers		
Below grade level		
At or above grade level		
Text Type		
Literary		
Informational		
Special Features		
Automaticity with print		
Prior knowledge and interest		
Discussion about texts		
Collaborative learning		
Writing emphasis		
Graphic representation		
Student control of reading process		
Student ownership of strategy		

your explanation. Does anyone have any questions they think are answered in this paper?

S2: How do you put together a paper airplane?

S1: What are the steps in making a model airplane?

T: Both of you noticed that the paper is about making an airplane. It tells the steps. In fact, all explanations answer two or three very general questions. One is, What are the steps?

Continue in this manner, using other students' samples to point out specific features of each type of text structure; questions the texts are designed to answer; and the key words and phrases that provide signals to the reader about the text structure used.

3. Students are guided again to produce explanation, comparison/contrast, and problem/solution texts. For these papers they use questions they have learned for the various text structures to guide their gathering of information. Students are encouraged to elaborate on the information they gather by integrating it with information from their own background knowledge of other text sources.

Using Think Sheets in the Writing Process

4. After completing a thematic unit, such as an animal unit in science, ask students to write a report on a related topic, such as an animal of their choice.

   Discuss with students that writing a research report is not just a matter of copying a book and that think sheets will be provided to help them work through the process.

   To encourage appropriate planning activities, provide a prewriting think sheet with fill-in sentences and questions relevant to planning, such as the following:

My topic is . . . Some things I already know that I can include in my paper are . . . Some ideas that I would like to put into my paper to make it interesting to my reader are . . . Who will read my paper? My audience will be interested in reading about this topic because . . . I will put my ideas into this order . . .

Once students are ready, provide them organizing think sheets that will help them think about information to include in their papers by focusing on the different types of writing that answer different sets of questions. These sheets also remind students to check themselves to ensure that all relevant information has been included. Organizing think sheets should have different sets of questions appropriate to each text structure. The Comparison/Contrast Organizing Think Sheet includes the following questions: What are two things that I am trying to compare and contrast? On what basis will I compare and contrast these ideas? In what ways are my two things alike? Different? What key words would be helpful for signaling my reader about the kind of paper I am writing? Where can I use these words?

Provide students with the third think sheet (on lined, colored paper) for writing the first draft. Encourage them to consider their other think sheets in writing their first draft.

Give students their fourth and fifth think sheets (Edit and Peer Editor) to support students' self-editing and encourage peer editing, respectively. The Edit and Peer Editor Think Sheets have three similar sections. First, the author/editor focuses on the content of the paper, considering parts that are especially interesting and clear and parts that may need revision. The second section focuses students' attention on the organization, asking students to check whether they have included information to answer the questions. The third section focuses on planning the next step in writing, which is a peer editing session (help I would like from my editor. . .) or revisions to the draft (parts I plan to change are . . .).

The Peer Editor Think Sheet helps students perform text analysis procedures useful for both writing and reading. For example, as the author reads a comparison/contrast paper, the editor considers questions such as the following: What does this paper compare and contrast? On what basis are they being compared and contrasted? What is one thing the author could do to make clearer what is being compared or contrasted? List two ways they are alike. List two ways they are different.

The Revision Think Sheet encourages students to take ownership of the revision plan by considering questions such as the following: What suggestions have others given me to improve my paper? What do I plan to do to make my paper more interesting? Easier to follow? What will I add? What will I remove? Students are prompted to return to their first draft to make their changes prior to final copy.

Relevant English–Language Arts Content Standards

Grades Five Through Eight: Writing Strategies

1.0   Students write clear, coherent, and focused essays. The writing exhibits the students' awareness of the audience and purpose. . . . Students progress through the stages of the writing process as needed.

Grades Five Through Eight: Writing Applications

2.0   Students write narrative, expository, persuasive, and descriptive essays. . . . Student writing demonstrates a command of standard American English and the research, organizational, and drafting strategies outlined in Writing Standard 1.0.

Grades Five Through Eight: Reading Comprehension

2.0   Students read and understand grade-level-appropriate material. They describe and connect the essential ideas, arguments, and perspectives of the text by using their knowledge of text structure, organization, and purpose.

Grades Nine Through Twelve: Reading Comprehension

2.0   Students read and understand grade-level-appropriate material. They analyze the organizational patterns, arguments, and positions advanced.

Further Resources

Raphael, Taffy E.; Becky W. Kirschner; and Carol Sue Englert. "Expository Writing Program: Making Connections between Reading and Writing," *The Reading Teacher*, Vol. 41 (April 1988), 790–95.

Raphael, Taffy E., and Elfrieda H. Hiebert. *Creating an Integrated Approach to Literacy Instruction*, San Diego: Harcourt Brace College Publishers, 1996.

Tutoring as a High-Impact Intervention

Tutoring as a high-impact intervention is an approach designed to accelerate the reading development of faltering readers in the upper grades. The 30-minute daily tutoring sessions over a six- to eight-week period rely primarily on the use of interesting informational texts. The approach consists of (1) easy reading; (2) writing; and (3) more challenging reading. It is based on careful observation of the student's instructional reading level and provides instruction on strategies for coping with challenging words and texts.

Goals

1. Provide many opportunities for a student to read a wide variety and quantity of informational texts (including texts initially perceived by the student as too difficult) for eventual transfer to successful classroom reading.

2. Help less competent readers learn how to enact processing similar to that used automatically by more competent readers, such as anticipating, self-correcting, summarizing, resolving new words or unfamiliar phrases, detecting when meaning is lost or not fitting, making connections, and building background knowledge.

3. Help students improve their spelling and understanding of the spelling system; rekindle their enthusiasm for writing; and observe their own rapid literacy development.

Teacher Preparation

1. Administer a conventional word recognition test by using graded word lists, beginning with words that will be very easy for the student and continuing until the student begins to make errors (or until you judge that the student is becoming frustrated).

Record all attempts, observing strategies used by the student, to deal with unfamiliar or unknown words.

2. Administer a formal or informal spelling assessment to investigate the student's control over both regular and irregular words in isolation and in context.

3. Assess the student's oral reading of expository text (passages of 250 to 350 words). Administer selections until three levels of difficulty have been identified: independent (student can correctly read 95 to 100 words in a 100-word passage), instructional (90 to 94), frustration (89 words or fewer). Observe the student's level of engagement. For example, consider the student's ability to monitor independently his or her reading, including signs of a self-initiated search for further information when meaning was lost or a problem was solved.

4. Use information from these assessments to compile a variety of texts likely to be useful for fostering the student's success in the classroom, using classroom teachers and librarians as consultants. Select texts that are at both the student's independent and instructional reading levels. These include both (1) texts that are easy enough for students to experience success; and (2) texts that offer enough difficulty so that you can observe at what point reading "breaks down." Seek out interesting, informational articles to expose the student to a wide variety of topics, genres, and writing styles within the 30-minute lesson. Most texts should be one to three pages, and some should include attractively presented photographs, maps, diagrams, and the like. Avoid the sterile, contrived texts that are often given to special needs readers. Include some texts that are transitional between narrative and informational, such as a biography, autobiography, travelogue, interview, and diary.

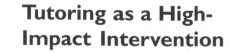

STRATEGY INDEX

Student Audience
Beginning readers
Below grade level
At or above grade level

Text Type
Literary
Informational

Special Features
Automaticity with print
Prior knowledge and interest
Discussion about texts
Collaborative learning
Writing emphasis
Graphic representation
Student control of reading process
Student ownership of strategy

5. Gather together pencils, a spiral notebook with unlined pages for the tutor's use, and materials for your own recordkeeping.

6. Go into each tutoring session with one or two ideas about how to elicit some good writing from students.

Instructional Procedures

1. During the introductory segment of each tutoring session, the student reads text that will be relatively easy. Begin building trust by ensuring that the initial texts are easy enough so that the student experiences success. In future sessions this introductory segment will include rereading a familiar selection from the previous day for practice and fluency.

2. During the middle of the tutoring session, turn the spiral notebook so that the binding is at the top. Have the student generate a few sentences on the bottom half of the notebook. To do so engage the student in a short conversation about a topic of interest to him or her. It may be taken from the reading or not. Showing genuine interest in the conversation, move into writing by giving the student a prompt, such as "Let's write a message about that, and I will help you." Say also, "If you don't know a word, you can try writing it at the top of the page, and I'll help you spell it correctly. Then you can include it in your message below." The student writes in pencil so the spelling can be corrected.

When the student is spelling a problematic word, have him or her say the word slowly as he or she writes it. From your knowledge of the student's spelling errors, immediately write the word correctly to prevent errors and to make the reading experience less frustrating for the student. For example, if the student previously wrote "helpet," intervene the next time by asking the student

what two letters should go at the end. Invite the student to check the written message against your correctly written copy. Once the message has been written correctly, have the student read it aloud. If the student's daily writing still contains errors, print or type the misspelled word correctly and have him or her read it aloud the next day to avoid further spelling confusion. Gradually increase the length of the message and introduce the student to other genres and topics.

During the writing portion of the lesson, weave explicit instruction about important words and spelling patterns into the session. Try to identify the most significant errors and common sources of confusion rather than attack every error. Supply the correct spelling for the student without making this step laborious and tedious. Give the student memorable examples that will help him or her generalize to other words. For example, to help the student with the word *instead*, point out an easier, rhyming word such as *bread* or *head*. One useful procedure is to have students create graphically connected networks of words following similar or related patterns, such as *explore, exploit, exit, exercise*. Students keep them in a file with tabs for reference. Note high-frequency words the student is consistently misspelling, such as "gon" for *gone*, which simply must be memorized. Do not interrupt the flow of comprehension to work on such issues during the reading portion of the lesson. Save them for the writing portion of the lesson.

3. Work with a more challenging text during the third part of the lesson. Set students up for success by introducing some important information about the text prior to reading it. For example, say "I'm going to read a few sentences that will give you an idea of what this is about" or "I'm

going to tell you a few things about this selection, and you may ask me for help." Select only some of the most important points about the article to discuss with the student. Be sure to point out and explain text types that may be new to the student, such as the interview or journal entry format.

As students experience success and grow in confidence, increase the difficulty of the new texts introduced in this part of the lesson. Be sure that the gradient of text difficulty from one session to the next is steep enough to ensure acceleration without dampening the student's enthusiasm.

4. Record important observations about the students' current competencies throughout the session, considering ways to help the students make significant progress toward greater reading independence.

General Guidelines

Consider the following suggestions:

- Select every task with the goal of accelerating learning and increasing fluency in reading.

- Incorporate powerful demonstrations of how to detect problems and work to solve them, ensuring clear, memorable examples. Look for instances in which the student can make use of the ability to solve problems; if the opportunities do not exist, look for better, more memorable examples.

- If tutoring bogs down, simply read a paragraph or sentence.

- Do not try to pre-teach all the vocabulary all of the time. Consider how important the word is, whether it is essential to understanding the passage, and whether it will be useful in the word networks.

- Minimize teacher and student talk; maximize time for reading and writing.

- Provide systematic, comprehensive intervention based on diagnosed needs.

Relevant English–Language Arts Content Standards

Grades One Through Four: Word Analysis, Fluency, and Systematic Vocabulary Development

1.0 Students understand the basic features of reading. They select letter patterns and know how to translate them into spoken language by using phonics, syllabication, and word parts. They apply this knowledge to achieve fluent oral and silent reading.

Grades One Through Twelve: Reading Comprehension

2.0 Students read and understand grade-level-appropriate material.

Grades One Through Four: Reading Comprehension

2.0 They draw upon a variety of comprehension strategies as needed (e.g., generating and responding to essential questions, making predictions, and comparing information from several sources).

Further Resources

Barr, Rebecca; Marilyn W. Sadow; and Camille L. Z. Blachowicz. *Reading Diagnosis for Teachers: An Instructional Approach* (Second edition). New York: Longman, 1990.

Gaffney, J. S.; J. M. Methven; and S. Bagdasarian. "Assisting Older Students to Read Expository Text in a Tutorial Setting: A Case for a High-Impact Intervention," *Reading and Writing Quarterly,* 2000.

Methven, Jeanette, and Janet Gaffney. "A Late Intervention Project: Tutoring to Improve Reading." Paper presented at the National Reading Conference, Center for the Study of Reading, University of Illinois at Urbana-Champaign, 1993.

Working Through Reading Stances

Working through reading stances is an approach to guiding students through literature and into critical analysis. It involves four major, recursive stances: (1) *being out and stepping in* (responding initially); (2) *being in and moving through* (extending understanding); (3) *stepping back and rethinking what one knows* (reflecting on previous knowledge); and (4) *stepping out and objectifying the experience* (developing an extended interpretation or analysis).

Goals

1. Provide students with practice in thinking and reasoning more fully about the literature they are reading by helping them to clarify the ideas presented and to connect them to their background experience and prior knowledge of other literary works.

2. Provide students with opportunities to write in-depth interpretations and analyses of specific literary pieces after they have used prewriting and discussion to work through the four stances.

Teacher Preparation

1. Identify a high-quality literary selection, such as a poem, short story, drama, or novel, that is both appropriate to your students and likely to engage them.

2. Choose the approach for collecting students' written responses (e.g., blank paper, reader response journals, or teacher-made response sheets).

Instructional Procedures

1. Introduce the selection in a way that will engage your students' interest and background experience. Explain to students that you will be prompting them to respond and reflect in different ways during the reading process. Briefly describe the stances (or phases) of the reading process as (1) an initial response; (2) a fuller or extended understanding; (3) reflection and rethinking about previous understandings; and finally (4) an extended interpretation or analysis.

2. Ask students to read the selection on their own. (You may wish to start them off by reading the first few paragraphs aloud.)

3. *Being out and stepping in* (responding initially). As students read, ask them to make notes of their initial response to the literary piece on blank paper or in their response journals. In this stance the reader attempts to make initial acquaintance by asking questions, making associations, and trying to establish a context for understanding the piece. This stance usually occurs as the reading begins or when the reader encounters the unexpected or unfamiliar vocabulary or information at any point in the reading. Readers will try to get acquainted with the characters, plot, and setting and understand how they interrelate. Students will need to use information from the text together with their background knowledge to "step in" to the piece.

4. *Being in and moving through* (extending understanding). When students become immersed in their reading of the selection, encourage them to continue to make note of their extended understandings. In this stance students use their previous images, prior knowledge, and the text itself to further their creation of meaning.

5. When students finish reading, prompt them to write an extended response revealing their increasing understanding of the characters, situations, feelings, and action. To do this, students may use their own personal reactions (already noted in their

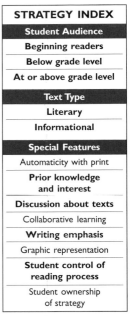

STRATEGY INDEX
Student Audience
Beginning readers
Below grade level
At or above grade level
Text Type
Literary
Informational
Special Features
Automaticity with print
Prior knowledge and interest
Discussion about texts
Collaborative learning
Writing emphasis
Graphic representation
Student control of reading process
Student ownership of strategy

initial response) or their natural empathy with a character or they may otherwise weave parts of the selection together, such as relating the title to a significant event.

6. *Stepping back and rethinking what one knows* (reflecting on previous knowledge). Direct students to examine their notes to see whether there were any moments in which they stepped outside their reading for a moment and used their growing understandings as a way to reflect on their own experience or their own knowledge of the world or other literary works. Prompt students to write or discuss new insights or understandings that may have occurred to them as a result of their reading.

7. *Stepping out and objectifying the experience* (developing an extended interpretation or analysis). Readers are now ready to reflect on and react to the ideas, the author's use of language, or to the reading experience itself. At this point students should be encouraged and stimulated to reason and write more fully about what they have read. Decisions about how to shape the next instructional activity will be influenced by (1) the text itself; (2) the students' responses, prewriting, and discussion thus far; and (3) an appropriate interpretive or analytical activity most likely to engage students and stretch their thinking about, and critical analysis of, their reading. For specific extended activities, see the Literary Response and Analysis strand (3.0) in the *English–Language Arts Content Standards*.

As students work through multiple readings on a related theme, you may wish to use think sheets as a way to help them integrate ideas from different sources for their writing. Model how each of several books, though different, addresses some similar topics or themes. Ask students to brainstorm possible topics and the single topic they wish to pursue. As they read several books on a chosen topic, have them take notes on their think sheets as preparation for essay writing by drawing ideas from books they have read, their dialogue journals, and classroom discussion.

Relevant English–Language Arts Content Standards

Grades Four Through Eight: Literary Response and Analysis

3.0 Students read and respond to historically or culturally significant works of literature that reflect and enhance their studies of history and social science. They clarify the ideas and connect them to other literary works. The selections in *Recommended Readings in Literature, Kindergarten Through Grade Eight* illustrate the quality and complexity of the materials to be read by students.

Grades Nine Through Twelve: Literary Response and Analysis

3.0 Students read and respond to historically or culturally significant works of literature that reflect and enhance their studies of history and social science. They conduct in-depth analyses of recurrent themes. The selections in *Recommended Literature, Grades Nine Through Twelve* illustrate the quality and complexity of the materials to be read by students.

Grade Eight: Writing Applications

2.3c [Students] write research reports [that] use a variety of primary and secondary sources and distinguish the nature and value of each.

Grades Nine Through Twelve: Writing Applications

2.2 [Students] write responses to literature [that] (a) demonstrate a comprehensive grasp of the significant ideas of literary works; (b) support important ideas and viewpoints through accurate and detailed references to the text or to other works.

Further Resources

Langer, J. A. "The Process of Understanding Literature." Report Series 2.1. New York: Center for the Learning and Teaching of Literature, University of Albany, 1989.

Raphael, Taffy E., and Elfrieda H. Hiebert. *Creating an Integrated Approach to Literacy Instruction.* San Diego: Harcourt Brace College Publishers, 1996.

Sample

"What I Learned"

Think Sheets from Multiple Readings

From *Red Scarf Girl*

When governments change, people change to match the belief system of the government in charge to avoid persecution. Sometimes having wealth and being successful can be seen as a threat to others. Like Anne Frank, Ji-li had hard decisions to make and her family's lives were in jeopardy. Both Anne Frank and Ji-li Jiang showed indomitable courage under fire.

From *The Terrible Things*

People can be taken away and persecuted by others without a valid reason. People try to rationalize why it is acceptable to punish and torture others who are different and they rejoice when they are left alone. Many people watched this happen and did nothing.

From *Anne Frank: The Diary of a Young Girl*

Anne Frank wrote her feelings and thoughts down to help her through a horrible time. She made the words and thoughts of a teenager important and valuable. Some people risked their lives to help others, while others watched the persecution and did not help. The Holocaust resulted in the deaths of Anne's family and herself.

Writing-Reading Workshop

The writing-reading workshop is a combination of the writing workshop and the reading workshop.

The writing workshop is a comprehensive instructional approach in which students are provided time in class to write, choices of topics and genres, access to materials, opportunities for peers to respond to their writing, and teacher-directed instruction and demonstrations in lessons and conferences. The approach involves giving students the options available to real-world authors, including daily time for writing, conferences with teachers and peers during drafting, pacing set by the writer, and opportunities to publish what they write.

The reading workshop is a comprehensive instructional approach in which students are provided time in class to read, choices of books and other materials, access to books and materials, opportunities for interaction with peers about their reading, and instruction and demonstrations through lessons and conferences.

Goals of the Writing-Reading Workshop

1. Provide opportunities for integrating the language arts. (See "Goals of the Writing Workshop" and "Goals of the Reading Workshop" noted separately below.)
2. Provide opportunities for students to use skills and strategies within a variety of written applications and reading contexts.

Teacher Preparation for the Writing-Reading Workshop

1. Decide which day(s) of the week to devote to the reading workshop and which day(s) to devote to the writing workshop.
2. Identify procedures for integrating activities from the reading and

writing workshops, such as folder pockets for organizing writing, spelling, reading, and homework; writing-reading notebooks for students to maintain a handbook of writing and reading mini-lessons with a table of contents; think sheets for students to bring together ideas and themes from multiple sources to create their own writing.

Goals of the Writing Workshop

1. Help students produce a broad range of quality writing that reflects their depth of understanding about given genres and is based on the students' reading of the genre in question.
2. Help students produce writing in a wide variety of genres, such as short stories, poetry, book reviews, letters to the editor, parodies, profiles, and essays.

Teacher Preparation for the Writing Workshop

1. Prepare classroom routines, procedures, and materials needed for the writing workshop. Materials include "Rules and Expectations for the Writing Workshop"; paper of different sizes, weights, and colors; writing implements; supplies and equipment; dictionaries and other reference materials; lists of types of writing; editing checklists; lists of written conventions as an aid in proofreading; peer writing conference records; personal spelling lists, weekly word study forms, and spelling review procedures; students' writing records; and students' permanent writing folders or portfolios.
2. Identify or create writing and reading surveys; quotations for the walls of a writing-reading workshop; high-quality student and published writing to serve as illustrative models of genres and strategies; and other resources that will be useful for direct

instruction in grammar, spelling, language, and the craft of writing.

Instructional Procedures for the Writing Workshop

1. Explain to students that they will be learning how to write by following the example of real-world authors. Procedures include scheduling daily time for writing, convening conferences with teachers and peers during the draft stage, allowing writers to set the pace, and publishing what they write. Most significantly, students decide what they will write during the writing workshop. Review workshop routines with students, including procedures for weekly, independent word study and spelling reviews.

2. Allow students to select topics on which they wish to write. Provide examples of possible topics and kinds of writing likely to engage your students, such as short stories; biographies and profiles; essays; editorials; autobiographical incidents; research reports; pamphlets and brochures; feature articles; reports of sports events; books for younger children; book commercials; parodies; speeches; eulogies; tributes; interviews; memoirs; web pages; computer programs; and reviews of books, CDs, plays, magazines, movies, and shows. If students encounter difficulty, question, model, and ask, "What do you care about? What do you know? What do you know about that others don't?" Share your own writing with students, and provide them with examples of student and published writing in the genres students undertake.

3. Allow students to spend sustained time on individual pieces of writing as they work through multiple drafts and edit and proof their work. Students' commitment to their own ideas and purposes should stimulate them to work hard to craft significant writing.

4. Meet with students in individual conferences for editorial suggestions as they work through the stages of the writing process: drafting, revising, editing, rewriting, and proofreading. Make note of their most frequent difficulties and weaknesses so that they can be addressed in subsequent lessons. Encourage students to participate in peer reviews as critics to their author peers and for further revisions of their own drafts.

5. Start the class by conducting brief lectures about procedures, conventions, craft, genres, grammatical structures, and topic development based on careful observations and analyses of student writing. On overhead transparencies illustrate how to work through problems that arise with different types of writing.

6. Establish weekly routines for independent word study and focused spelling instruction. Begin by teaching students how to proofread for and correct misspellings in their own writing. Students create their personal spelling lists based on several sources: (1) words they are not sure of; (2) misspellings they find; (3) words that students notice in their reading; and (4) words provided by the teacher. On an appointed day every week, students prepare their weekly word study lists, which they take from their personal spelling lists. On that day spelling lessons are focused on topics such as the history of English and word origins; spelling strategies; procedures for studying words; spelling resources; words that follow basic patterns; words that follow common rules; personal survival words; spelling demons; foreign words; contractions; commonly misspelled homonyms; and meanings of prefixes, suffixes, and roots. On a later day in the week,

work is collected on independent word studies, and students participate in a spelling review. For this review students find a partner, exchange word study lists, and administer spelling reviews in pairs following a classroom procedure for spelling reviews.

7. Search for ways to publish students' work once they have completed their final composition. Publishing efforts may include the following: individually bound books; individual pieces handwritten or typed, then printed or photocopied; individual pieces of writing as gifts for people whom writers care about; submissions to class magazines, school literary magazines, and yearbooks; submissions to local newspapers; submissions to magazines that publish student writing; announcements on the intercom or in an assembly; submissions to the principal's weekly newsletter; posters and other literary creations for classroom bulletin boards and school corridors.

At the end of the year, ask students to assess their entire body of work and describe their growth.

Goals of the Reading Workshop

1. Help students develop a love of books, appreciation for more serious literature, and understandings about literary craft.

2. Extend, enrich, and deepen students' reflections about literature by encouraging written correspondence with the teacher and by providing a genuine, interested audience who will write back to the students about their responses and reflections.

Teacher Preparation for the Reading Workshop

1. Develop a classroom library with high-quality literature and popular titles. Write a letter inviting students to write back about books, and place the letter in a notebook for each student.

2. Prepare classroom materials and establish routines and procedures for recordkeeping needed for the reading workshop. Make available to students "Rules and Expectations for the Reading Workshop," organizers for reading lists and homework, forms for personal glossaries, reading attitude surveys, student reading records, forms for dialogue journals, illustrative book reviews, and book commercials.

Instructional Procedures for the Reading Workshop

1. Begin with a book talk about old favorite books as well as new additions to your classroom library. Ask students to give book talks (i.e., talk about a book each one is reading or has read). Schedule frequent book talks and book reviews throughout the year. Encourage students to borrow books from their school and community libraries.

2. Direct students to select their own books, and allow regularly scheduled time for in-class reading. Observe students and meet with them in conferences to ensure that each student has chosen the right book to begin the year's reading. Require at least one-half hour of independent reading every weeknight.

3. Provide students opportunities for guided discussion and social interaction about the books they are reading. Be responsive to what the student is doing. Discussion is necessary to maintain student interest and extend student learning into higher realms of literacy development. Model the value of self-selected reading by talking about the books you are reading.

4. Provide students with notebooks containing a letter from you inviting

them to write back about books. Exchange letters that describe accounts of your processes as readers, speculations on authors' processes as writers, suggestions for revisions in what has been read, connections between different books, and connections between books and background experiences.

5. Present explicit lessons based on knowledge of students' strengths and needs that address writing techniques, styles, genres, authors, and the structural features of literature. Have students take note of such mini-lessons in their writing-reading notebooks.

6. Encourage students to progress through the year from popular titles to more serious literature. Require students to make daily or regular entries in their dialogue journals and carry on regular correspondence. Encourage students to draw ideas for the writing workshop from their reading.

7. Ask students at the end of the year to write a reflective essay assessing their work for the year and describing their reading growth.

Relevant English–Language Arts Content Standards

Grades Five Through Eight: Word Analysis, Fluency, and Systematic Vocabulary Development

1.0 Students use their knowledge of word origins and word relationships, as well as historical and literary context clues, to determine the meaning of specialized vocabulary and to understand the precise meaning of grade-level-appropriate words.

Grades Nine Through Twelve: Word Analysis, Fluency, and Systematic Vocabulary Development

1.0 Students apply their knowledge of word origins to determine the meaning of new words encountered in reading materials and use those words accurately.

Grades Five Through Eight: Reading Comprehension

2.0 Students read and understand grade-level-appropriate material. They describe and connect the essential ideas, arguments, and perspectives of the text by using their knowledge of text structure, organization, and purpose. The selections in *Recommended Readings in Literature, Kindergarten Through Grade Eight* illustrate the quality and complexity of the materials to be read by students. In addition, by grade eight, students read one million words annually on their own, including a good representation of grade-level-appropriate narrative and expository text (e.g., classic and contemporary literature, magazines, newspapers, online information).

Grades Nine Through Twelve: Reading Comprehension

2.0 Students read and understand grade-level-appropriate material. They analyze the organizational patterns, arguments, and positions advanced. The selections in *Recommended Literature, Grades Nine Through Twelve* (1990) illustrate the quality and complexity of the materials to be read by students. In addition, by grade twelve, students read two million words annually on their own, including a wide variety of classic and contemporary literature, magazines, newspapers, and online information.

Grades Five Through Eight: Writing Applications

2.0 Students write narrative, expository, persuasive, and descriptive text of at least 500 to 700 words in each genre. Student writing demonstrates a command of standard American English and the research, organizational, and drafting strategies outlined in Writing Standard 1.0.

Grades Nine Through Twelve: Writing Applications

2.0 Students combine the rhetorical strategies of narration, exposition, persuasion, and description to produce text of at least 1,500 words each. Student writing demonstrates a command of standard American English and the research, organizational, and drafting strategies outlined in Writing Standard 1.0.

Further Resources

Allen, Janet. *It's Never Too Late: Leading Adolescents to Lifelong Literacy*. Portsmouth, N.H.: Heinemann, 1995.

Atwell, Nancie. *In the Middle: New Understandings about Reading, Writing, and Learning*. Portsmouth, N.H.: Boynton/Cook Publishers, 1998.

Calkins, Lucy M. *The Art of Teaching Writing*. Portsmouth, N.H.: Heinemann, 1994.

Graves, Donald H. *Writing: Teachers and Children at Work*. Portsmouth, N.H.: Heinemann, 1983.

Muschla, Gary R. *Reading Workshop Survival Kit*. West Nyack, N.Y.: The Center for Applied Research in Education, 1997.

Example of the Writing-Reading Workshop Technique

The following paragraph represents an example of writing that reflects a student's thoughts on a literary selection.

As I read *To Kill a Mockingbird* by Harper Lee, I realized the importance of really paying attention to the story from the beginning to the end. By doing this I was able to fully understand the complexity of the plot and the characters. I could organize and follow the events and the perspectives of the different characters.

The author showed me through the details and actions in the literature that injustice can happen to anyone at any time regardless of the truth as it is presented. This book makes you think about the lessons you should teach when you are raising your own children. The author showed me that our justice system has faults that still exist today and that there are consequences for all choices both good and bad. Since I have read this book I think twice before I do something. I think about the consequences and this influences my decisions.

Strategy List

Strands in the English–Language Arts Content Standards

Reading

1.0—Word Analysis, Fluency, and Systematic Vocabulary Development
2.0—Reading Comprehension (Focus on Informational Materials)
3.0—Literary Response and Analysis

Writing

1.0—Writing Strategies
2.0—Writing Applications (Genres and Their Characteristics)

VOCABULARY DEVELOPMENT

Analogy Graphic Organizer

The analogy graphic organizer provides a visual framework for students to analyze important relationships among concepts and to identify the similarities and differences between a new concept and something with which they are already familiar.

Goals

1. Expand student understanding of important concepts.
2. Help students understand how an analogy can be used to illustrate the similarities and differences between a new concept and something familiar to them.

Teacher Preparation

1. Try to determine what students already know about possible analogous relationships involving a concept you want to introduce.
2. Select one concept familiar to students that can be used to develop an analogous relationship to the new concept.

Instructional Procedures

1. Discuss with students what an analogy is and provide an example, such as the following: Gills are to fish as lungs are to people.
2. Elicit from students a list of specific characteristics that the two concepts you have chosen have in common.
3. Elicit a similar list of differences.
4. Discuss with students the categories that form the basis for the relationship between the concepts.
5. Encourage students to use the analogy graphic organizer to write a summary describing the similarities and differences between the two concepts.
6. Demonstrate how the analogies can be used as retrieval clues or mnemonic (i.e., memory assistance) devices to help students recall information.

Relevant English–Language Arts Content Standards

Grades Five Through Eight: Word Analysis, Fluency, and Systematic Vocabulary Development

1.0   Students use their knowledge of word origins and word relationships, as well as historical and literary context clues, to determine the meaning of specialized vocabulary and to understand the precise meaning of grade-level-appropriate words.

Grade Eight: Word Analysis, Fluency, and Systematic Vocabulary Development

1.1   [Students] analyze idioms, analogies, metaphors, and similes to infer the literal and figurative meanings of phrases.

Further Resources

Buehl, Doug. *Classroom Strategies for Interactive Learning.* Schofield: Wisconsin State Reading Association, 1995.

Cook, Doris, *Strategic Learning in the Content Areas.* Madison: Wisconsin Department of Public Instruction, 1989.

Sample

Analogy Graphic Organizer

NEW CONCEPT	FAMILIAR CONCEPT
Decimals	**Fractions**

Similarities

Both express whole numbers and parts of a whole number.

The amounts they express may be the same.

Both may have a value less than one, equal to one, or more than one.

The four operations of adding, subtracting, multiplying, and dividing can be performed on both decimals and fractions.

Any fraction can be expressed as a decimal.

Differences

Fractions have a numerator and a denominator.

Decimals use a decimal point to separate the whole numbers from the parts.

Fractions are written as two numbers separated by a horizontal or diagonal line.

Operations on fractions require a set of algorithmic steps different from those for whole numbers and decimals.

Relationship Categories

Forms

Amounts expressed

Operations

Algorithms

Concept Wheel/Circle

The concept wheel/circle is an instructional technique that builds on students' background knowledge, encourages brainstorming and discussion, and visually displays the connection between previous conceptual knowledge and the new word.

Goals

1. Promote growth in vocabulary, conceptual understandings, and comprehension.
2. Activate and extend the background knowledge of students.

Teacher Preparation

1. Select an important concept to teach.
2. Have dictionaries available.

Instructional Procedures

1. Introduce the concept to students, writing the word on the chalkboard.
2. Ask students to generate a list of other words or phrases that come to mind when they think of the target word.
3. Lead a class discussion on students' responses.
4. Write a list of words from their responses that fit appropriately with the target word on the chalkboard.
5. Direct students to find a definition of the word in the textbook, glossary, or dictionary.
6. Read the definition of the target word and direct students to compare their generated list of words with the definition.
7. Direct students to look over the words on the board very carefully and with the definition in mind to decide on at least three words from the list that will help them remember the target word.
8. Tell students to write their selected words in the concept wheel to help them remember the concept (see example).

Relevant English-Language Arts Content Standards

Grade Seven: Vocabulary and Concept Development

1.3   Clarify word meanings through the use of definition, example, restatement, or contrast.

Grade Eight: Vocabulary and Concept Development

1.3   Use word meanings within the appropriate context and show ability to verify those meanings by definition, restatement, example, comparison, or contrast.

Further Resources

Rupley, William H.; John W. Logan; and William D. Nichols. "Vocabulary Instruction in a Balanced Reading Program," *The Reading Teacher*, Vol. 52 (December 1998/January 1999), 340.

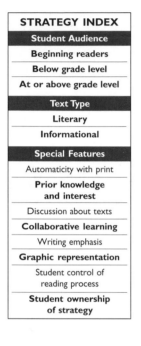

STRATEGY INDEX
Student Audience
Beginning readers
Below grade level
At or above grade level
Text Type
Literary
Informational
Special Features
Automaticity with print
Prior knowledge and interest
Discussion about texts
Collaborative learning
Writing emphasis
Graphic representation
Student control of reading process
Student ownership of strategy

Example of a Concept Wheel

Photosynthesis

light
combining
food making
chlorophyll
sun
green leaves
solar energy
oxygen
carbon dioxide

Photosynthesis	Light
Chlorophyll	Food making in plants

LINK

LINK is a preparation-for-learning strategy that prompts students to brainstorm what they will encounter in a reading selection and direct their own discussion of what they already know about a topic. The acronym stands for *List, Inquire, Note,* and *Know*.

Goals

1. Help students link their prior knowledge with the information they will be studying.
2. Prompt students to anticipate content and make associations, and motivate them to study new material carefully.

Teacher Preparation

Select an important concept or term in the material on which you intend to focus. Be sure it is a word that will trigger a response from the students.

Instructional Procedures

1. Display the term or concept on an overhead transparency or a chalkboard.

List

2. Ask the students to list on paper, within three minutes, words associated with the concept.
3. Display their responses on the overhead transparency or chalkboard. To ensure maximum participation, ask for one response from each student in the class. You may want to call on less active participants first to increase chances of their involvement. Allow students to offer a second idea after everyone has responded.

Inquire

4. Students ask other students about items on the list. The teacher's role at this stage is largely passive and neutral. The purpose of this activity is to allow students to share and elaborate on their understandings. Let *them* discover their errors and difficulties.

Note

5. Turn off the overhead projector or erase words on the chalkboard. Then instruct the students to turn over their papers and write down everything that comes to mind from prior experience and class discussion in response to the term or concept on the board. Limit the time for brainstorming to one minute. One variation is to have students write a definition of the concept.

Know

6. Students are now ready to read the passage. After reading, they may be asked to note what they now know after they have encountered new material.

Relevant English–Language Arts Content Standards

Grade Four: Reading Comprehension

2.3 [Students] make and confirm predictions about text by using prior knowledge and ideas presented in text itself.

Grades One Through Twelve: Reading Comprehension

2.0 Students read and understand grade-level-appropriate material.

Further Resources

Buehl, Doug. *Classroom Strategies for Interactive Learning.* Schofield: Wisconsin State Reading Association, 1995.

Cook, Doris. *Strategic Learning in the Content Areas.* Madison: Wisconsin Department of Public Instruction, 1989.

Vaughan, Joseph L., and Thomas H. Estes. *Reading and Reasoning Beyond the Primary Grades.* Boston: Allyn and Bacon, 1986.

ABOLITIONISM

slavery	black people	Africans	North	South
antislavery	slave masters	cruelty	Civil War	conflict
"North Star"	Frederick Douglass	Canada	Lincoln	Harriet Tubman
overseers	John Brown	prejudice	lashing	*Uncle Tom's Cabin*
abolish	slave revolts	Quakers	protest	Underground Railroad

Student Brainstorm:

Abolitionism is the desire to abolish slavery. Before the Civil War many black people in the South were slaves. The Quakers (a religious group) in the North were against slavery and helped slaves escape to the North into Canada. Some abolitionists, like John Brown, led slave revolts; others, like Harriet Tubman, led slaves to freedom in the North. They were able to do this by using a system of signals, stops, and hiding places. This system was known as the Underground Railroad. A newspaper published and written by Frederick Douglass called the North Star often contained coded messages that helped people make their way to freedom.

List-Group-Label

List-group-label is an activity that combines brainstorming and categorization as a way to help students organize concepts. Although it works best when students have some background knowledge related to the concepts, the activity can be used to introduce or review concepts.

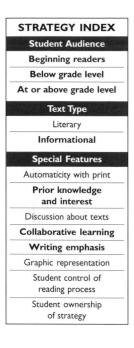
Goals

1. Stimulate meaningful word associations among terms that are part of the same category of concepts.

2. Help students distinguish super-, sub-, and coordinate relations among grade-appropriate words.

3. Activate students' background knowledge prior to reading a passage.

Teacher Preparation

Identify a topic or overarching concept for generating student responses.

Instructional Procedures

1. Write the topic on the chalkboard or on an overhead transparency.

2. Elicit from the entire class all the words or phrases students can associate with the topic. Accept and record all responses at this point. A list of 20 to 30 words should be generated.

3. Divide the class in small groups and have students group the words that have been listed on the basis of something they have in common. In this step words that do not belong will usually be recognized and deleted.

4. Once categories of words have been identified, students decide on a label for each group.

5. This activity can be extended by adding a writing exercise in which students summarize what they have learned about the topic.

Relevant English–Language Arts Content Standards

Grade One: Word Analysis, Fluency, and Systematic Vocabulary Development

1.17 Classify grade-appropriate categories of words (e.g., concrete collections of animals, foods, toys).

Grade One: Reading Comprehension

2.6 Relate prior knowledge to textual information.

Grade Three: Word Analysis, Fluency, and Systematic Vocabulary Development

1.5 Demonstrate knowledge of levels of specificity among grade-appropriate words and explain the importance of these relations (e.g., *dog/mammal/animal/living things*).

Further Resources

Alverman, D. E., and S. F. Phelps. *Content Reading and Literacy*. Boston: Allyn and Bacon, 1994.

Taba, Hilda. *Teacher's Handbook for Elementary Social Studies*. Reading, Mass.: Addison-Wesley, 1967.

Sample List-Group-Label Exercise

Angles

The list-group-label strategy may be applied in a geometry class, as follows:

Step 1. **Free associations** (*by whole class*)

point	circumference	obtuse
line	semicircle	radius
diameter	center	compass
arc	vertex	ray
protractor	*pi*	sides
acute	right	endpoint
		ratio

Step 2. **Grouping and labeling** (*by students as a class, in pairs, or in small groups*)

Terms about angles: vertex, sides, ray, endpoint

Devices for measurement: compass, protractor

Terms about circles: chord, arc, circumference, diameter, semicircle, radius, center, pi

Types of angles: acute, right, obtuse

Used in formula for *pi:* circumference, diameter, ratio

Units of length: point, line endpoint, ray, line segment

Step 3. **Sample writing exercise** (*by students in groups or pairs*)

Angles are figures formed by two rays that have the same endpoints. The endpoint is called the vertex. The rays are called the sides of the angles.

Peer Vocabulary Teaching

Peer vocabulary teaching is a strategy in which students learn to identify the most crucial words in a reading selection; justify selecting that word; enter the word on a personal word list; use word analysis and/or context clues to infer the meaning of the word; consult the dictionary to obtain a definition when necessary; and then teach the word and its meaning to a peer through a selected memory device or cue.

Goals

1. Involve students with active processing of, and multiple exposures to, words while providing them with both definitions and contextual information as needed.
2. Integrate vocabulary learning with content instruction; provide vocabulary-building activities in a nonthreatening context; and structure learning activities to build background.

Teacher Preparation

1. Select a variety of excerpts from classroom materials to use for explicit instruction in how to identify crucial terms in different kinds of passages.
2. Develop a format for students' personal word list entries for student glossaries.

Instructional Procedures

1. Explain to students that they need to develop the ability to identify crucial terms in what they read (that is, words whose meanings they must know to understand a particular text). Words that are introduced in a leading sentence and repeated in various ways are important and appropriate for dictionary work. Other words likely to be crucial are italicized terms, words in boldface, terms used in headings, words used in introductions and summaries, words defined by the author, and terms in graphics and glossaries.

2. Select an excerpt from the reading being studied by the class. Instruct students to read the excerpt and underline those unfamiliar words that they believe they must know to comprehend the text. Students then compare their responses and discuss the criteria they used to select the words. This can be helpful in illustrating differences between the selection criteria for different types of reading assignments. For example, in a short story it may be crucial that the words relating to the plot be understood; in a chapter from a textbook, words that appear in the introduction may be targets of intensive study.

3. Ask students to select one word from a chapter the class is studying and enter it into their personal word lists. They must have a reason for choosing that particular word, that is, a way of demonstrating the importance of the word in the reading selection.

4. Instruct students to use their knowledge of word part analysis (affixes and roots) or their understanding of the sentence-level and general contexts to infer a reasonable meaning for the word. If those approaches do not work, students will then look the word up in the dictionary. Students complete their personal word list entries.

5. Have each student choose a strategy, such as an image, word map, context clue, word part, or significant idea, to teach the meaning of the word to another student.

6. Allow all students the next day to share in class their word lists and the reasons for their selections.

7. Divide all students in the class into pairs. They alternately teach their word and learn the word of their partner. This should lead to a good discussion of the criteria for crucial terms, and it also gives students the

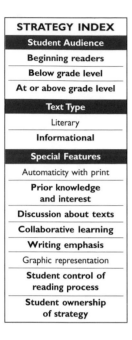

STRATEGY INDEX

Student Audience
Beginning readers
Below grade level
At or above grade level

Text Type
Literary
Informational

Special Features
Automaticity with print
Prior knowledge and interest
Discussion about texts
Collaborative learning
Writing emphasis
Graphic representation
Student control of reading process
Student ownership of strategy

opportunity to compare the effectiveness of the different vocabulary identification and study strategies used by their classmates. The cycle repeats on a regular basis.

Relevant English–Language Arts Content Standards

Grades Five Through Eight: Word Analysis, Fluency, and Systematic Vocabulary Development

1.0 Students use their knowledge of word origins and word relationships, as well as historical and literary context clues, both to determine the meaning of specialized vocabulary and to understand the precise meaning of grade-level-appropriate words.

Grades Nine Through Twelve: Word Analysis, Fluency, and Systematic Vocabulary Development

1.0 Students apply their knowledge of word origins to determine the meaning of new words encountered in reading materials and use those words accurately.

Further Resources

Haggard, M. R. "The Vocabulary Self-collection Strategy: Using Student Interest and Word Knowledge to Enhance Vocabulary Growth," *Journal of Reading,* Vol. 29 (1986), 634–42.

Johnson, Denise, and Virginia Steele. "So Many Words, So Little Time: Helping College Learners Acquire Vocabulary-building Strategies," *Journal of Adolescent and Adult Literacy,* Vol. 39 (February 1996), 348–57.

Nation, I. S. P. *Teaching and Learning Vocabulary.* New York: Newbury House, 1990.

Reyes, Maria L., and Linda A. Molner. "Instructional Strategies for Second-Language Learners in the Content Areas," *Journal of Reading,* Vol. 35 (October 1991), 96–103.

Stahl, S. "Three Principles of Effective Vocabulary Instruction," *Journal of Reading,* Vol. 29 (1986), 662–71.

Example of Peer Vocabulary Teaching

Word	What I Think It Means	Clues (Context or Structure)	Dictionary Definition (only if needed)
Mobilize	To move from place to place	Now the American government faced the problem of how to mobilize or *assemble* an army that could help the Allies.	
Protectorate	In need of protection	Protect'-orate	A country or region that is protected and partially controlled by a more powerful country.
Reparations	Payment for damage during war time	The European Allies wanted to *reward* themselves and punish Germany by taking German territory and *large sums of money* called reparations.	

Rating Vocabulary

Rating vocabulary is an activity in which students rate their knowledge of words before they read, after they read, and after they discuss the words. Most appropriately used at the beginning of a lesson or unit, this strategy encourages students to think metacognitively about their conceptual background for each word being introduced.

Goals

1. Prior to reading, help students determine whether words in a reading selection are familiar or unfamiliar.

2. Encourage students to think about words they encounter in print and to respond strategically to those that are unfamiliar.

Teacher Preparation

1. Identify and, if necessary, prioritize the most important words in a lesson or unit.

2. Develop a Rating Vocabulary activity sheet following the format of the example below.

Instructional Procedures

1. Give students a copy of the Rating Vocabulary activity sheet and explain that they will think about the words at three different points: before reading, after reading, and after discussing the words.

2. Explain the rating criteria: A plus sign (+) indicates students are sure they know the meaning of the word; a minus sign (−) indicates they are sure they do not know the meaning of the word; and a question mark (?) indicates they are uncertain about the meaning of the word.

3. Read the words aloud to the whole class or have the students read the words silently. Pause after each word and have the students rate the words on the activity sheet.

4. Have the students read the selection silently. When they have finished reading, students rate the words again in the "After Reading" column.

5. Break into small groups in which students share their ratings by discussing what each word means, which words they knew prior to reading, and which words they figured out while reading.

6. Have students complete the last column of the activity sheet. Write on the board or on a transparency any words that a group still does not understand.

7. Elicit from students the strategies they used to determine the meaning of words that were initially unknown.

Relevant English–Language Arts Content Standards

Grade Three: Word Analysis, Fluency, and Systematic Vocabulary Development

1.6 Use sentence and word context to find the meaning of unknown words.

Grade Four: Word Analysis, Fluency, and Systematic Vocabulary Development

1.3 Use knowledge of root words to determine the meaning of unknown words within a passage.

Grade Five: Word Analysis, Fluency, and Systematic Vocabulary Development

1.2 Use word origins to determine the meaning of unknown words.

Grade Six: Word Analysis, Fluency, and Systematic Vocabulary Development

1.4 Monitor expository text for unknown words or words with novel meanings by using word, sentence, and paragraph clues to determine meaning.

Grade Seven: Word Analysis, Fluency, and Systematic Vocabulary Development

1.3 Clarify word meanings through the use of definition, example, restatement, or contrast.

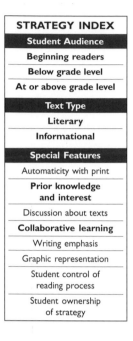

STRATEGY INDEX

Student Audience
Beginning readers
Below grade level
At or above grade level

Text Type
Literary
Informational

Special Features
Automaticity with print
Prior knowledge and interest
Discussion about texts
Collaborative learning
Writing emphasis
Graphic representation
Student control of reading process
Student ownership of strategy

Grade Eight: Word Analysis, Fluency, and Systematic Vocabulary Development

1.3 Use word meanings within the appropriate context and show ability to verify those meanings by definition, restatement, example, comparison, or contrast.

Further Resources

Rothstein, Vicki, and Rhoda Zacker Goldberg. *Reading and Vocabulary Language Lessons for the Curriculum, Grades K–6: Thinking Through Stories.* East Moline, Ill.: Linguisystems, 1993.

Sample Activity Sheet for Rating Vocabulary

Unit: Revolutionary War

+ = I knew it	− = I don't know it	? = I'm not sure

	Before Reading	After Reading	After Discussion
1. Redcoat	+		
2. Flintlock	?	+	
3. Boycott	−	?	+
4. Minutemen	?	+	
5. Hessians	−	?	+
6. Patriot	+		
7. Loyalist	?	?	+
8. Casualties	?	+	
9. Independence	+		
10. Townshend Acts	−	?	+
11. Intolerable Acts	−	?	+
12. Proclamation of 1763	−	?	+

Semantic Feature Analysis

Semantic feature analysis is an activity in which students identify important characteristics of a category of concepts, compare specific features of individual concepts in the category, and then distinguish between those specific features. The use of a matrix helps students see the similarities and differences between the concepts.

Goals

1. Reinforce and expand concepts previously introduced as part of a reading selection or content area lesson.

2. Clarify frequently confused terms that are part of the same category of concepts.

3. Help students become aware of similarities and differences between concepts within a specific category.

Teacher Preparation

1. Identify a category of concepts in the subject you are teaching.

2. Select several terms within the category and two or three features that some of the terms share.

3. Create a matrix with the terms you have selected in the left column and the features they share across the top. Leave space in the column and across the top for additional terms to be added.

Instructional Procedures

1. Use an overhead transparency of the matrix to demonstrate how a semantic feature analysis works by coding the first concept. Use a plus sign (+) if the concept exhibits a feature and a minus sign (–) if it does not.

2. Elicit from students how they would code the remaining concepts in your example and record their responses on the transparency.

3. Distribute copies of the matrix to each student and have students brainstorm additional concepts and features that fit the category. Have students enter the new concepts and features on their copy of the matrix as you add them to the transparency.

4. Have students work in pairs to complete the matrix. Discuss the decisions students make regarding their codings and the similarities and differences between the concepts.

Relevant English–Language Arts Content Standards

Grade Two: Reading Comprehension

2.5 Restate facts and details in the text to clarify and organize ideas.

Grade Four: Reading Comprehension

2.5 Compare and contrast information on the same topic after reading several passages or articles.

Grade Five: Reading Comprehension

2.4 Draw inferences, conclusions, or generalizations about text and support them with textual evidence and prior knowledge.

Further Resources

Johnson, D., and P. D. Pearson. *Teaching Reading Vocabulary* (Second edition). New York: Holt, Rinehart & Winston, 1984.

Example of Semantic Feature Analysis

Animal	Spinal Column	Lungs	Mammary Glands	Four Legs	Mollusk	Reptile	Mammal
Snail	−	−	−	−	+	−	−
Alligator	+	+	−	+	−	+	−
Clam	−	−	−	−	+	−	−
Lizard	+	+	−	+	−	+	−
Whale	+	+	+	−	−	−	+
Snake	+	+	−	−	−	+	−
Shark	+	−	−	−	−	−	−

Semantic Word Map

A semantic word map allows students to conceptually explore their knowledge of a new word by mapping it with other related words or phrases similar in meaning to the new word.

Goal

Help students acquire a clearer definition of a concept by learning the connections among several related words.

Teacher Preparation

1. Select a concept and anticipate students' background knowledge.
2. Reflect on important related ideas, events, characteristics, and examples for discussion.

Instructional Procedures

1. Introduce the concept.
2. Have students brainstorm many words regarding the concept.
3. Record their words on the board.
4. Extend the discussion around words that suggest larger related categories, ideas, events, characteristics, and examples.
5. Remind students which words on the list are likely to be most useful as the larger, organizing ideas.
6. Direct students to work together in small groups to decide which words belong under the appropriate categories and to discuss the reasons for their decisions.
7. Give students about 10 minutes to complete their word maps. Walk around the room observing each group's progress, assisting when needed.
8. Allow all groups to present their semantic word maps and their reasons for choosing each word for the appropriate category.

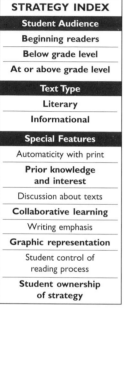
Variation

1. Model the process of creating a semantic word map by identifying a common Greek, Latin, or Anglo-Saxon word root; its core meaning; and the common base form of the root, such as *astron,* star: *aster, astro.* (In addition to standard classroom dictionaries, a dictionary of word origins will also be useful.)

   Examples:
   - *bene*—good, well: *bene, beni*
   - *civis*—citizen: *cit, civ*
   - *liber*—free: *lib*
   - *malus*—bad, evil: *mal, mali*

2. Write the word root and its meaning on the board and draw a circle around it.
3. Have students brainstorm as many words as they can think of that share that root (*astrology, astronomy, asteroid, astronaut, astronomer, astrologer, astroturf, Astrodome*).
4. As students call out the words, write them on the board on lines radiating from the center, pointing out their meanings in relation to the root.
5. Demonstrate how to remodel the word map by creating clusters under broader categories, such as persons, things, fields of study.
6. Select a useful word root central to the understanding of one or more key concepts.
7. Have students work independently or in small groups to create their own semantic word maps as demonstrated above.
8. Encourage students to present their word maps orally to explain the new words they have learned and the word associations that will help them remember the target concept.
9. Direct students to proceed with the reading.
10. Incorporate Greek, Roman, and Norse mythology in semantic word maps to help students relate the

meaning of a new word to its mythical origin (e.g., the word *protean* is derived from the name of the sea god Proteus, who could assume various shapes).

Guidelines from Research

1. Select for vocabulary instruction words from texts students will read in the classroom.

2. Engage students in learning new words to help them retain the words and deepen their understanding of new vocabulary. Provide students multiple opportunities to use new words in their speaking, listening, reading, and writing activities.

3. Build a conceptual base for learning new words. Use analogies, language features, and other relationships to known words to activate students' background knowledge of concepts related to new vocabulary.

4. Provide various instructional strategies (mental pictures, visual aids, kinesthetic associations, smells, tastes) to help students retain word knowledge.

Relevant English–Language Arts Content Standards

Grade Seven: Vocabulary and Concept Development

1.2 Use knowledge of Greek, Latin, and Anglo-Saxon roots and affixes to understand content-area vocabulary.

1.3 Clarify word meanings through the use of definition, example, restatement, or contrast.

Grade Eight: Vocabulary and Concept Development

1.3 Use word meanings within the appropriate context and show ability to verify those meanings by definition, restatement, example, comparison, or contrast.

Grades Nine and Ten: Vocabulary and Concept Development

1.3 Identify Greek, Roman, and Norse mythology and use the knowledge to understand the origin and meaning of new words (e.g., the word *narcissistic* drawn from the myth of Narcissus and Echo).

Grades Eleven and Twelve: Vocabulary and Concept Development

1.4 Apply knowledge of Greek, Latin, and Anglo-Saxon roots and affixes to draw inferences concerning the meaning of scientific and mathematical terminology.

Further Resources

Rupley, William H.; John W. Logan; and William D. Nichols. "Vocabulary Instruction in a Balanced Reading Program," *The Reading Teacher*, Vol. 52 (December 1998/January 1999), 340.

Example of Semantic Word Map

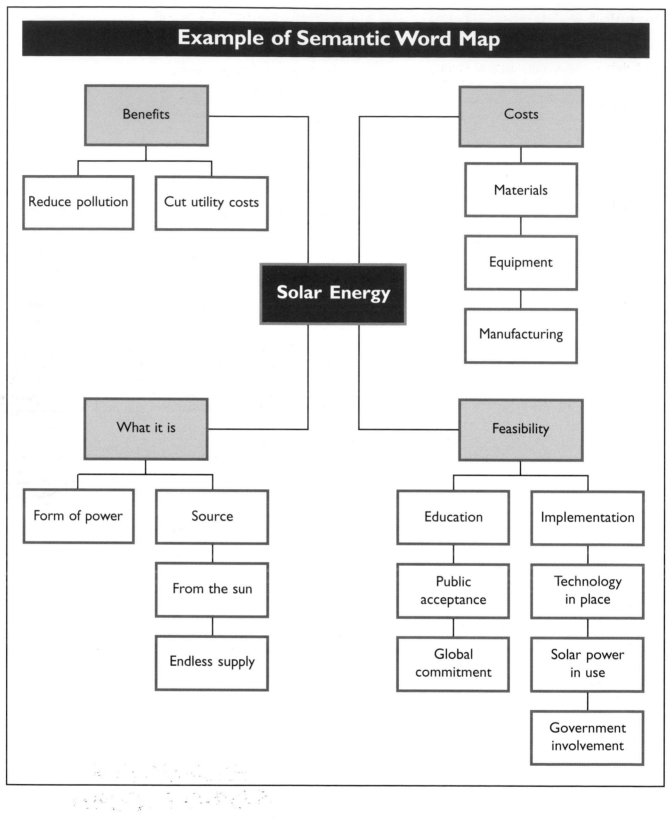

Vocab-Lit Study Sheet

Vocab-lit study sheet is a technique for helping students understand literary elements through vocabulary study. It emphasizes understanding aspects of one's own vocabulary and concept development (metacognition).

Goals

1. Guide students to an understanding that literary forms have elements with a symbolic and literal meaning.
2. Help students discern different levels of meaning to understand and appreciate what they are reading.
3. Facilitate students' development of vocabulary strategies.

Teacher Preparation

Choose words from the assigned reading that are closely related to the theme of the literature being read and could serve as springboards for a discussion of literary elements.

Instructional Procedures

1. Divide the class into small groups. Introduce significant words from the assigned reading and assign one word for each small group to consider.
2. Model for the students how to complete the vocab-lit study sheet.
   a. After writing the word on the study sheet, each student indicates his or her own understanding of the group's word.
   b. Group members reveal the level of understanding they checked. Those with greater knowledge should discuss their understanding with group members.
   c. The group then checks the way in which the word is used in the assigned reading and writes the appropriate sentence on the study sheet.
   d. Guide the students in a discussion of what they learned from reflecting on the word's meaning in this context and instruct them to complete the study sheet.

Relevant English–Language Arts Content Standards

Grades One Through Four: Literary Response and Analysis

3.0   Students read and respond to a wide variety of significant works of children's literature. They distinguish between the structural features of the text and the literary terms or elements (e.g., theme, plot, setting, characters).

Grades Five Through Eight: Word Analysis, Fluency, and Systematic Vocabulary Development

1.0   Students use their knowledge of word origins and word relationships, as well as historical and literary context clues, to determine the meaning of specialized vocabulary and to understand the precise meaning of grade-level-appropriate words.

Further Resources

Chase, Ann C., and Frederick A. Dufelmeyer. "Vocab-lit: Integrating Vocabulary Study and Literature Study," *Journal of Reading,* Vol. 34 (November 1990), 188–93.

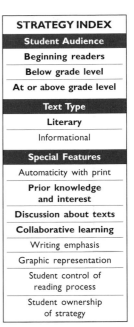

STRATEGY INDEX
Student Audience
Beginning readers
Below grade level
At or above grade level
Text Type
Literary
Informational
Special Features
Automaticity with print
Prior knowledge and interest
Discussion about texts
Collaborative learning
Writing emphasis
Graphic representation
Student control of reading process
Student ownership of strategy

Sample Vocab-Lit Study Sheet

Word	My knowledge	Group strategy	Context
	Unknown _____ Acquainted _____ Established _____	Experience _____ Context _____ Dictionary _____	
Definition		**What we learned**	

Word	My knowledge	Group strategy	Context
	Unknown _____ Acquainted _____ Established _____	Experience _____ Context _____ Dictionary _____	
Definition		**What we learned**	

Word	My knowledge	Group strategy	Context
	Unknown _____ Acquainted _____ Established _____	Experience _____ Context _____ Dictionary _____	
Definition		**What we learned**	

Word	My knowledge	Group strategy	Context
	Unknown _____ Acquainted _____ Established _____	Experience _____ Context _____ Dictionary _____	
Definition		**What we learned**	

Wide Reading

Wide reading is a method to ensure that students read large quantities of print regularly. Students are provided a wide selection of reading materials, time for reading in class, opportunities to talk and write about their reading, and explicit role models demonstrating enjoyment of reading.

Goal

Promote overall improvement in vocabulary development, reading comprehension, reading frequency, and reading for enjoyment as a lifetime habit.

Teacher Preparation

1. Create a book-rich environment with titles in an appropriate range of reading levels, genres, authors, and topics, making every effort possible to increase students' access to books.

2. Plan how students will document their reading and record their comments and how you will find out their reactions to wide reading.

Instructional Procedures

1. Explain to all students, including students learning English as a second language, that research has shown the value of free reading in developing vocabulary, language, and literacy.

2. Share your own "reading history" with students.

3. Explain to students that time will be regularly scheduled for wide reading. Explain the schedule and the following rules:

   • The entire class (both students and teacher) reads.

   • There are no interruptions.

4. Provide students access to large quantities of interesting, age-appropriate books.

5. Provide class time for reading, have students document what they are reading, and encourage them to write comments or letters to you in response to their reading.

6. Meet with students about their reading, talk to them about their reading habits and attitudes, and help them set their goals.

7. Make sure every student is productively engaged in reading. Help struggling readers find appropriate materials, and allow them to find a partner and read aloud or read along with an audio tape.

8. Model a book talk after wide reading has become a regular activity in the classroom, and encourage students to share their reading with the rest of the class.

9. Show students that reading is enjoyable by doing the following:

   • Demonstrate that you read for enjoyment every day.

   • Talk about the benefits of reading.

   • Give book talks or short oral readings.

   • Have students give brief book talks or book commercials.

   • Invite older students and entertaining adults to give book talks.

   • Talk about things from reading that make you curious.

   • Compare a book with a movie.

   • Mention intriguing ideas suggested by a book.

10. Give students a questionnaire on their reactions to the wide reading activity after several weeks so that program weaknesses can be remedied.

11. Help students become aware of their own growth as readers.

12. Invite parents to extend the wide reading activity into the home setting and encourage students to read at home.

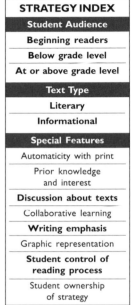

STRATEGY INDEX

Student Audience
Beginning readers
Below grade level
At or above grade level

Text Type
Literary
Informational

Special Features
Automaticity with print
Prior knowledge
and interest
Discussion about texts
Collaborative learning
Writing emphasis
Graphic representation
**Student control of
reading process**
Student ownership
of strategy

Relevant English–Language Arts Content Standards

Grades Five Through Eight: Reading Comprehension

2.0 Students read and understand grade-level-appropriate material. . . . The selections in *Recommended Readings in Literature, Kindergarten Through Grade Eight* illustrate the quality and complexity of the materials to be read by students. In addition, by grade eight, students read one million words annually on their own, including a good representation of grade-level-appropriate narrative and expository text (e.g., classic and contemporary literature, magazines, newspapers, online information).

Grades Nine Through Twelve: Reading Comprehension

2.0 In addition, by grade twelve, students read two million words annually on their own, including a wide variety of classic and contemporary literature, magazines, newspapers, and online information.

Further Resources

Anderson, Richard C. *Research Foundations for Wide Reading*. Paper commissioned by the World Bank. Urbana-Champaign: Center for the Study of Reading, University of Illinois, 1992.

Gambrell, Linda B. "Creating Classroom Cultures That Foster Reading Motivation," *Reading Teacher,* Vol. 50 (September 1996), 14–23.

Pilgreen, Janice L. *The SSR Handbook: How to Organize and Manage a Sustained Silent Reading Program*. Portsmouth, N.H.: Heinemann-Boynton/Cook, 2000.

Pilgreen, Janice, and Stephen Krashen. "Sustained Silent Reading with English as a Second Language High School Students: Impact on Reading Comprehension, Reading Frequency, and Reading Enjoyment," *School Library Media Quarterly,* Vol. 22 (Fall 1993), 21–23.

Tierney, Robert J.; John E. Readence; and Ernest K. Dishner. *Reading Strategies and Practices: A Compendium*. Boston: Allyn and Bacon, 1995.

Sample Wide Reading Record

Date	Title	Author	Genre	Reading Level

Comments:

Date	Title	Author	Genre	Reading Level

Comments:

Date	Title	Author	Genre	Reading Level

Comments:

Date	Title	Author	Genre	Reading Level

Comments:

Date	Title	Author	Genre	Reading Level

Comments:

Strategy List

Strands of the English–Language Arts Content Standards

Reading

1.0—Word Analysis, Fluency, and Systematic Vocabulary Development

2.0—Reading Comprehension (Focus on Informational Materials)

3.0—Literary Response and Analysis

Writing

1.0—Writing Strategies

2.0—Writing Applications (Genres and Their Characteristics)

Phonemic Awareness Training

Phonemic awareness training helps students understand that speech is composed of a series of individual sounds; for example, *cat* is a word made up of a series of sounds, or phonemes, */k/, /a/,* and */t/.* Phonemic awareness tasks require children to analyze or manipulate the units of speech rather than focus on meaning. Phonemic awareness is usually mastered during literacy acquisition in kindergarten and the primary grades. Phonemic awareness training is recommended *only* for those upper grade students who have demonstrated significant delays in acquiring phonological fundamentals of early literacy skills as revealed by a diagnostic assessment. Such training is typically used with upper grade students as part of an intensive reading intervention and should last no more than ten minutes at the beginning of a lesson.

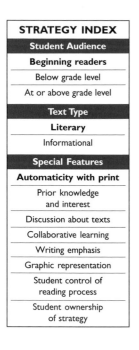

STRATEGY INDEX

Student Audience

Beginning readers

Below grade level

At or above grade level

Text Type

Literary

Informational

Special Features

Automaticity with print

Prior knowledge and interest

Discussion about texts

Collaborative learning

Writing emphasis

Graphic representation

Student control of reading process

Student ownership of strategy

Goals

1. Help students learn how to break down and manipulate speech so that they will understand the relationship of the letters in the writing system to the phonemes in speech.

2. Develop sufficient phonemic awareness in a student delayed in this area so that she or he is more likely to benefit from reading instruction, which, in turn, heightens phonemic and language awareness.

Teacher Preparation

1. Plan the precise focus and sequence of each phonemic awareness activity.

2. Gather or create any necessary materials, such as cards with pictures.

Instructional Procedures

• Before beginning phonemic awareness training for a particular stage, explain what the activity involves and why it is important for sounding out words.

• Drills increase in difficulty from one stage to the next. Day one may begin with stages 1, 2, and 3; day two may continue with stages 2, 3, and 4; and so forth.

• In most cases students should *initially* attend to phonemes (sounds units), not their orthographic representations (letters used in spelling).

• Be prepared for individual differences and avoid making rigid judgments about students based on their responses to these tasks.

• Shift to print-based activities in which students can use their skills in meaningful contexts as quickly as possible.

• Be sure to produce sounds clearly for students.

Stage 1. Phoneme Production/ Replication

1. Have the student produce and distinguish similar phonemes: /b/, /p/; /k/, /g/; /t/, /d/; /f/, /v/; /ng/, /nk/; /sh/, /ch/; /e/, /i/

2. Have the student describe differences for troublesome pairs, noting how each sound is formed in the mouth (e.g., /th/ compared with /f/).

Stage 2. Phoneme Isolation

1. Ask students what is the first sound in a given word (e.g., /b/ *band*). For a group of words, ask, "What's the sound that starts these words: *turkey, time,* and *tape?*" Answer: /t/

2. Ask students to identify the last sound in a word (e.g., *much* /ch/). For a group of words, ask, "What's the sound that ends these words: *check, fake,* and *week?* Answer: /k/

3. Ask students to identify the middle sound in a word (e.g., *mitt* /i/). For a group of words, ask, "What's the sound in the middle of these words: *treat, feel,* and *beak?*" Answer: /ee/

Stage 3. Phoneme Segmentation and Counting

1. Have student say the speech sounds (phonemes) that can be heard in a word that you pronounce orally (e.g., *jeep* /j/ /e/ /p/).

2. Ask the student how many speech sounds (phonemes) she or he can hear in a given word (e.g., jeep → 3).

3. Ask students to clap and count the syllables of their first and last names together (if reinforcement is needed and is age-appropriate).

4. Determine the number of syllables in a name, and ask students to hold two fingers horizontally under their chins so they can feel the chin drop for each syllable. To maximize this effect, encourage students to elongate or stretch each syllable.

5. Have students consciously practice segmenting words into sounds every time they learn to spell a new word in writing and spelling activities.

Stage 4. Phoneme Blending

1. Tell students to blend a set of sounds together to make a word (e.g., /r/ /o/ /k/ [rock]). Give other examples to provide practice.

2. Tell students that you will present a word in a category (such as an animal) sound by sound (e.g., "d-o-g"). Pronounce the words by articulating each of the sounds separately. When the student guesses the word, she or he will name a word for someone else sound by sound.

3. Have students practice blending every time they sound out and blend together a new word encountered in print.

Stage 5. Rhyming Words

1. Tell students to say a word that rhymes with a given word (e.g., *weak—streak, freak, creek, leak*).

2. Have students produce as many words as they can think of that rhyme with a given word or prompt.

Stage 6. Phoneme Deletion

1. Have students practice saying other words without their initial phonemes. Examples: Say *band* without the /b/ (*and*). Say *truck* without the /r/ (*tuck*). Say *stripe* without the /st/ (*ripe*). Say *cable* without the /c/ (*able*).

2. Say the name of a student without the initial sound (e.g., [R]-obert) and have students figure out whose name has been called and what sound is missing.

3. Advance to initial blends, final phonemes, final blends, and initial consonant clusters.

Stage 7. Phoneme Substitution

1. Tell the student to say a word and change the first sound to another. For example: Say *can;* now change the first sound in *can* to /p/. (*pan*)

   Other initial phoneme substitution tasks are:
   Hop /p/ → (*pop*); *meal* /r/ → (*real*); *bet* /j/ → (*jet*); *cope* /s/ → (*soap*)

2. Advance to final and then medial phonemes.

   Say *his.* Now change the last sound to /t/. (*hit*)

   Say *his.* Now change the middle sound to /a/ (short *a*). (*has*)

See the guidelines suggested on pages 96 to 100 of the *Reading/Language Arts Framework for California Public Schools.*

Relevant English–Language Arts Content Standards

Grade One: Word Analysis, Fluency, and Systematic Vocabulary Development

1.4 Distinguish initial, medial, and final sounds in single-syllable words.

1.6 Create and state a series of rhyming words, including consonant blends.

1.7 Add, delete, or change target sounds to change words (e.g., change *cow* to *how; pan* to *an).*

1.8 Blend two to four phonemes into recognizable words (e.g., /c/a/t = *cat;* /f/l/a/t/ = flat).

1.9 Segment single syllable words into their components (e.g., /c/a/t = cat).

Further Resources

Adams, Marilyn, and Barbara Foorman. "The Elusive Phoneme," *American Educator*, Vol. 22 (Spring/Summer 1998), 18–22.

Greene, Jane F. "Language! Effects of an Individualized Structured Language Curriculum for Middle and High School Students," *Annals of Dyslexia,* Vol. 46 (1996), 97–121.

Greene, Jane F. *Sounds and Letters for Readers and Spellers.* Longmont, Colo.: Sopris West, 1998.

Joseph, Laurice M. "Word Boxes Help Children with Learning Disabilities Identify and Spell Words," *The Reading Teacher,* Vol. 52 (December 1998/January 1990), 348–56.

Reading/Language Arts Framework for California Public Schools. Sacramento: California Department of Education, 1999.

Stahl, Steven A.; Ann M. Duffy-Hester; and Katherine A. D. Stahl. "Theory and Research into Practice: Everything You Always Wanted to Know about Phonics (But Were Afraid to Ask)," *Reading Research Quarterly,* Vol. 33 (July/ August/September 1998), 338–55.

Teaching Reading: A Balanced, Comprehensive Approach to Teaching Reading in Prekindergarten Through Third Grade. Sacramento: California Department of Education. 1996.

Yopp, Hallie. "Developing Phonemic Awareness in Young Children," *The Reading Teacher,* Vol. 9 (May 1992), 696–703.

Phonemic and Syllable Awareness Training

Phonemic and syllable awareness training helps students to become aware of units within words. Activities include clapping the syllables in words, representing syllables with index cards, counting and representing phonemes with small paper squares on each index card, and finally showing students how sounds map on to letter combinations by using the small squares on the index cards. Only words that pose a difficulty to students are selected for focused instruction, and those chosen serve as examples of a common spelling pattern that is illustrated for the students. Phonemic and syllable awareness training is typically used with upper grade students only as part of an intensive reading intervention together with practice in reading connected text.

Goals

1. Help readers pronounce words accurately during reading.
2. Help students apply understandings of spelling patterns and word families.

Teacher Preparation

1. Use a diagnostic tool to determine whether the student would be likely to benefit from this procedure (for examples of such tools, see pages 218 and 220 of the *Reading/Language Arts Framework*. Identify words within the listening vocabulary of the student for the training. Focus only on those word patterns that consistently cause confusion for the student in reading and writing. Look for a word that illustrates the target spelling pattern and provide additional words to serve as examples of the pattern.
2. Gather together 5" x 8" index cards (to represent the syllables) and a stack of small paper squares (to represent the phonemes).

Instructional Procedures

1. Explain to students who have a demonstrated need for work in syllable awareness that printed words can be broken down into smaller parts and that these smaller parts are called syllables.

    a. Say the words, emphasizing the syllables by clapping.

    b. Ask students to clap the syllables with you.

    c. Discuss with students the benefits of becoming aware of syllables.

2. Provide students with several index cards (5" x 8") on which they can write the syllables of words. Also make available a supply of small squares that students can use to represent individual phonemes within syllables.

    a. Pronounce a multisyllabic word for students (an example of a common spelling pattern).

    b. Ask students to place an index card on their desk for each syllable.

    c. Demonstrate as appropriate.

3. Pronounce the first syllable and help students segment its phonemes, counting them and representing them within the index card with appropriate small squares (no letters on the small squares). Proceed through the remaining syllables.

4. Put letters on the squares and show students the printed word.

5. Show students how sounds map onto letters represented by small squares on the index cards. Write down examples of other words following the same spelling pattern.

6. Provide students with opportunities to practice reading connected text in materials containing the words just

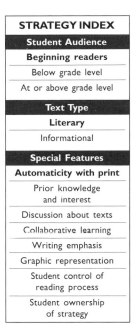

STRATEGY INDEX		
Student Audience		
Beginning readers		
Below grade level		
At or above grade level		
Text Type		
Literary		
Informational		
Special Features		
Automaticity with print		
Prior knowledge and interest		
Discussion about texts		
Collaborative learning		
Writing emphasis		
Graphic representation		
Student control of reading process		
Student ownership of strategy		

studied. The materials should be age-appropriate, and the students should be able to read 90 to 95 percent of the words on a given page. Look for transfer of this skill to new texts.

See the guidelines suggested on pages 96 to 100 of the *Reading/Language Arts Framework for California Public Schools.*

Relevant English–Language Arts Content Standards

Grade Two: Word Analysis, Fluency, and Systematic Vocabulary Development

1.1 Recognize and use knowledge of spelling patterns (e.g., diphthongs, special vowel spellings) when reading.

Grades Two and Three: Word Analysis, Fluency, and Systematic Vocabulary Development

1.3 Decode regular multisyllabic words.

Grade Three: Word Analysis, Fluency, and Systematic Vocabulary Development

1.1 Know and use complex word families when reading (e.g., -*ight)* to decode unfamiliar words.

Further Resources

Bear, Donald R., and others. *Words Their Way: Word Study for Phonics, Vocabulary, and Spelling Instruction.* Englewood Cliffs, N.J.: Prentice-Hall, Inc., 1996.

Reading/Language Arts Framework for California Public Schools, Kindergarten Through Grade Twelve. Sacramento: California Department of Education, 1999.

Teaching Reading: A Balanced, Comprehensive Approach to Teaching Reading in Prekindergarten Through Third Grade. Sacramento: California Department of Education, 1996.

Williams, J. P. "Teaching Decoding with an Emphasis on Phoneme Analysis and Phoneme Blending," *Journal of Educational Psychology,* Vol. 72 (1980), 1–15.

Phonemic and Syllable Analysis Training

Phonemic and syllable analysis training teaches students to observe syllables in words; identify vowel letters and letter combinations and match them with sounds; write the word by breaking it into syllables; say the word by blending the syllables together; and check the pronunciation for sense and a match with their listening vocabulary. This procedure is recommended only for students who have a demonstrated need for work in syllable analysis. Phonemic and syllable analysis training is typically used with upper grade students only as part of an intensive reading intervention together with practice in reading connected text.

Goal

Help readers pronounce words accurately while reading.

Teacher Preparation

1. Use a diagnostic tool to determine whether the student would be likely to benefit from this procedure. (To diagnose the specific difficulty of a reader, see pages 218 and 220 of the *Reading/Language Arts Framework* for ways to measure progress in reading.)
2. Identify several printed multisyllabic words within the listening vocabulary of the student.
3. Prepare several sentences containing multisyllabic words within the listening vocabulary of the student.

Instructional Procedures

1. Explain to students who have a demonstrated need for work in syllable analysis and who have at least a moderate awareness of syllable structures in spoken words that printed words can be broken down into smaller parts just as spoken words can be broken down.
   a. Display printed words broken down into syllables.
   b. Point to each syllable as you say it, stretching out the word.
   c. Explain that each syllable has at least one vowel letter/sound.
   d. Blend the syllables together orally while running your finger under the entire word.
2. Provide students with several printed multisyllabic words within their listening vocabularies and help them pronounce these words.
   a. Ask students to underline or highlight vowels and/or vowel combinations (letters) in one of the words.
   b. Ask students to say the syllables in the word, stretching out the word while pointing to the vowel letters in each syllable that correspond to the vowel sounds.
   c. Ask students to rewrite the word by using dots to indicate the syllable breaks.
   d. Work through several more examples.
3. Provide students with several more multisyllabic words in their listening vocabularies (do not pronounce them).
   a. Ask students to highlight the vowel letters and write each word by using dots between syllables.
   b. Ask students to pronounce each syllable slowly.
   c. Ask students to blend the syllables together, looking at the entire word.
4. Provide students with sentences that include one or more multisyllabic words.
   a. Demonstrate how to analyze the words in context.

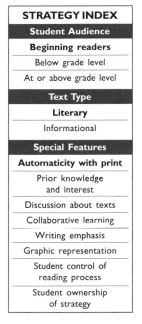

STRATEGY INDEX
Student Audience
Beginning readers
Below grade level
At or above grade level
Text Type
Literary
Informational
Special Features
Automaticity with print
Prior knowledge and interest
Discussion about texts
Collaborative learning
Writing emphasis
Graphic representation
Student control of reading process
Student ownership of strategy

b. Emphasize that pronunciations must be checked against listening vocabulary and against sense in context.

5. Look for transfer of this skill to online encounters with similar words. Give students opportunities to practice in texts that are not too easy and not too difficult for them.

See the guidelines suggested on pages 96 to 100 of the *Reading/Language Arts Framework for California Public Schools.*

Relevant English–Language Arts Content Standards

Grade One: Word Analysis, Fluency, and Systematic Vocabulary Development

1.2   Use knowledge of vowel digraphs and *r*-controlled letter-sound associations to read words.

Grade Two: Word Analysis, Fluency, and Systematic Vocabulary Development

1.1   Recognize and use knowledge of spelling patterns (e.g., diphthongs, special vowel spellings) when reading.

1.3   Decode two-syllable nonsense words and regular multisyllable words.

Grade Three: Word Analysis, Fluency, and Systematic Vocabulary Development

1.2   Decode regular multisyllabic words.

Further Resources

Reading/Language Arts Framework for California Public Schools, Kindergarten Through Grade Twelve. Sacramento: California Department of Education, 1999.

Teaching Reading: A Balanced, Comprehensive Approach to Teaching Reading in Prekindergarten Through Third Grade. Sacramento: California Department of Education, 1996.

Williams, J. P. "Teaching Decoding with an Emphasis on Phoneme Analysis and Phoneme Blending," *Journal of Educational Psychology,* Vol. 72 (1980), 1–15.

Analogy-Based Word Learning and Phonics

Analogy-based word learning and phonics is a procedure for teaching students to decode words they do not know by using words or word parts they do know. It involves (1) drawing analogies between the known and unknown; and (2) teaching beginning readers decoding procedures for key words with common phonogram patterns and word parts. The four steps under "Instructional Procedures for Analogizing" describe a useful process for helping students in the upper grades to sound out novel and difficult words they may encounter in text. "Instructional Procedures for Decoding Key Words" represents an analogy-based system for teaching phonics, which is designed to help students learn letter/sound connections in easy words that can then be used for decoding other words with similar spelling patterns. Although analogizing may help a broad range of students, the basic steps for learning key words are more likely to be provided only in the context of a reading intervention. Whatever approach teachers use for basic decoding should be systematic and explicit and should be tailored to the needs of individual students through thoughtful, in-depth assessments.

Goals

1. Help students apply word-learning procedures in reading connected text.

2. Guide students' practice to develop metacognitive awareness and control over their own word learning.

3. Enhance students' enthusiasm for exploring letter-sound matches in unfamiliar words by reviewing what they have learned about words.

Teacher Preparation

1. Identify the appropriate instructional procedure (drawing analogies or word learning) to use with particular students or groups of students based on careful observation of their oral reading and other diagnostic information.

2. Prepare a Word Pattern Wall, a Talk-to-Yourself Chart, a Partner-Sharing Chart, a Making Words Chart, and illustrative examples as appropriate to your students. The Word Pattern Wall should illustrate phonic patterns.

Instructional Procedures for Analogizing

1. Explain to students that one way to learn how to read and understand words they do not know is by using similar or related words or word parts they do know. Model for students how to figure out the meaning of a new word (*medic*) by thinking about the meaning of a familiar word (*medical*).

2. Ask students to read *be*, *send*, and *table*. Compare and contrast these words with the word parts in the more difficult word *de/pend/able* to help them decode and pronounce this word. Provide students with additional examples to illustrate the process of analogizing.

3. Provide students who encounter a new and difficult word with an easier word they are likely to know that contains a clue to the pronunciation or meaning of the new word. Encourage students to practice this approach independently when they stumble on an unfamiliar word.

4. Build on the strengths and the knowledge base of upper grade students, which is likely to be considerably greater than that of primary grade students.

Instructional Procedures for Decoding Key Words

1. Explain to students that becoming full alphabetic readers—connecting letters and sounds in words—is

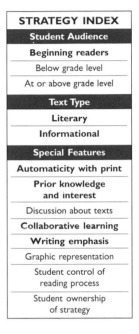

STRATEGY INDEX

Student Audience
Beginning readers
Below grade level
At or above grade level

Text Type
Literary
Informational

Special Features
Automaticity with print
Prior knowledge and interest
Discussion about texts
Collaborative learning
Writing emphasis
Graphic representation
Student control of reading process
Student ownership of strategy

necessary if they are to become good readers. Challenge them to become thoughtful and analytic word detectives.

2. Pronounce a new word, and have students analyze the sounds. Then place the word on the chalkboard. Hearing a word without first seeing it makes it easier for students to detect and correctly identify the number of sounds.

3. Model how to analyze words fully through self-talk:

   First we stretch out the word so that we can hear all the sounds in the word. As we stretch out each sound, we hold up a finger to count the number of sounds. Next we look at the word and count the letters. Do we have the same number of letters as sounds, or will it take more than one letter to represent some of the sounds? Next we figure out what letters match the sounds. Listen as I analyze stop, /s/, /t/, /o/, /p/. *I hear four sounds. I see four letters.*

   That means each letter will probably have a sound. The *o* has a different sound from the one I hear in *go*. In *go* the *o* is not in the middle as it is in *stop*. The *o* in *stop* has the same sounds as in *not*, and the *o* is in the middle of two consonants as it is in *stop*. The spelling pattern is ——*op*. Some words that rhyme with *stop* are . . ." (See the Talk-to-Yourself Chart.)

4. Provide guided practice following the steps noted previously. They routinely require students to:
   • Stretch out sounds in words;
   • Analyze and talk to themselves about letter-sound matches;
   • Identify the spelling pattern and rhyming words; and
   • Summarize what they have learned about sounds and letters.

5. Have students assess themselves to determine whether they have learned the key words for the week. They talk to themselves about each word by following the six steps on the Talk-to-Yourself Chart. Then the word is covered, and students listen to each sound and write the corresponding letter or letters on a card. If necessary, the teacher models stretching out the word and talking to himself or herself about it as the students reflect on each word.

6. Add a partner-sharing component. After the self-assessment, students find another word on the word pattern wall that has the same kind of sounds and letters as the word they wrote on the card. Students share with partners what they have learned by following the statements on the Partner-Sharing Chart.

7. Once students have analyzed key words, they practice changing one letter in the words to create new words. The teacher might say, "My word is *fun*. My new word is *fin*. I made this word because I know the word pattern wall word *pig*. *Pig* is like *fin* because the only vowel in the word is between two consonants, so the vowel in *pig* and *fin* probably makes the same sound. Using the statements shown in the Making Words Chart, students share their newly discovered words with their partners and discuss what they know about sounds and letters that explain the changes they made.

8. Students also spell the key words. At first they practice with the assistance of Elkonin boxes, a drawn rectangle divided into sections or boxes that correspond to sounds heard in words. Students place in each individual box all the letters needed to represent one sound. For example, three boxes would be used to spell *dog*. Three boxes would also be used to spell *right*, with the letters *igh* placed in the middle box. Later in the week, students spell the words from memory without the use of boxes.

9. Each day students apply what they have learned about words by reading texts that contain words with familiar spelling patterns. The text they read is either a predictable rhyme written by the teacher or an easy-reading trade book. These texts are first read to students as they point and follow, then they echo and do a choral reading. Finally, students read all or parts of the text on their own. In addition, students are given a predictable rhyme to read to someone at home.

10. At the conclusion of the lesson, students share what they have learned about their language and record it in their What-I-Know-About-My-Language journal to share with their parents at home.

Guidelines for Basic Reading Interventions

The *Reading/Language Arts Framework for California Public Schools* offers the following recommendations:

1. Adopt a program of documented effectiveness that teaches students the fundamentals of systematic decoding and sequentially extends their abilities to read and write more complicated word types and text structures.

2. Administer measures of assessment and assign to students the materials and programs that will enable them to read successfully (with 90 to 95 percent accuracy).

3. Design and schedule special instruction to maximize resources.

4. Schedule a sufficient amount of time for reading instruction and protect that time.

5. Monitor student progress and adjust the instruction and time allocations accordingly.

For further detail see pages 96 to 100 of the *Reading/Language Arts Framework*.

Relevant English–Language Arts Content Standards

Grade One: Word Analysis, Fluency, and Systematic Vocabulary Development

1.10 Generate the sounds from all the letters and letter patterns, including consonant blends and long- and short-vowel patterns (i.e., phonograms), and blend those sounds into recognizable words.

1.12 Use knowledge of vowel digraphs and *r*-controlled letter-sound associations to read words.

1.15 Read common word families (e.g., -ite, -ill, -ate).

Grade Three: Word Analysis, Fluency, and Systematic Vocabulary Development

1.10 Know and use complex word families when reading (e.g., -ight) to decode unfamiliar words.

Further Resources

Ehri, L. C. "Phases of Development in Reading Words," *Journal of Research in Reading*, Vol. 18 (1995), 116–25.

Elkonin, D. B. "U.S.S.R.," in *Comparative Reading*. Edited by J. Downing. New York: Macmillan, 1973, pp. 551–79.

Gaskins, Irene W., and others. "Procedures for Word Learning: Making Discoveries about Words," *The Reading Teacher*, Vol. 50 (December 1996/January 1997), 312–27.

Reading/Language Arts Framework for California Public Schools, Kindergarten Through Grade Twelve. Sacramento: California Department of Education, 1999.

Stahl, Steven A.; Ann M. Duffy-Hester; and Katherine A. D. Stahl. "Theory and Research into Practice: Everything You Always Wanted to Know about Phonics (But Were Afraid to Ask)," *Reading Research Quarterly*, Vol. 33 (July/August/September 1998), 338–55.

Sample
Word Pattern Wall

Week 1	in	and	up	
Week 2	king	long	jump	
Week 3	let	pig	day	
Week 4	truck	black	not	
Week 5	cat	it	go	look
Week 6	red	fun	he	
Week 7	name	swim	my	map
Week 8	car	vine	see	can
Week 9	tent	round	skate	ten
Week 10	old	frog	right	
Week 11	slide	stop	tell	her
Week 12	an	smash	brave	
Week 13	cow	sleep	scout	
Week 14	for	all	saw	
Week 15	had	kick	snail	glow
Week 16	boat	think	nest	
Week 17	treat	make	thank	
Week 18	mice	little	more	
Week 19	ship	clock	wash	station
Week 20	skunk	whale	boy	baby
Week 21	squirt	school	could	
Week 22	caught	coin	talk	
Week 23	page	lew	flu	
Week 24	use	bug	rain	
Week 25	pal	fur	place	
Week 26	phone	queen	write	
Week 27	knife	plane	guess	
Week 28	babies	tax	delicious	

Sample
Talk-to-Yourself Chart

The word is_____.

Stretch the word.

I hear_____sounds.

I see _____letters because _____.

(Students reconcile the number of letters they see with the number of sounds they hear.)

The spelling pattern is_____.

This is what I know about the vowel: _____.

Another word on the word pattern wall with the same vowel sound is _____.

Sample
Partner-Sharing Chart

Person 1:

My word is _____.

My word from the word pattern wall is _____.

The words are alike because _____.

Do you agree?

Why or why not?

Sample
Making Words Chart

Person 1:

My word is_____.

My new word is_____.

I made this word because I know_____.

Do you agree?

Person 2:

Give one of these answers:

Yes/No, because_____.

Exchange roles.

Applying Word Knowledge in Context

Applying word knowledge in context is a strategy in which students use contextual clues and word knowledge to identify unknown words. Teaching the strategy involves an introduction, modeling, and ongoing reinforcement.

Goals

1. Help students use spelling cues, vocabulary knowledge, and context clues for the efficient application of word analysis in reading.

2. Give students an effective means of developing and extending their vocabulary.

Teacher Preparation

1. Select an interesting passage containing a target vocabulary word needed for comprehension of the passage and photocopy the passage on an overhead transparency.

2. Identify a word in the passage for which students can use root, suffix, prefix, and context clues for determining the meaning.

Instructional Procedures

1. Elicit from students their thoughts and ideas about approaching an unknown word that is important to the overall meaning of what they are reading. Encourage students to take the following steps:

   a. Examine the context first to see if you can get a sense of the word.

   b. You will probably need to examine the word for meaningful parts—base, root, prefixes, or suffixes.

   c. If there is a prefix, take it off first.

   d. If there is a suffix, take it off second.

   e. Look at the base or root to see if you know it or if you can think of a related word (a word that has the same base or root).

   f. Reassemble the word, thinking about the meaning contributed by the base or root, the suffix, and then the prefix—this should give you a more specific idea of what the word is.

2. Try out this meaning in the sentence; check whether it makes sense in the context.

3. Look up the word in the dictionary if it still does not make sense or if you were unable to break the word down into affixes and base (and if it is still critical to the meaning of the overall passage).

4. Display the following text on a transparency:

   To say that Kim was *disillusioned* when at last she saw their vacation island would be putting it mildly. It did not look like the travel poster at all—there wasn't much of a beach, and what there was seemed to have stringy seaweed all over it. A cold wind blew without letup.

   Model the strategy by thinking aloud.

   "I don't know this word (pointing to *disillusioned*), so I'll think about the context. It sounds as though Kim isn't too happy. She was expecting something else, whatever it was like in the poster, but here she's found a disappointing beach with stringy seaweed all over it. And to top it off, it's cold! So this word (pointing again to *disillusioned*) may have something to do with being unhappy. Let's think about the word—it looks as though there's a prefix, *dis-*. That leaves *illusioned*, and *–ed* is a suffix, so I'll take that off. That leaves *illusion*. I've heard of that. I think it's when something isn't real. *Dis-* usually means "not" or the opposite of

STRATEGY INDEX

Student Audience
Beginning readers
Below grade level
At or above grade level

Text Type
Literary
Informational

Special Features
Automaticity with print
Prior knowledge and interest
Discussion about texts
Collaborative learning
Writing emphasis
Graphic representation
Student control of reading process
Student ownership of strategy

something. So Kim was "not illusioned"? Hmm . . . let's see if that fits the context. . . . She expected something else, but it was not the way the island *really* was—maybe her expectation was an illusion, not real."

5. Reinforce this process with students on an ongoing basis as needed.

6. Point out to students that many authors of textbooks try to provide a rich context to support new vocabulary. Helpful features for deciphering meaning and finding topics include italics, boldface, glossaries, footnotes, graphics, various indexes, illustrations, and so on.

Relevant English–Language Arts Contents Standards

Grades Five Through Eight: Word Analysis, Fluency, and Systematic Vocabulary Development

1.0 Students use their knowledge of word origins and word relationships, as well as historical and literary context clues, to determine the meaning of specialized vocabulary and to understand the precise meaning of grade-level-appropriate words.

Grades Nine Through Twelve: Word Analysis, Fluency, and Systematic Vocabulary Development

1.0 Students apply their knowledge of word origins to determine the meaning of new words encountered in reading materials and use those words accurately.

Further Resources

Adams, Marilyn J. *Beginning to Read: Thinking and Learning about Print.* Cambridge, Mass.: MIT Press, 1990.

Bear, Donald R., and others. *Words Their Way: Word Study for Phonics, Vocabulary, and Spelling Instruction.* Englewood Cliffs, N.J.: Prentice-Hall, Inc., 1996.

Stahl, Steven A., and T. Gerard Shiel. "Teaching Meaning Vocabulary: Productive Approaches for Poor Readers," *Reading and Writing Quarterly: Overcoming Learning Disabilities,* Vol. 8 (1992), 223–42.

Cloze Procedure

The cloze procedure is a reading test that consists of selected passages of text in which words have been systematically deleted. Readers must fill in the blanks left in the text. Words can be deleted in ways that require readers to employ specific reading strategies or context clues.

Goals

1. Practice using context clues to successfully determine the missing words in a passage.
2. Develop an understanding of why context is important.

Teacher Preparation

1. Depending on the purpose of the activity, prepare the text as follows:
   a. Letters and letter clusters should be deleted to encourage the use of graphophonic clues (i.e., those derived from letter-sound relationships).
   b. Function words, such as conjunctions, prepositions, and pronouns, help students focus on syntactic clues.
   c. Content words, such as nouns and verbs, require the use of semantic clues.
2. Delete every fifth word or the type of word on which you have chosen to focus. However, leave the first sentence intact so that readers can develop a sense of the context of the passage.
3. Generally, a passage of 200 to 300 words is appropriate because it is long enough to get a sense of the readers' typical processing behavior. However, a 100- to 200-word passage is adequate for younger students or for students using the cloze procedure for the first time.

4. For most students, passages written at their instructional level provide the appropriate level of difficulty. However, English language learners may find the task more difficult than native speakers of English because familiarity with English language patterns may affect one's ability to fill in the blanks correctly.

Instructional Procedures

1. Demonstrate on a practice passage how to use context clues.
2. Ask students to complete the entire passage by using the context clues in the passage and their knowledge of the topic, text structure, and word order in English.
3. Have students compare their responses after completing the cloze procedure and encourage other students to discuss the context clues they used to make their guess.
4. Reveal the words that were deleted and give students time to compare their answers with the original choices.

Relevant English–Language Arts Content Standards

Grade Three: Word Analysis, Fluency, and Systematic Vocabulary Development

1.6   Use sentence and word context to find the meaning of unknown words.

Grade Five: Word Analysis, Fluency, and Systematic Vocabulary Development

1.5   Understand and explain the figurative and metaphorical use of words in context.

Grade Six: Word Analysis, Fluency, and Systematic Vocabulary Development

1.4   Monitor expository text for unknown words or words with novel meanings by using word, sentence, and paragraph clues to determine meaning.

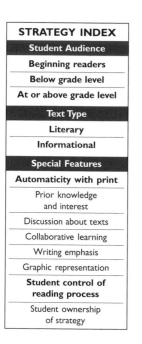

STRATEGY INDEX

Student Audience
Beginning readers
Below grade level
At or above grade level

Text Type
Literary
Informational

Special Features
Automaticity with print
Prior knowledge and interest
Discussion about texts
Collaborative learning
Writing emphasis
Graphic representation
Student control of reading process
Student ownership of strategy

Grades Nine and Ten: Word Analysis, Fluency, and Systematic Vocabulary Development

1.2 Distinguish between the denotative and connotative meanings of words and interpret the connotative power of words.

Further Resources

Hornsby, David; Jo-Ann Parry; and Deborah Sukarna. *Teach On: Teaching Strategies for Reading and Writing Workshops.* Portsmouth, N.H.: Heinemann, 1992.

Johns, Jerry L., and others. *Celebrate Literacy! The Joy of Reading and Writing.* Bloomington, Ind.: ERIC Clearinghouse on Reading and Communication Skills, 1992.

Contextual Redefinition

Contextual redefinition is a strategy for showing students the importance of context in ascertaining meaning. It is useful in those instances in which difficult terms can be defined by the context in which they occur.

Goals

1. Help students realize that context can provide additional clues to the meaning of words and engage students in using context to discover the meaning of unknown words.

2. Help faltering readers experience the thinking processes involved in deriving a definition from context as students model appropriate reading behavior for one another.

Teacher Preparation

1. Select a few words students will encounter in text that are essential for comprehending important concepts and yet may be difficult for students as they read.

2. Provide a context with clues of definition or description for each word. If such a context already exists in the text, use that context instead of creating one. If the text lacks a sentence or short paragraph containing clues for a given word, create one that will provide significant information about the meaning of the word.

Instructional Procedures

1. Present the words in isolation. Using an overhead transparency or chalkboard, ask students to provide a meaning for each word. Students then support their choices and, as a group, arrive at a consensus on what they believe is the best meaning. Examples are as follows:
   • vapid
   • lummox
   • piebald

2. Present the words in a sentence. Using the sentence or short paragraph previously developed, present the word in its appropriate context, as in these examples:
   • Even though she intended to discuss a lively issue, her conversation with me was *vapid*, lacking animation and force.
   • As a result of his ungainly, slovenly appearance, Bill was often unjustly labeled a *lummox*.
   • Though described as *piebald* because of its spotted black and white colors, the horse was still considered beautiful by many horse lovers.

3. Ask students to offer suggestions for the meaning of each word and defend their definitions. This process exposes less able readers to the thinking processes involved in deriving a definition from context as students model appropriate reading and thinking behavior for one another.

4. Have students or groups of students consult a dictionary to verify the choices offered by class members.

Relevant English–Language Arts Content Standards

Grade Three: Word Analysis, Fluency, and Systematic Vocabulary Development

1.6   Use sentence and word context to find the meaning of unknown words.

Grade Five: Word Analysis, Fluency, and Systematic Vocabulary Development

1.5   Understand and explain the figurative and metaphorical use of words in context.

Grade Six: Word Analysis, Fluency, and Systematic Vocabulary Development

1.4   Monitor expository text for unknown words or words with novel meanings by using word, sentence, and paragraph clues to determine meaning.

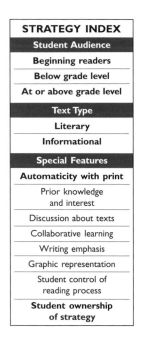

STRATEGY INDEX
Student Audience
Beginning readers
Below grade level
At or above grade level
Text Type
Literary
Informational
Special Features
Automaticity with print
Prior knowledge and interest
Discussion about texts
Collaborative learning
Writing emphasis
Graphic representation
Student control of reading process
Student ownership of strategy

Grades Nine and Ten: Word Analysis, Fluency, and Systematic Vocabulary Development

1.2 Distinguish between the denotative and connotative meanings of words and interpret the connotative power of words.

Further Resources

Cunningham, J. W.; P. M. Cunningham; and S. V. Arthur. *Middle and Secondary School Reading.* New York: Longman, 1981.

Moore, David W.; John E. Readence; and Robert J. Rickelman. *Prereading Activities for Content Area Reading & Learning.* Newark, Del.: International Reading Association, 1989.

Readence, J. E.; T. W. Bean; and R. S. Baldwin. *Content Area Reading: An Integrated Approach* (Second edition). Dubuque, Iowa: Kendall Hunt, 1985.

Structural Scavenger Hunt

A structural scavenger hunt is an instructional approach in which students search for and write down words containing particular word parts, predict meanings from their knowledge of the word part and the context, and present their findings to the class.

Goal

Help students recognize unfamiliar words when reading text by using their knowledge of word parts in conjunction with contextual and phonic information.

Teacher Preparation

1. Prepare memorable examples of the following terms: prefix, suffix, affix, root word, and base word.

2. Prepare a list of words for sorting according to a particular instructional focus.

Instructional Procedures

1. Teach students some basic structural terms: prefix, suffix, affix, root word, and base word. With well-chosen examples, show students how word parts work:

   • The basic part of a word is called a root or base (e.g., *whole* in *unwholesome*).

   • A part added before the root is called a prefix (e.g., *pre* as in *presupposition*).

   • A part added after the root is called a suffix (e.g., *-ible* as in *unintelligible*).

   • An affix is a word part such as a suffix or prefix.

2. Ask students to sort a list of well-chosen words by prefix, root or base, and suffix.

3. Name and show a particular word part(s) useful to know for its frequency in text or relevance to a topic under study. Show students a cluster of words with that word part.

4. Ask students to look for words containing the word part (root, prefix, or suffix) over the course of the day or the next several days. Students write down any words containing the word part, including their contexts, as they find them and predict a meaning for each word by using knowledge of the word part and contextual information.

5. Have students present their findings to the class as you present your own findings.

6. Reinforce the necessity of using contextual information to verify the predicted meaning of a word that has been analyzed.

Relevant English–Language Arts Content Standards

Grade Three: Word Analysis, Fluency, and Systematic Vocabulary Development

1.4   Know common roots and affixes derived from Greek and Latin and use this knowledge to analyze the meaning of complex words (e.g., *international*).

1.8   Use knowledge of prefixes (e.g., *un-, re-, pre-, bi-, mis-, dis-*) and suffixes (e.g., *-er, -est, -ful*) to determine the meaning of words.

Grade Four: Word Analysis, Fluency, and Systematic Vocabulary Development

1.3   Use knowledge of root words to determine the meaning of unknown words within a passage.

Determining word meanings through the use of word parts is also central to the following vocabulary and concept development standards: Grade five, 1.4; grade six, 1.4; grade seven, 1.2; grade eight, 1.3; grades nine and ten, 1.1; grades eleven and twelve, 1.2

Further Resources

Durkin, D. *Strategies for Words* (Second edition). Boston: Allyn and Bacon, 1981.

Underwood, Terry. "Thirty Ways to Improve Reading in the Intermediate and Middle Grades (Grades 4-8: Assumptions, Instructions, Assessments)." Sacramento: California State University, Summer 1997 (unpublished manuscript).

STRATEGY INDEX

Student Audience
Beginning readers
Below grade level
At or above grade level

Text Type
Literary
Informational

Special Features
Automaticity with print
Prior knowledge and interest
Discussion about texts
Collaborative learning
Writing emphasis
Graphic representation
Student control of reading process
Student ownership of strategy

Word Sorts

Word sorts is a systematic program of word study. It is an approach to vocabulary growth and spelling development guided by an informed interpretation of spelling errors and other literacy behaviors.

Goals

1. Help students perceive word patterns quickly and accurately in order to recognize, produce, and understand written language.
2. Facilitate accurate, rapid word recognition through opportunities to engage in meaningful reading and to examine the same words, both in and out of context.

Teacher Preparation

1. Choose words for sorting in the subject matter students are learning. Sorting can be done for any phonetic pattern, such as initial sounds, rhyming words, vowel patterns, or multisyllabic patterns. For more advanced readers, sorting may be based on word parts that provide clues to the meaning or grammatical function of a word. The first few times, choose words based on three categories that are very different from one another so that students experience success and understand what they are doing. (This is called a *closed sort*.) As students become more sophisticated, they may determine the categories, and the teacher's choice of words would allow for a variety of categories. (This is called an *open sort*.) Choose an open or closed sort depending on how sophisticated you want it to be.
2. Choose the way you want to present the words, depending on the group that will be doing the word sorting. For example, use cards for groups; a chalkboard or cards and a pocket chart for an entire class; or photocopied lists for individuals, partners, or small groups. Sources of words may include lists of high-frequency words, a content word wall, or classroom books. Word sorts can also be done in the form of popular games such as Word Concentration™, Go Fish™ for Words, and Word Rummy™.

Instructional Procedures

1. Establish a category and demonstrate how to sort words by using the most feasible procedure for your classroom. You may draw columns on the chalkboard, on a sorting board, or on individual chalkboards; or fold plain paper to create columns.
2. Select a key word for the label of the category. Students read both the key word and the new word each time a new example is categorized. An "Other" column may be added for words that do not fit any of the categories because they neither look nor sound the same. This can especially draw attention to words such as *have* or *said* that do not sound like most of the words with these spelling patterns.
3. Note that in all word sorts, it is important to find ways to develop the students' speed and automaticity as they sort. A variation that promotes automaticity is the blind sort, in which the teacher or leader calls out words that have already been sorted but that are not shown to the students (thus blind). Students indicate which column the word belongs in before seeing the word. After working with words in sorts and blind sorts, do a *blind writing sort,* in which the teacher or leader calls out the previously sorted words and the students write the words in the appropriate column before seeing them. Then show the word so that students can confirm their spelling and categorization.

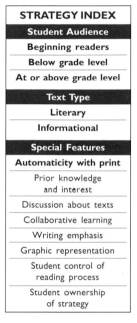

STRATEGY INDEX

Student Audience
Beginning readers
Below grade level
At or above grade level

Text Type
Literary
Informational

Special Features
Automaticity with print
Prior knowledge and interest
Discussion about texts
Collaborative learning
Writing emphasis
Graphic representation
Student control of reading process
Student ownership of strategy

4. Follow a word sort with a *word hunt* as a bridge into student reading and writing. Post charts of the categories the class has worked on, and have students hunt for words that fit the patterns. They then add the words they find to the charts or even to word notebooks that they keep. This is a good way to draw students' attention to spelling patterns in the materials they are reading.

Guidelines for Word Sorts

1. *Look for what students use but confuse.* After noting features in students' spelling that are consistently present and correct, look for features that are used inconsistently to determine areas that need strengthening.

2. *Step backward in order to step forward.* In setting up categories, contrast something new with something that is already known. If, for example, you are beginning to introduce a new sound or pattern, be sure to present it in contrast to a familiar sound or pattern. Begin with activities in which the students will likely experience success.

3. *Use words students can read.* Words should come from all sources that students can read: language experience stories, recent readings, words from poems, words in spelling books, and so on. Choose words to sort that students can easily pronounce and can read immediately out of context. This is especially important for English learners.

4. *Sort words on the basis of contrasting features.* Contrasts are essential to students learning to categorize items. For example, words that double the consonants are contrasted with those that do not.

5. *Sort by sight and sound.* Students examine words by how they are spelled, how they sound, and what they mean. Note the distinctions in meaning of the following words, categorized by sound:

pail	pale	there	their
tail	tale	where	wear
mail	male	here	hear
sail	sale		

6. *Begin with obvious contrasts first.* Whenever students begin the study of a new feature, teachers choose distinctive key words. For example, homographs illustrate how a syllable stress in the same word signals different grammatical functions. The following categories highlight a common relationship between syllable stress and word function for many homographs.

Stress in First Syllable	Stress in Second Syllable
subject (noun, adjective)	subject (verb)
conduct (noun)	conduct (verb)
rebel (noun, adjective)	rebel (verb)
console (noun, adjective)	console (verb)

7. *Do not hide exceptions.* Place so-called irregular words in a miscellaneous category. For example, in looking at long-vowel patterns, students find these exceptions: *give, have,* and *love;* yet it is no coincidence that they all have a *v,* and they form a consistent pattern.

8. *Return to meaningful texts.* After sorting, students need to return to meaningful texts to hunt for other examples to add to the sorts. These hunts extend the analysis to more difficult vocabulary. For example, after sorting a list of words by meaning, make sure the same words are reorganized into categories that reflect spelling patterns. Words that are spelled with ——*er,* ——*or,* and

——ar endings are examples from an integrated language arts unit.

——*er*	——*or*	——*ar*
commander	major	cellar
officer	captor	peculiar
anger	victor	spectacular
soldier	honor	
deserter	favor	
prisoner	clamor	

Students scan the pages of their texts to find multisyllabic words ending in *——y*, which leads to interesting discoveries when the words are sorted by sound and part of speech. Examples are as follows:

Noun	*Adjective*	*Adverb*
country	sorry	seriously
cemetery	silly	horribly
custody	starry	hurriedly
celery	happy	certainly
gypsy	pretty	happily

See the guidelines suggested on pages 96 to 100 of the *Reading/Language Arts Framework for California Public Schools.*

Relevant English–Language Arts Content Standards

Grade Three: Word Analysis, Fluency, and Vocabulary Development

1.1 Know and use complex word families when reading (e.g., *-ight*) to decode unfamiliar words.

1.4 Use knowledge of antonyms, synonyms, homophones, and homographs to determine the meanings of words.

1.8 Use knowledge of prefixes (e.g., *un-, re-, pre-, bi-, mis-, dis-*) and suffixes (e.g., *-er, -est, -ful*) to determine the meaning of words.

Grades Four Through Six: Word Analysis, Fluency, and Vocabulary Development

1.1 Read aloud narrative and expository text fluently and accurately and with appropriate pacing, intonation, and expression.

Further Resources

Bear, Donald R., and others. *Words Their Way: Word Study for Phonics, Vocabulary, and Spelling Instruction.* Englewood Cliffs, N.J.: Prentice-Hall, Inc., 1996.

Bear, Donald R., and Shane Templeton. "Explorations in Developmental Spelling: Foundations for Learning and Teaching Phonics, Spelling, and Vocabulary," *The Reading Teacher,* Vol. 52 (November 1998), 222.

Cunningham, Patricia M. *Phonics They Use: Words for Reading and Writing.* Boston: Allyn and Bacon, 1991.

Cunningham, Patricia M., and Dorothy P. Hall. *Making Big Words.* Parsippany, N.J.: Good Apple, Inc., 1994.

Cunningham, Patricia M., and Dorothy P. Hall. *Making Words.* Parsippany, N.J.: Good Apple, Inc., 1994.

Invernizzi, Marcia; Mary P. Abouzeid; and Janet W. Bloodgood. "Integrated Word Study: Spelling, Grammar, and Meaning in the Language Arts Classroom," *Language Arts,* Vol. 74 (March 1997), 185–92.

Cross-Age Reading

Cross-age reading is a technique in which nonfluent readers prepare for an oral reading performance for a younger child. Preparing for the performance is a lesson in itself. A complete lesson involves storybook selection; practice with repeated oral readings; small-group coaching on how to talk about the book with a younger child; small-group coaching on how to improve the oral reading performance; the oral reading performance with a younger child; reflection about the quality of storybook reading interactions; and practice with specific strategies to help students improve subsequent readings.

STRATEGY INDEX
Student Audience
Beginning readers
Below grade level
At or above grade level
Text Type
Literary
Informational
Special Features
Automaticity with print
Prior knowledge and interest
Discussion about texts
Collaborative learning
Writing emphasis
Graphic representation
Student control of reading process
Student ownership of strategy

Goals

1. Help older, faltering readers improve their reading fluency, focus on comprehension, and develop additional strategies for effective reading.
2. Improve attitudes toward school and learning for both older readers and younger students.

Teacher Preparation

1. Identify faltering oral readers in need of extra oral reading practice, and make arrangements for linking them with younger students.
2. Locate a collection of appropriate books from the school or classroom library, and select storybooks for modeling specific strategies.

Instructional Procedures

Preparation

1. Help each student select an appropriate book for cross-age reading. Guide students to select books that they personally like and that contain elements younger children would enjoy, including illustrations.

2. Encourage students to become more fluent readers by allowing time for repeated readings of the books during class. This might involve a silent reading at first, followed by one or more oral readings in pairs to prepare for the "performance."

3. Help the students decide how to introduce and discuss a book with younger children. Focus on questions and comments that would help involve the child in the performance.

Prereading Collaboration

4. Meet with a small group of student readers/performers for 10 to 15 minutes and encourage students to read aloud with the group to get feedback on the fluency and expressiveness of their oral reading and on their use of questions and comments. Thus students have another reason for improving their oral reading performances.

Cross-Age Reading

5. Match readers with younger children and observe the oral reading performance of each student, encouraging them to assume the role of expert readers.

Postreading Collaboration

6. Meet with readers/performers after each cross-age reading session to allow them to reflect on the quality of the storybook reading interactions. During this time help students develop strategies they would use to improve subsequent readings. For example, model how you relate personal experience and background knowledge at different stages of your own storybook reading. This may involve (a) predicting what may happen in the story based on prior knowledge suggested by the title, genre of the book, and artwork; (b) understanding motives and

actions of characters in the story by relating similar personal experiences to the text; and (c) stopping at various points in the story to predict what may happen next. Engage students by asking clarifying questions and relating their own personal experience to the story. Encourage students to use this strategy with their young audience by asking questions before, during, and after the reading that would activate children's background knowledge.

7. Note that the mental modeling component in step 6 should lead students immediately back to the preparation in step 1 as they begin to plan their next storybook readings.

Variation: If there are no younger students near the school, this procedure can be approximated by having students record their oral performances on audiotapes for younger children.

Relevant English–Language Arts Content Standards

Grade One: Word Analysis, Fluency, and Systematic Vocabulary Development

1.16 [Students] read aloud with fluency in a manner that sounds like natural speech.

Grades One Through Four: Literary Response and Analysis

3.0 Students read and respond to a wide variety of significant works of children's literature.

Grade Four: Reading Comprehension

2.2 [Students] use appropriate strategies when reading for different purposes (e.g., full comprehension, location of information, personal enjoyment).

Further Resources

Labbo, Linda D., and William H. Teale. "Cross-Age Reading: A Strategy for Helping Poor Readers," *The Reading Teacher*, Vol. 43 (February 1990), 362–69.

Easy Reading to Build Fluency

Easy reading to build fluency uses silent reading in class with specific procedures to motivate less able readers to read the books they can read.

Goals

1. Develop fluency among students for whom reading is a labored, word-by-word, sometimes syllable-by-syllable, process.
2. Dignify students' reading of books that are appropriate for them in difficulty although intended for a younger audience.

Teacher Preparation

1. Schedule independent reading time when students can choose books (including nonfiction) and interact with others about what they read from books.
2. Collect, on a rotating basis, a variety of easy books, including nonfiction picture books, alphabet books, and choral selections containing repeating patterns, rhythms, and rhymes. Make available other needed equipment, such as audiotape recorders.

Instructional Procedures

1. Model, by reading aloud, the use and enjoyment of easy books. For example, share an abundance of books having pattern, rhythm, and repetition, and explain why you like them.
2. Legitimize easy reading by creating a program or opportunities for older students to read to younger buddies. It is important to ensure that the age difference between the less able reader and the listener is sizeable and that the pairings are arranged so that the older, less able reader is not paired with a younger child who reads better than he or she does.

3. Have students choose easy books and practice reading them for a tape recording to be given to a friend. Or add the tape to a collection of audiotapes in the classroom library.
4. Use carefully selected easy books, including picture storybooks, as springboards to lively discussion with the entire class.
5. Broaden the perception of what is considered acceptable reading materials. Language experience activities may provide good opportunities to transcribe popular cheers, songs, chants, stories, and firsthand experiences for the classroom library.
6. Make the expanding world of nonfiction books more available and more familiar to students. Point out that much of what is known about science and history has been learned from simple books. Nonfiction and fiction books should be read to students regularly. For example, *Tadpole Diary* (see "Further Resources") may be interesting and informative to a middle grade student.

Language Experience Approach

For beginning readers and English learners whose background experiences may have little in common with the content of commercially prepared reading materials:

1. Expose students to an experience that may serve as the subject of dictation and writing. It may be a field trip, an experience at school, or something else with which students will be familiar.
2. Discuss the experience or topic with students to generate ideas and words.
3. Record what the student or students dictate. Individual student stories may be recorded in notebooks. Group dictations should be recorded on a flip chart.
4. Read the story back to the students, pointing to every word when the dictation is finished.

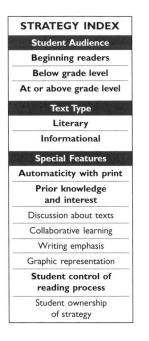

STRATEGY INDEX
Student Audience
Beginning readers
Below grade level
At or above grade level
Text Type
Literary
Informational
Special Features
Automaticity with print
Prior knowledge and interest
Discussion about texts
Collaborative learning
Writing emphasis
Graphic representation
Student control of reading process
Student ownership of strategy

5. Give the story to the student and ask him or her to:

   a. Read it silently, skipping words she or he does not know.

   b. Read it a second time, underlining all the words she or he knows.

   c. Read it orally to the teacher, who pronounces every word the student does not know.

6. Have the student read the same story twice on the next day: first quickly and the second time underlining all words she or he knows with a color different from the one used the day before. (The story may also serve as a useful context for other kinds of skill instruction.)

7. Direct students to create posters or word banks of known words. To extend the word building, have students use the words in a different way each day (e.g., categorizing, making sentences, sorting according to initial or ending sounds).

8. Collect copies of students' dictated stories and encourage students to read their stories fluently and with expression to other students.

Relevant English–Language Arts Content Standards

Grade One: Word Analysis, Fluency, and Systematic Vocabulary Development

1.16 Read aloud with fluency in a manner that sounds like natural speech.

Grade Two: Word Analysis, Fluency, and Systematic Vocabulary Development

1.6 Read aloud fluently and accurately and with appropriate intonation and expression.

Grade Three: Word Analysis, Fluency, and Systematic Vocabulary Development

1.3 Read aloud narrative and expository text fluently and accurately and with appropriate pacing, intonation, and expression.

Grades Four Through Six: Word Analysis, Fluency, and Systematic Vocabulary Development

1.1 Read narrative and expository text aloud with grade-appropriate fluency and accuracy and with appropriate pacing, intonation, and expression.

Further Resources

Allen, R.V., and C. Allen. *Language Experience Activities.* Boston: Houghton Mifflin, 1967.

Cunningham, Patricia M. *Phonics They Use: Words for Reading and Writing.* Boston: Allyn and Bacon, 1991.

Dixon, Carol N., and Denise Nessel. *Language Experience Approach to Reading and Writing.* Englewood Cliffs, N.J.: Alemany Press, 1983.

Drew, D. *Tadpole Diary.* London: Rigby Inc., 1987.

Fielding, Linda, and Cathy Roller. "Making Difficult Books Accessible and Easy Books Acceptable," *The Reading Teacher,* Vol. 45 (May 1992), 678–85.

Paired Reading

Paired reading is a technique in which a parent, volunteer, or older student reads, along with a student who is a nonautomatic decoder or word-by-word reader, a book of the student's choosing. The helper adjusts his or her oral participation according to the difficulty that the student experiences, offering just that support needed to maintain a fluent, oral reading.

Goals

1. Help students make a significant gain in oral reading fluency and comprehension.
2. Provide reading practice for struggling decoders in a warm, encouraging environment with a model of fluent reading.

Teacher Preparation

1. Gather together a diverse collection of books with an appropriate range of levels of difficulty and with appeal to struggling, nonfluent readers.
2. Decide who will be designated and trained to be the helper in the paired reading; how and when the training will be conducted; and when, where, and how long the daily paired reading will take place.

Instructional Procedures

1. Explain to students likely to benefit from paired reading (only those who are halting, word-by-word readers and struggling decoders) that it will give them practice reading smoothly, which will improve their reading abilities.
2. Explain that five to 15 minutes will be devoted to paired reading (in home or in school) daily over a designated period, such as three months.
3. Invite each student participating in paired reading to select a book for reading aloud.

4. Have both the helper and the reader read the story or other text aloud together. Neither must go too fast. Helpers should keep their speed as fast or as slow as the reader's.
5. Note that the reader must read every word. If the reader struggles and then gets it right, the helper should show pleasure. Do not let the reader struggle for more than five seconds.

   If the reader struggles too long or struggles and gets the word wrong, then the helper (1) says it correctly; and (2) makes sure the reader then says it correctly too.

   The helper makes sure the reader looks at the words. It is best if the reader points with a finger to the word while reading.
6. When reading together, the reader may feel confident enough to read alone. The paired readers should agree on a way for the reader to ask the helper to be quiet, such as a knock, a sign, or a squeeze. (The reader should avoid verbal cues, or she will lose track of the reading.) The helper immediately stops reading aloud.

   If the reader struggles for more than five seconds or struggles and gets the word wrong, the helper reads the word aloud correctly. The helper then makes sure the reader pronounces the word correctly. If possible, the helper should record the miscues the reader makes so they can be analyzed by the teacher. Or the readers themselves may record their miscues in a personal word log.

   Both go on reading aloud together until the reader again feels confident enough to read alone and again asks the helper to be quiet. Signed contracts between students and parent (or helper) may be used along with record sheets noting date, book chosen, time spent, comments, signatures, and so on.

STRATEGY INDEX
Student Audience
Beginning readers
Below grade level
At or above grade level
Text Type
Literary
Informational
Special Features
Automaticity with print
Prior knowledge and interest
Discussion about texts
Collaborative learning
Writing emphasis
Graphic representation
Student control of reading process
Student ownership of strategy

Relevant English–Language Arts Content Standards

Grade One: Word Analysis, Fluency, and Systematic Vocabulary Development

1.16 Read aloud with fluency in a manner that sounds like natural speech.

Grade Two: Word Analysis, Fluency, and Systematic Vocabulary Development

1.6 Read aloud fluently and accurately and with appropriate intonation and expression.

Grade Three: Word Analysis, Fluency, and Systematic Vocabulary Development

1.3 Read aloud narrative and expository text fluently and accurately and with appropriate pacing, intonation, and expression.

Grades Four Through Six: Word Analysis, Fluency, and Systematic Vocabulary Development

1.1 Read aloud narrative and expository text fluently and accurately and with appropriate pacing, intonation, and expression.

Further Resources

Rasinski, Timothy V., and Anthony D. Fredericks. "The Akron Paired Reading Project," *The Reading Teacher,* Vol. 44 (March 1991), 514–15.

Stanovich, K. E. "Matthew Effects in Reading: Some Consequences of Individual Differences in the Acquisition of Literacy," *Reading Research Quarterly,* Vol. 21, 360–406.

Topping, K. "Paired Reading: A Powerful Technique for Parent Use," *The Reading Teacher,* Vol. 40 (March 1987), 608–14.

Reading Aloud

Reading aloud provides students a shared book experience in which the teacher models appropriate phrasing, inflection, and fluency to help students be successful in reading.

Goals

1. Model good reading, motivate independent reading, build vocabulary, enrich background experiences, expose subtleties of the characters and meaning in text, introduce different authors and their works, expose students to a variety of writing styles, and introduce a variety of genres (e.g., poetry, fantasy, nonfiction).

2. Introduce words and concepts to students above their reading level and above those encountered in everyday speech; stimulate students to read more and to read at higher levels of comprehension; and provide repeated exposure to meaningful language as both English learners and monolingual students develop English proficiency and specific content knowledge.

Teacher Preparation

1. Select books suited to your students' interests and language and maturity levels. Consider folktales; concept books; books with illustrations large enough to be seen by a group from a short distance; books about compelling issues that generate discussion; books with dramatic tension and dialogue that help to move the action forward; books that invite interaction, have an identifiable pattern or a repeating refrain, contain rhymes and sensory images, and are humorous and clever; and books of particular interest to the group.

2. Contact your library-media teacher and public librarian for personal recommendations and bibliographies of good books for reading aloud. For further recommendations, contact Library Services, Los Angeles Unified School District, which has an ongoing evaluation program (Focus on Books) for identifying outstanding books for reading aloud.

Instructional Procedures

1. Explain to students the instructional benefits of reading aloud regardless of their age. Some benefits are enumerated under "Goals."

2. Read a variety of fiction and nonfiction books and other literature frequently to students. In some cases you may wish to work with groups of five to seven students so that everyone can see the pictures and the print easily. Provide a variety of opportunities for students to interact with one another and the teacher about the reading. The language interactions of teachers and peers centering on the text will serve as models for English learners.

3. Use verbal and nonverbal cueing strategies while reading to increase to the maximum students' (especially English learners') understanding. Verbal cueing strategies include using pauses for dramatic effect to indicate a change in events; exaggerating intonation to emphasize important words and concepts; using dramatic language and changing the pitch, volume, or linguistic stress to indicate voices of different characters; and changing the volume to indicate a change in mood. Nonverbal cueing strategies include pointing to illustrations or parts of illustrations; using facial expressions to indicate various characters or changes in a single character's mood; and using gestures to accompany the main actions and events in the story.

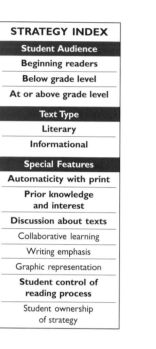

STRATEGY INDEX

Student Audience
Beginning readers
Below grade level
At or above grade level

Text Type
Literary
Informational

Special Features
Automaticity with print
Prior knowledge and interest
Discussion about texts
Collaborative learning
Writing emphasis
Graphic representation
Student control of reading process
Student ownership of strategy

4. Involve all students in the story by asking questions appropriate to their individual levels of language acquisition. Questions to clarify the meaning of words, to develop concepts, to encourage both literal and inferential comprehension of the story, and to relate the story to the students' background and experiences all help to involve the students.

5. Read aloud books with a pattern, refrain, or predictable sequence and encourage students to repeat the refrain to complete the pattern. Such books help develop an understanding of patterns of language. Consistency of plot and language patterns allows students with limited English skills to use and practice vocabulary and language patterns in an interesting, meaningful manner.

6. Point out the connections to the text when reading a book with many illustrations. Illustrated books are especially helpful to English learners trying to make sense of the language. In addition, provide cueing strategies. Books that are both well illustrated and predictable provide the ideal opportunity for English learners to understand and acquire language and concepts.

7. Ask students thought-provoking questions throughout the story. During the reading, frequently ask students to report on what has just occurred, predict what might come next, state why they think that will happen next, and project themselves into the story, imagining how they would feel and what they might say. Such activities help English learners who have basic communication skills in English but need to develop academic language.

8. Read and reread favorite stories and let students listen to them on tapes or records while following along in the book. Repeated hearing of the same story reinforces vocabulary and language patterns and establishes

sequence of events in students' minds. By sharing knowledge of a familiar book, an English learner may use a memorized chunk of language, such as "What's this?" to get another student who is more fluent in English to provide labels for objects or events pictured.

9. Provide related follow-up activities using a variety of formats and manipulative materials. Have students retell the story by using the language patterns they have heard. Develop specific aspects of vocabulary and comprehension.

Relevant English–Language Arts Content Standards

Kindergarten: Literary Response and Analysis

3.0   Students listen and respond to stories based on well-known characters, themes, plots, and settings. The selections in *Recommended Readings in Literature, Kindergarten Through Grade Eight* illustrate the quality and complexity of the materials to be read by students.

Grades One Through Four: Literary Response and Analysis

3.0   Students read and respond to a wide variety of significant works of children's literature.

Grades Five Through Twelve: Literary Response and Analysis

3.0   Students read and respond to historically or culturally significant works of literature that reflect and enhance their studies of history and social science.

Further Resources

Hough, Ruth A.; Joanne R. Nurss; and D. Scott Enright. "Story Reading with Limited English Speaking Children in the Classroom," *The Reading Teacher* (February 1986), 510–14.

Krashen, Stephen D. *The Power of Reading: Insights from the Research.* Englewood, Colo.: Libraries Unlimited, Inc., 1993.

Teaching Reading: A Balanced, Comprehensive Approach to Teaching Reading in Prekindergarten Through Grade Three. Sacramento: California Department of Education, 1996.

Trelease, Jim. *The Read-Aloud Handbook.* New York: Penguin, 1995.

Repeated Reading

Repeated reading is a simple rehearsal strategy useful for nonautomatic decoders and word-by-word readers, not for students who are already reading fluently. It consists of rereading a short, meaningful passage several times until a satisfactory level of fluency is reached and then repeating the procedure with a new passage. Rereading can be done through independent practice or by reading with assistance along with an audiotape.

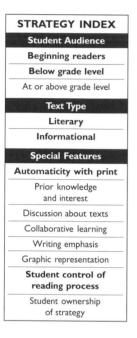

STRATEGY INDEX

Student Audience
Beginning readers
Below grade level
At or above grade level

Text Type
Literary
Informational

Special Features
Automaticity with print
Prior knowledge
and interest
Discussion about texts
Collaborative learning
Writing emphasis
Graphic representation
Student control of
reading process
Student ownership
of strategy

Goals

1. Increase fluency and automaticity for slow and halting readers to free their attention for comprehension.

2. Help students become more willing and able to undertake reading new material.

Teacher Preparation

1. Extract passages from many different kinds of reading materials likely to be of interest to your students: core literature texts, trade books, language experience texts, newspaper articles, and student writing.

2. Prepare graphs or charts for recording the reading speed and number of word recognition errors to show visible proof of progress for students participating in repeated reading.

3. Note that you may wish to set up a special area either in the classroom or in the school library where students can go to practice reading. For the unassisted procedure, provide a timing device (such as a stopwatch), a reading chart, and reading materials so students can keep records of how fast they read each time they practice.

Instructional Procedures for Independent, Unassisted Repeated Reading

1. Engage students in a discussion of how athletes develop skill at their sports. Bring out the fact that athletes spend considerable time practicing basic skills until they develop speed and smoothness in their activity. Explain that repeated reading constitutes this same type of practice.

2. Have students select easy stories or books of interest to them. It may be helpful initially to use graded reading passages or graded word lists with some students to determine texts of appropriate difficulty.

3. Mark off short selections (50 to 300 words) for practice in the material selected by each student, depending on the reading skill of the student.

4. Have the student read the short selection aloud to you or an assistant. Record the reading speed and number of word recognition errors on a graph. Monitor the word recognition level of the passages. On the first reading, the student should read with 85 percent accuracy or better before starting to practice; otherwise, the passage may be too difficult.

5. Direct the student to the practice center or to his or her seat to practice reading the selection while the next student reads to the assistant. You may wish to instruct the student to use a stopwatch and keep records of words read per minute (WPM) for each reading practice. The reading practice may be done silently, but the testing is done orally.

6. Repeat the procedure with each student until he or she reaches a reading rate of 85 to 100 WPM. Keep the practice passages at the same level of difficulty until acceptable rates of speed and accuracy are reached on the first or second reading. Then give the student more difficult passages.

7. Have the student go on to the next passage. As the student gains more reading skills, the length of the passage can be increased.

Teacher Preparation for Assisted Repeated Reading by Audiotapes

1. Establish a collection of books on tape with the following characteristics: high interest, appropriate pacing, good language patterns, appropriate sound effects, clear cues for page turning, and lack of cultural biases.

2. Set up a special area in the classroom or in the school library where students can go to practice reading stories. Provide a tape recorder, book, audiotape, and chart for students to record how many times they listen to the book.

3. Develop a list of 20 words from the story for each book in the practice center so that students can independently test into a book at the appropriate level. Provide guidelines such as the following: *If you know more than 15 words, the book is probably too easy; eight or fewer, the book is probably too hard.* Prepare written instructions.

Instructional Procedures for Assisted Repeated Reading by Audiotapes

1. Students visit the school library to choose a book (with an audiotape) that is not too easy or too difficult.

2. Students test into a book by reading a list of 20 words drawn from the story, using the guidelines previously established (see step 3 noted above) to determine whether the book is too easy or too difficult.

3. In an area of the library (or classroom) set aside for rereading practice, students read along with a tape several times each day until they can read the story smoothly by them-

selves (about 15 to 20 readings in total).

4. When the student is ready, she or he either reads the entire book to an adult or, if the book is too long, prepares several pages to read aloud. She or he also takes the word test taken before beginning the book (see step 3 of "Teacher Preparation for Assisted Repeated Reading").

5. If the student can read the book easily and knows all the words on the word list, she or he receives a written commendation and chooses another book to start practicing.

Additional Guidelines

1. When students are reading with few errors but below 45 WPM, use the assisted, read-aloud approach with an audiotaped model of the passage. The model gives students support and a sense of the proper phrasing and speed of fluent reading.

2. As soon as students reach a rate exceeding 60 WPM on their first reading of a practice passage, use the independent repeated reading procedure (unassisted). These students need more practice than support.

3. Predetermining the mastery level for speed seems to be particularly appropriate for very slow word-by-word readers and remedial students— 85 WPM has been used successfully with older remedial students. The students move to a new passage once they reach the goal (a set rate of speed) on the passage they have been practicing.

4. Setting a specific number of rereadings rather than a criterion seems appropriate for students who are reading at relatively high rates of speed and accuracy. Three to five rereadings for each passage is a good goal for mastery, according to several researchers.

5. Some teachers have students divide a story into segments of 100 words each. Students practice each part until they reach the criterion (typically, one minute). Then they proceed to the next segment. When they have completed all the parts, they can read the entire story fluently.

6. Accuracy of reading, while desirable, is not essential. What is essential is speed. Poor readers who are being tested for both accuracy and speed often become fearful of making errors and lose speed. Speed is the preferred indicator of automaticity; therefore, speed is emphasized in repeated reading.

Instructional Procedures for Paired Repeated Reading

Paired repeated reading is an easy-to-manage variation in which students read a short passage aloud three times and then evaluate their own and their partner's reading. This procedure typically takes 10 to 15 minutes.

1. Students select and read silently a 50-word passage from the story (trade book, student-produced story, core literature) they are working with in direct instruction.

2. Students choose a partner and decide who will read first.

3. One student reads orally while the other keeps a record of errors and the time. The student who records may also ask comprehension questions.

   Or the reader reads his or her passage three times and evaluates how well he or she reads after each time (the listener tells the reader how his or her reading has improved after the second and third readings).

4. The students exchange roles and repeat step 3.

Relevant English–Language Arts Content Standards

Grade One: Word Analysis, Fluency, and Systematic Vocabulary Development

1.16 Read aloud with fluency in a manner that sounds like natural speech.

Grade Two: Word Analysis, Fluency, and Systematic Vocabulary Development

1.6 Read aloud fluently and accurately and with appropriate intonation and expression.

Grade Three: Word Analysis, Fluency, and Systematic Vocabulary Development

1.3 Read aloud narrative and expository text fluently and accurately and with appropriate pacing, intonation, and expression.

Grades Four Through Six: Word Analysis, Fluency, and Systematic Vocabulary Development

1.1 Read narrative and expository text aloud with grade-appropriate fluency and accuracy and with appropriate pacing, intonation, and expression.

Further Resources

Dowhower, Sarah L. "Repeated Reading: Research into Practice," *The Reading Teacher* (March 1989), 502–7.

Morris, Darrell; Criss Ervin; and Kim Conrad. "A Case Study of Middle School Reading Disability," *The Reading Teacher,* Vol. 49 (February 1996), 368–77.

Samuels, S. Jay. "The Method of Repeated Readings," *The Reading Teacher,* Vol. 50 (February 1997), 376–81.

Samuels, S. Jay; Nancy Schermer; and David Reinking. "Reading Fluency: Techniques for Making Decoding Automatic," in *What Research Has to Say About Reading Instruction.* Edited by S. J. Samuels and A. E. Farstrup. Newark, Del.: International Reading Association, 1992, pp. 124–43.

Sight Word Study

Sight word study is a multiple-step technique for teaching students sight words (those that occur with high frequency and lack predictable spelling patterns, such as *some, through,* and *been*). This technique is appropriate only for students with a demonstrated need in this area and may be modified to serve individual needs.

Goals

1. Help students recognize high-frequency words quickly and easily to read with fluency.
2. Help students write high-frequency words quickly, easily, and accurately in their own compositions.

Teacher Preparation

1. Choose the word(s) for instructional focus based on close observation and records of students' reading and writing.
2. Find samples of running text containing multiple occurrences of the word(s).

Instructional Procedures

1. Discuss with students who have a demonstrated need for improvement in sight word recognition the reasons for studying sight words.
2. Demonstrate the meaning of *high frequency* by having students highlight a particular sight word throughout a text.
3. Present the word to be learned orally in a sentence.
4. Read the word to students as it appears in a sentence that they can see (highlighted or underlined).
5. Write only the word on a chalkboard or transparency, and point out the irregularities.

6. Ask students the following questions:
   - What is the first letter?
   - What is the last letter?
   - How many letters are in the word?
7. Focus attention on the letters.
   - Spell the word aloud.
   - Trace the word (in the air, in sand, on sandpaper).
8. Have students read the word aloud in phrases and sentences.
9. Have students look for the word in running text, highlight or underline each occurrence of the word in text, and make a simple chart showing how many times they found the word in text.
10. Have students make a list of high-frequency words they know and add new words to the list for convenient reference during writing.
11. Put the words on cards and place them in a box or on a ringholder for students who have difficulty learning words. Review the words frequently. Have the students spend a few additional minutes learning one or two of the words they found especially difficult. Have them write the word or words several times.
12. Play card games, such as Concentration™, with the words.
13. Have the students sort words (by first letter, last letter, or some other feature).

See the guidelines suggested on pages 96 to 100 of the *Reading/Language Arts Framework for California Public Schools.*

Relevant English–Language Arts Content Standards

Kindergarten: Word Analysis, Fluency, and Systematic Vocabulary Development

1.15 Read simple one-syllable and high-frequency words (i.e., sight words).

STRATEGY INDEX
Student Audience
Beginning readers
Below grade level
At or above grade level
Text Type
Literary
Informational
Special Features
Automaticity with print
Prior knowledge and interest
Discussion about texts
Collaborative learning
Writing emphasis
Graphic representation
Student control of reading process
Student ownership of strategy

Grade One: Word Analysis, Fluency, and Systematic Vocabulary Development

1.11 Read common, irregular sight words (e.g., *the, have, said, come, give, of*).

Further Resources

McNinch, G. H. "A Method for Teaching Sight Words to Disabled Readers," *The Reading Teacher,* Vol. 35 (1981), 269–72.

Pinnell, Gay Su, and Irene C. Fountas. *Help America Read.* Portsmouth, N.H.: Heinemann, 1997.

Reading/Language Arts Framework for California Public Schools, Kindergarten Through Grade Twelve. Sacramento: California Department of Education, 1999.

Underwood, Terry. "Thirty Ways to Improve Reading in the Intermediate and Middle Grades (Grades 4-8: Assumptions, Instructions, Assessments)." Sacramento: California State University, Summer/1997 (unpublished manuscript).

SELECTED REFERENCES

Some of the references cited in this material may no longer be in print or otherwise available. The publication data were supplied by the Professional Development and Curriculum Support Division. Questions about the availability of materials or the accuracy of the citations should be e-mailed to Beth Breneman (*bbrenema@cde.ca.gov*).

Adams, Marilyn J., and Bertram C. Bruce. 1982. "Background Knowledge and Reading Comprehension," in *Reader Meets Author/Bridging the Gap*. Edited by Judith A. Langer and M. T. Smith-Burke. Newark, Del.: International Reading Association, pp. 2–25.

Allington, Richard, and Anne McGill-Franzen. 1993. "What Are They to Read? Not All Children, Mr. Riley, Have Easy Access to Books," *Education Week* (October 3), 26.

Almasi, J. 1994. "The Nature of Fourth Graders' Sociocognitive Conflicts in Peer-led and Teacher-led Discussions of Literature," *Reading Research Quarterly*, Vol. 29 (October, November, December), 304–7.

Anderson, N. 1991. "Individual Differences in Strategy Use in Second Language Reading," *Modern Language Journal*, Vol. 75, 460–72.

Barr, Mary A. 1995. *California Learning Record: A Handbook for Teachers, Grades 6–12*. San Diego: University of California, San Diego.

Barr, Mary A., and others. 1999. *Assessing Literacy with the Learning Record: A Handbook for Teachers, Grades K–6*. Portsmouth, N.J.: Heinemann.

Barr, Rebecca; Marilyn W. Sadow; and Camille L. Z. Blachowicz. 1990. *Reading Diagnosis for Teachers: An Instructional Approach* (Second edition). New York: Longman.

Beaugrande, Robert de. 1984. "Learning to Read Versus Reading to Learn: A Discourse-Processing Approach," in *Learning and Comprehension of Text*. Edited by Heinz Mandle, Nancy L. Stein, and Tom Trabasso. Hillside, N.J.: Erlbaum, 159–91.

Beck, Isabel, and M. McKeown. 1991. "Conditions of Vocabulary Acquisition," in *Handbook of Reading Research* (Vol. 2). Edited by R. Barr and others. White Plains, N.Y.: Longman, pp. 789–814.

Brown, Rachel; Pamela Beard El-Dinary; and Michael Pressley. 1997. "Balanced Comprehension Instruction: Transactional Strategies Instruction," in *Balanced Instruction: Strategies and Skills in Whole Language*. Edited by Ellen McIntyre and Michael Pressley. Norwood, Mass.: Christopher-Gordon Publishers, Inc.

Burke, Jim. 1999. *I Hear America Reading*. Portsmouth, N.H.: Heinemann.

The California Reading Initiative and Special Education in California. 1999. Sacramento: California Department of Education.

Campbell, J., and others. 1996. *NAEP 1994 Reading Report Card for the Nation and the States*. Washington, D.C.: U.S. Department of Education.

Carnine, Silbert, and E. J. Kame'enui. 1990. *Direct Instruction Reading*. Columbus, Ohio: Merrill Publishing Company.

Chamot, Anna Uhl, and Michael O'Malley. 1994. *The CALLA Handbook: How to Implement the Cognitive Academic Language Learning Approach*. Reading, Mass.: Addison-Wesley Longman.

Claggett, Fran. 1996. *A Measure of Success: From Assignment to Assessment in English Language Arts*. Portsmouth, N.H.: Boynton Cook.

Consortium in Reading Excellence (CORE), Inc. 1999. *Assessing Reading: Multiple Measures for Kindergarten through Eighth Grade*, Novato: Arena Press.

Cook, Doris M. 1989. *Strategic Learning in the Content Classroom.* Madison: Wisconsin Department of Public Instruction.

Cunningham, Ann E., and Keith E. Stanovich. 1998. "What Reading Does for the Mind," *American Educator* (Spring/Summer), 8–15.

Educating English Learners for the Twenty-First Century: The Report of the Proposition 227 Task Force. 1999. Sacramento: California Department of Education.

English–Language Arts Content Standards for California Public Schools, Kindergarten Through Grade Twelve. 1998. Sacramento: California Department of Education.

"English Language Development Standards." In preparation. Sacramento: California Department of Education. Will be available in Spanish.

Every Child a Reader: The Report of the California Reading Task Force. 1995. Sacramento: California Department of Education.

Farr, Roger, and Robert Pritchard. 1994. "Assessment in the Content Areas: Solving the Assessment Puzzle," in *Content Area Reading and Learning: Instructional Strategies.* Edited by Diane Lapp, James Flood, and Nancy Farnan. Boston: Allyn and Bacon.

Feathers, Karen M. 1993. *Infotext: Reading and Learning.* Scarborough, Ontario: Pippin Publishing Corporation.

Fielding, Linda G., and P. David Pearson. 1994. "Reading Comprehension: What Works," *Educational Leadership* (February), 62–67.

Fitzgerald, Jill. 1995. "English-as-a-Second-Language Learners' Cognitive Reading Processes: A Review of Research in the United States," *Review of Educational Research*, Vol. 65 (Summer), 145–90.

Gambrell, Linda B. 1996. "Creating Classroom Cultures That Foster Reading Motivation," *The Reading Teacher*, Vol. 50 (September), 14–23.

Guide to the California Reading Initiative: 1996 Through 1999 (Third edition). 1999. Sacramento: California State Board of Education.

Implementing the Components of the California Reading Initiative: A Blueprint for Teachers of Early Reading Instruction (Second edition). 1996. Prepared by the California County Superintendents Educational Services Association—Curriculum and Instructional Steering Committee. Sacramento: CCSESA.

Jago, Carol. 1999. *Nikki Giovanni in the Classroom.* Urbana, Ill.: National Council of Teachers of English.

Jago, Carol. 2000. *With Rigor for All: Teaching the Classics to Contemporary Students.* Portland, Maine: Calendar.

Joyce, James. 1934. *Ulysses.* New York: Modern Library.

Keen, Ellin, and Susan Zimmerman. 1997. *Mosaic of Thought: Teaching Comprehension in a Reader's Workshop.* Portsmouth, N.H.: Heinemann.

Krashen, Stephen. 1993. *The Power of Reading.* Englewood, Colo.: Libraries Unlimited, Inc.

Learning to Read, Reading to Learn: Resource Guide. 1996. Washington, D.C.: American Federation of Teachers.

Lenski, S.; M. A. Wham; and J. L. Johns. 1999. *Reading and Learning Strategies for Middle and High School Students.* Dubuque, Iowa: Kendall-Hunt.

McKenna, Michael C., and Richard D. Robinson. 1990. "Content Literacy: A Definition and Implications," *Journal of Reading*, Vol. 34 (November), 184–86.

Moats, Louisa Cook; Alice R. Furry; and Nancy Brownell. 1999. *Learning to Read, Components of Beginning Reading Instruction K–8.* Sacramento: California State Board of Education.

Moats, Louisa Cook. 1998. "Teaching Decoding," *American Educator,* Vol. 22, Nos. 1–2 (Spring/Summer), 42–49, 95–96.

Moats, Louisa Cook. 1996. "Wanted: Teachers with Knowledge of Language," *Topics in Language Disorders,* Vol. 16, No. 2 (February), 73–86.

Moran, Carrol, and Josefina Villamil Tinajero. 1997. "Strategies for Working with Overage Students," in *The Power of Two Languages: Literacy and Biliteracy for Spanish-Speaking Students.* Edited by Josefina Villamil Tinajere and Alma Flor Ada. New York: McGraw-Hill.

Morris, Darrell; Criss Ervin; and Kim Conrad. 1996. "A Case Study of Middle School Reading Disability," *The Reading Teacher,* Vol. 39 (February), 368.

Paris, Scott G.; Marjorie Y. Lipson; and Karen K. Wixson. 1983. "Becoming a Strategic Reader," *Contemporary Educational Psychology,* Vol. 8, 293–316.

Pearson, P. David, and others. 1990. *Developing Expertise in Reading Comprehension.* Technical Report No. 512. Champaign, Ill.: University of Illinois, Center for the Study of Reading.

Practical Ideas for Teaching Writing as a Process at the Elementary School and Middle School Levels. 1996. Edited by C. B. Olson. Sacramento: California Department of Education.

Practical Ideas for Teaching Writing as a Process at the High School and College Levels. 1997. Edited by C. B. Olson. Sacramento: California Department of Education.

Pressley, Michael, and Peter Afflerbach. 1995. *Verbal Protocols of Reading: The Nature of Constructively Responsive Reading.* Hillsdale, N.J.: Erlbaum.

Read All About It! Readings to Inform the Profession. 1999. Sacramento: California State Board of Education.

Readence, J. E.; T. W. Bean; and R. S. Baldwin. 1998. *Content Area Literacy: An Integrated Approach* (Sixth edition). Dubuque, Iowa: Kendall-Hunt.

Reading Engagement: Motivating Readers Through Integrated Instruction. 1997. Edited by John T. Guthrie and Allan Wigfield. Newark, Del.: International Reading Association.

Reading/Language Arts Framework for California Public Schools, Kindergarten Through Grade Twelve. 1999. Sacramento: California Department of Education.

Recommended Literature, Grades Nine Through Twelve. 1990. Sacramento: California Department of Education.

Recommended Readings in Literature, Kindergarten Through Grade Eight (Revised annotated edition). 1996. Sacramento: California Department of Education.

Scarcella, Robin C. 1996. "Secondary Education in California and Second Language Research: Instructing ESL Students in the 1990s," *The CATESOL Journal,* Vol. 9, No. 1, 129–52.

Scarcella, Robin. 1990. *Teaching Language Minority Students in the Multicultural Classroom.* Englewood Cliffs, N.J.: Prentice Hall Regents.

Schicfele, U. 1991. "Interest, Learning, and Motivation," *Educational Psychologist*, Vol. 16, 299–323.

Schoenbach, Ruth, and others. *Reading for Understanding: A Guide to Improving Reading in Middle and High School Classrooms.* San Francisco: Jossey-Bass, 1999.

Simpson, M. L. 1984. "The Status of Study Strategy Instruction: Implications for Classroom Teachers," *Journal of Reading*, Vol. 28, 136–42.

Stanovich, Keith E. 1997. "Twenty-Five Years of Research on the Reading Process: The Grand Synthesis and What It Means for Our Field." Oscar S. Causey Research Award address presented at the National Reading Conference, Scottsdale, Arizona, December.

Stewart, J. 1996. "The Blackboard Bungle: California's Failed Reading Experiment," *L.A. Weekly*, Vol. 18, No. 14, 22–29.

Strategic Teaching and Learning: Cognitive Instruction in the Content Areas. 1987. Edited by Beau Fly Jones, Annemarie S. Palincsar, Dona S. Ogle, and Eileen G. Carr. Alexandria, Va.: Association for Supervision and Curriculum Development.

Taylor, Theodore. 1969. *The Cay.* New York: Doubleday.

Teaching Reading: A Balanced, Comprehensive Approach to Teaching Reading in Prekindergarten Through Third Grade. 1996. Sacramento: California Department of Education.

Vaca, Richard. 1997. "The Benign Neglect of Adolescent Literacy," *Reading Today* (February/March), 3.

Vaughn, Joseph L., and Thomas H. Estes. 1986. *Reading and Reasoning Beyond the Primary Grades.* Boston: Allyn and Bacon.

Programs

CORE

PAT Strategic
ee twisted learners

WestEd — Reading
Strategic for Un
Literacy
Reading
Apprenticesh
District
Admin
invited
first

- Words
- Rewards - Archer

Project
Success → Accelerated Reader
(Cat) → Scholastic Crest
tested → Language! Texted work

Corrective Reading

→ Not instructional program
Interventions
Response other than Spec. Ed

Smart Teacher
Smart System ← Hardest
Smart Curricula

Kate
Kense
Strate
Interd

SCOE

Program Design, Coordination
& Articulation

PDC

Reading
Cadre —
Skunk

Mapping a
Curricula

- 4 D Program
- Awareness Session
- Initial & Ongoing PD
- Coaching Support
- Program Mtlness
- Evaluation etc
- Reading Cadre etc

INDEX

98-035 003-0062-99 4-00 10M